WEATHERING THE STORM

WEATHERING THE STORM

Taiwan, Its Neighbors, and the Asian Financial Crisis

PETER C.Y. CHOW

BATES GILL

Editors

BROOKINGS INSTITUTION PRESS
Washington, D.C.

Copyright © 2000
THE BROOKINGS INSTITUTION
1775 Massachusetts Avenue, N.W., Washington, D.C. 20036
www.brookings.edu

Library of Congress Cataloging-in-Publication data
Weathering the storm : Taiwan, its neighbors, and the Asian financial
crisis / Peter C. Y. Chow, Bates Gill, editors.
p.   cm.
Includes bibliographical references and index.
ISBN 0-8157-1399-1
1. Financial crises—Taiwan.   2. Financial crises—East Asia.
3. East Asia—Economic conditions.   I. Chow, Peter C. Y.
II. Gill, Bates.   III. Title.

HB3722 .W43   2000   00-008805
330.95′0429—dc21   CIP

9 8 7 6 5 4 3 2 1

The paper used in this publication meets the minimum requirements of the American
National Standard for Information Sciences—Permanence of Paper for Printed
Library Materials, ANSI Z39.48-1984.

Typeset in Times Roman

Composition by Princeton Editorial Associates
Scottsdale, Arizona, and Roosevelt, New Jersey

Printed by R. R. Donnelley and Sons
Harrisonburg, Virginia

ß THE BROOKINGS INSTITUTION

The Brookings Institution is an independent organization devoted to nonpartisan research, education, and publication in economics, government, foreign policy, and the social sciences generally. Its principal purposes are to aid in the development of sound public policies and to promote public understanding of issues of national importance.

The Institution was founded on December 8, 1927, to merge the activities of the Institute for Government Research, founded in 1916, the Institute of Economics, founded in 1922, and the Robert Brookings Graduate School of Economics and Government, founded in 1924.

The general administration of the Institution is the responsibility of a Board of Trustees charged with safeguarding the independence of the staff and fostering the most favorable conditions for scientific research and publication. The immediate direction of the policies, program, and staff is vested in the president, assisted by an advisory committee of the officers and staff.

In publishing a study, the Institution presents it as a competent treatment of a subject worthy of public consideration. The interpretations or conclusions in such publications are those of the author or authors and do not necessarily reflect the views of the other staff members, officers, or trustees of the Brookings Institution.

Foreword

With alarming alacrity, the promise of the "Asian economic miracle" and the "Pacific century" devolved into regionwide economic chaos in July 1997 and the onset of what has become known as the Asian financial crisis. One by one, many of the region's great economic success stories—Hong Kong, Indonesia, South Korea, Thailand—suffered damage to their financial markets, their currencies, and their economic well-being.

Even three years hence, the legacies of the Asian financial crisis still linger despite promising upturns on several fronts. Investor and consumer confidence has yet to return to previous levels, and even post–International Monetary Fund "success stories" such as South Korea remain embittered by the experience. The political fallout of the crisis in Indonesia—the loss of East Timor to an independence referendum and the fall of the Suharto regime—still manifests itself in a fragile new democracy in Jakarta and a United Nations protectorate in Dili. Even countries not directly affected by the crisis, such as China and Japan, still struggle with effects of the crisis and place their hopes in a return to more upbeat and prosperous regional economic times. Of course, what spread through the region in the summer and fall of 1997 went on to negatively affect other economies across the globe, Brazil and Russia most importantly.

With the distance of time, much can be learned from the events before, during, and after the crisis. Without laying blame or pointing fingers, all the relevant players in this drama—governments, private industry, and international lending institutions—need to draw appropriate comparative lessons if similar financial disasters are to be avoided as fledgling economies take wing in the new and fast-paced globalized economy. On the opposite side of the same coin, we should also be asking why some economies in the region—Taiwan's in particular—did not suffer from the worst ravages of the storm that swept through East Asia in 1997–98.

In early 1999, the Chung-Hua Institution for Economic Research and Professor Peter C. Y. Chow of New York University approached the Brookings Institution to convene a gathering of some of the world's leading comparative economists to address just such questions. Working with Robert Litan, director of the Brookings Economic Studies Program, and Bates Gill, director of the Brookings Center for Northeast Asian Policy Studies, Chow organized a conference at Brookings in April 1999 that took a unique and innovative approach: to compare, contrast, and draw policy lessons from the failures and successes of four key economies in the region—Indonesia, South Korea, Taiwan, and Thailand—in the face of the Asian financial storm. We are especially grateful to the Chung-Hua Institution for its initiative and support for this conference.

This volume results from the collective research presented at that conference. Building on the meticulous analysis of experts from both sides of the Pacific who participated in the conference and contributed chapters to the book, the editors present several key findings and recommendations in a concluding chapter, including a special focus on general principles for the stable liberalization of financial markets in developing economies. This work certainly meets its goal of providing much-needed new understanding and reasoned policy lessons to help the Asia-Pacific region meet its vast economic potential in the new millennium, and it will prove useful to national policymakers, international institutional lenders, and comparative economists alike.

The views expressed in this volume are those of the individual authors and should not be ascribed to the Chung-Hua Institution, or to the trustees, officers, or other staff members of the Brookings Institution.

MICHAEL H. ARMACOST
President

April 2000
Washington, D.C.

Preface

In order to derive useful policy lessons for emerging economies in East Asia and throughout the world, the Chung-Hua Institution for Economic Research in Taipei, the Brookings Institution Center for Northeast Asian Policy Studies, and the Brookings Institution Economic Studies Program jointly convened a conference in April 1999 entitled "The Asian Financial Crisis and the Role of Taiwan in the Region." Drawing together the featured presentations of nine prominent East Asian and American specialists, this volume presents the results of that successful conference.

Our hope in publishing this volume is to contribute further to analysts' understanding of the sources and lessons of the Asian financial crisis. We recommend the volume for use by academics and economic policymakers in governments, international organizations, and universities, both in the region and beyond, as they assess and implement strategies for more stable regional and global economic development.

In addition to presenting new comparative analyses across particular trouble spots in the Asian financial crisis—such as Indonesia, Korea, and Thailand—this volume makes a special contribution of its own by focusing on the role of Taiwan. Three important aspects of this approach bear our readers' careful attention. First, we conducted these comparative analyses of four key regional economies in the hope that their results could be used to guide policymakers by highlighting common problems and solutions for emerging economies in an increasingly globalized financial and economic marketplace. As they did in analyses they provided in response to the world debt crisis of the 1980s and the Mexican peso crisis in the early 1990s, academic analysts and policymakers alike must apply their expertise to gain global lessons from the Asian financial debacle. The specialists writing in this volume offer numerous policy-relevant recommendations and reforms that will be of use to national governments and international institutions alike as they seek to prevent the recurrence of such financial crises in the future.

Second, in examining Taiwan's relative success in weathering the storm of the financial crisis, this volume helps explain the widely varying degrees of performance of the region's affected economies and generates critical lessons for emerging economies as to managing internal and external financial shocks. Third, the volume points to important considerations about Taiwan's future economic role in the region. Given Taiwan's relative success in the face of the challenges of the crisis and its positive contributions to regional economic stability, in what ways can Taiwan further contribute in the future? In answering this question, the volume suggests ways in which Taiwan can positively affect regional economic integration and growth.

In closing, we thank the Chung-Hua Institution for Economic Research for its financial support and Robert Litan, director of the Brookings Institution Economic Studies Program, for his cooperation and guidance. We are also enormously grateful for the dedicated administrative and editorial support provided by Brookings colleagues Sun Kordel, Charlene Mui, and Steven Ocone, as well as the efforts of Princeton Editorial Associates on behalf of Brookings Institution Press.

Peter C. Y. Chow   Bates Gill
New York   *Washington, D.C.*

Contents

Part One

OVERVIEW

CHAPTER ONE

The Asian Financial Crisis and Its Aftermath

Peter C. Y. Chow

In past decades the rapid growth of Asia-Pacific economies generated a dynamism widely acknowledged as the new "center of gravity" for the world economy. Indeed, paying homage to the dramatic economic successes of the region, in 1993 the World Bank published a book entitled *The East Asian Miracle*.[1] But only four years after its publication the economies of most East Asian countries stunningly collapsed. Starting with the depreciation of the Thai baht in July 1997, the financial contagion spread to affect economies throughout the region and beyond. How could the enviable miracle in East Asia be undone in such a short time, and what policy lessons can be drawn from the experience? In spite of much research and writing on these questions, they continue to present difficult analytical puzzles. With the crisis largely behind us—and with the perspective that comes with time—this volume takes a fresh and unique approach to these pressing questions.

Even prior to their export booms in the first half of the 1990s, most economies in East and Southeast Asia had undertaken various degrees of financial liberalization to overcome previous decades of financial repression. The drive for globalization of financial markets also pushed fragile financial markets in developing Asian countries to integrate with well-functioning markets in the developed world. But was the financial crisis caused by the drive for liberaliza-

1. World Bank (1993).

tion undertaken in those countries? Is the globalization of financial markets to be blamed for causing the crisis? If so, why did the financial typhoon blast Indonesia, Korea, and Thailand, among others, but only glance off Taiwan? In addition, what has been the legacy of the crisis in the region, and what lessons can we draw from it to avoid a recurrence of the debacle both in the region and among emerging economies the world over? As an overview, this chapter summarizes how the contributors to this volume have tackled these critical questions.

Restructuring, Readjustments, and Recoveries

In the second section of the book we examine the problems and prospects for the three economies most heavily affected by the financial crisis: Korea, Indonesia, and Thailand.

Korea

As the eleventh largest economy in the world, Korea suffered enormously from the financial crisis in 1997. In chapter 2 Tatsuo Yanagita analyzes the major causes of the Korean financial crisis, with a particular focus on the "conditionality" requirements of the International Monetary Fund (IMF) and the country's subsequent path to recovery.

According to Yanagita, the seeds of the crisis were planted by the close tripartite relationship among the government, state banks, and Korean industrial conglomerates (chaebols). Starting in the late 1970s, these ties enabled the chaebols to obtain preferential policy loans at subsidized interest rates in order to develop heavy and chemical industries—a point also developed by Chen and Ku in chapter 5. In the early 1990s Korea still required its financial institutions to report long-term foreign loans to the government authorities concerned, but it did not require reporting of their short-term loans, which were regarded as trade-related financing. This mistaken policy, in turn, provided financial institutions with strong incentives to make short-term foreign loans, resulting in unsound foreign liabilities, thus exposing the Korean economy to external financial disruptions. With the 1997 economic recession and slowdown in exports, Korea began to experience an excruciating series of corporate bankruptcies, nonperforming loans, and bank failures and insolvencies, along with the ensuing financial disaster.

The IMF restructuring and conditionality requirements comprised three major components: macroeconomic policy, financial and corporate restructuring, and liberalization of current as well as capital accounts. Yanagita points out that fiscal policy played only a modest role in IMF conditionality because it was "intended to provide only limited support for a modest current account adjustment." The fiscal measures intended to fulfill this policy objective included widening the tax base for corporate and income tax, imposing a value-added tax, and reducing government expenditure. Monetary policy was assigned to stabilize the downward pressure of the Korean won in light of underlying economic fundamentals. Hence, a policy of tightening the money supply and raising interest rates ensued.

In the meantime, the IMF financial restructuring included "a clear and firm exit policy for financial institutions, strong market and supervisory discipline, and independence of the central bank," whereas corporate restructuring required the establishment of "transparent and efficient ties among government, banks, and business in order to upgrade their accounting, auditing, and disclosure standards." For liberalization of current and capital accounts, the IMF required the Korean government "to eliminate trade-related subsidies and the import diversification program, as well as streamline and improve transparency of import certification procedures." As to the capital account, Korea was asked to open money, bond, and equity markets to capital inflows, and to liberalize foreign direct investment. With regard to structural reforms, the IMF emphasized the rationalization of the banking system and called for a major restructuring of the chaebol system.

Yanagita reserves final judgment as to the efficacy of the IMF package, in spite of the modest recovery of the Korean economy. Relying on extensive empirical evidence, he argues that the conventional IMF conditionality approach failed in Korea. First, foreign investors, "by taking account of the expected rate of change in value of the won to the dollar," acquired assets denominated in Korean won. As a result, "foreign capital inflow slowed despite the high interest rates because the credit risk involved in the payment of principal was too high." Second, the savings rate in Korea had already reached 34 percent of the gross domestic product (GDP) in 1997. Hence, only limited value could be obtained by imposing a high interest rate to curtail consumption, raise savings, and improve the balance of payments. Moreover, a high interest rate resulting from tightened monetary policy would have a contractionary effect and impose additional debt burdens on the construction industry and small- and medium-size enterprises, which were already facing difficult straits.

As Yanagita notes, "the IMF should have encouraged the rescheduling of short-term debts into long-term debts instead of advising the imposition of a high interest rate."

Indonesia

As Steven Radelet relates in chapter 3, prior to the financial crisis in the 1990s, Indonesia already faced increasing short-term debts (especially in firms closely tied to political families), an overvalued currency, slow export growth, and a weak banking system. An implicit government guarantee of foreign loans made by the Indonesian government led to the provision of foreign loans for poor-quality projects without adequate risk analysis—raising the problem of "moral hazard." Other than saving the cost of borrowing (about 6 percentage points), the Indonesian crawling peg discouraged firms from hedging against foreign exchange exposure on their dollar-denominated loans. Liberalization in Indonesia enabled privately owned banks to compete with the state banks. But liberalization without appropriate supervisory and regulatory arrangements had disastrous results.

Sharing many of Yanagita's views, Radelet criticizes the IMF for its badly designed program in Indonesia. The IMF urged Indonesia to tighten its monetary policy, whereas creation of a budget surplus was set at the top of its agenda. Moreover, the IMF ordered bank closures without recognizing the lack of deposit insurance in Indonesia, and its offer of U.S.$3 billion in loans was too little to be effective in quelling the resulting panic. Radelet points out that Indonesian problems were not rooted in excessive aggregate demand in its macroeconomy, rendering the conventional IMF austerity program unsuitable. Mismanagement of the crisis by the IMF and the Suharto government, especially the ill-advised idea of establishing a currency board, aggravated the depth of the country's financial crisis, and, according to Radelet, caused economic contraction far greater than was either necessary or inevitable. Radelet also argues that strong U.S. Treasury criticism of Indonesian budget proposals in early 1998 helped contribute to the confusion and uncertainty and to the eventual downfall of Suharto.

Indonesia still must travel a long road to recover from its economic and political turmoil. Radelet summarizes the Indonesian situation by noting first how the mutual interdependence between political and economic stabilities turned from a "positive" to a "negative," and he concludes that Indonesia has little prospect of turning back for the foreseeable future. Second, he points out that the cost of restructuring the moribund banking system under a government recapitalization scheme may be well above 30 percent of GDP. But given its nonperforming loan rate of 60 to 75 percent, Radelet concludes that "even with the recapitalization, many banks remain illiquid and have little incentive to begin lending." Third, debt restructuring will be difficult owing to the reluctance of Indonesia's largest creditor—Japan, which suffers from its own long-term recession problems—to offer debt relief.

Fourth, in the wake of the crisis Indonesian exports grew in volume but declined in dollar terms due to the sharp depreciation of the rupiah (and probably due to low price elasticity of foreign demand). As Radelet makes clear, the relatively stagnant world price for oil and petroleum products—which account for 25 percent of Indonesian exports—further cut the country's revenues. Fifth, there is little room for trimming budget deficits in Indonesia because expenditures are highly rigid, yet tax revenues cannot be increased due to the collapse of its economy. With Indonesia facing a painful "Hobson's choice," Radelet warns of a long road to recovery for the fourth most populous nation in the world.

Thailand

In chapter 4 Frank Flatters suggests that Thailand may be the first into and fastest out of the Asian financial debacle. Noting a policy of "malign neglect," Flatters highlights the poor responsiveness of the Thai government in the face of private warnings from the IMF. He further describes the flawed policy choices that led the Thai government to defend the Thai baht between the third quarter of 1996 and February 1997. As a result, Thailand nearly exhausted its foreign exchange reserves, going from U.S.$40 billion in the third quarter of 1996 to U.S.$2.8 billion in June 1997. Hence, the depreciation of the baht on July 2, 1997, was inevitable. In addition, the indecisive policy of bailing out financial institutions—and the Thai government's inconsistent and confused signals to clean up the financial mess—exacerbated an already troubled situation. In retrospect, Flatters believes that the worst of the crisis could have been avoided.

The IMF program in Thailand focused on exchange rate management and financial market stability, and it included fiscal austerity and tightened monetary policy. However, contrary to its actions in the Korean and Indonesian cases, the IMF changed course in mid-1998: fiscal policy was shifted from the projected surplus to deal with the deficit, and monetary policy was aimed at

cutting interest rates and increasing credit. Regardless of the merits and de-
merits of the IMF-Thai collaboration on rescue programs, Flatters argues that
one major weakness underlying the IMF strategy was a miscalculation of
external effects, such as the effect of the regional spread of the crisis on the
Thai economy. In addition, he elaborates the problems for restructuring and
corporate governance that are posed in societies where the rule of law and legal
infrastructures are not well developed.

Flatters provides realistic and objective short- and long-term assessments of
the Thai economy. In the first instance, in spite of the promising introduction of
economic legal reforms, elements such as the questionable near-term effectiveness of fiscal policies, continued concerns as to Thailand's overall socio-
political stability, and a host of uncertain external factors make a short-term
recovery far from certain. In judging longer-term prospects Flatters draws
attention to three key points. First, the long-term cost of policy errors and
financial restructuring now stands at somewhere between 1 and 4 percent of
GDP. Moreover, the sunk cost and demolition of partially completed construction
projects will need to be absorbed out of future growth. Second, it is still too early
to predict the effectiveness of institutional and government reform, especially
constitutional reforms to eliminate "money politics," though they are already under
way. Last, Flatters notes that enhancing long-term competitiveness through
technological inputs will require substantial investment in human capital, infrastructure, and a competitive market system that will do away with entrenched
protectionism and corruption. Overcoming such challenges will be as difficult as it
is essential for Thailand's long-term economic success.

Taiwan Weathering the Storm

Relatively speaking, the economies of the East Asian countries were less
hurt by the financial storm than were the Southeast Asian countries. However,
among the East Asian countries there are differences in terms of their industrial
organization, financial structures, and speed of financial liberalization. Comparative studies of Korea and Taiwan can yield valuable lessons on dealing
with potential financial crises.

Comparing Korea and Taiwan

Both Korea and Taiwan were reputed for their miraculous economic growth
and were often favorably compared as two of the "Asian economic dragons."

But the financial crisis severely hit Korea, whereas Taiwan weathered the financial storm with relatively minor damage.

In chapter 5 Tain-Jy Chen and Ying-Hua Ku start off the third major section of the book by usefully providing a comparative analysis to help explain this apparent incongruity. First of all, although both embarked on economic success through investment in their heavy industries beginning in the late 1970s, their approaches and policy objectives were substantially different. Most important, the Korean approach made export growth and world-class position priorities for its heavy and chemical industries, whereas Taiwan aimed most of all at import substitution to serve its downstream labor-intensive exports. In addition, the Korean approaches were dominated by industrial conglomerates—the chaebols—and highly subsidized by preferential loans. But according to Chen and Ku, Taiwan's industrial structure was dominated by its export-oriented small- to medium-size enterprises. These authors argue that it was this approach to its heavy and chemical industries in the 1970s that was the primary cause of Korea's deep indebtedness, a problem from which it was unable to escape.

In their comparative analysis Chen and Ku also spell out the differences between Korea and Taiwan in terms of capital account liberalization and structural reform, both of which led to the different impacts on the two economies of the Asian financial crisis. Owing to differences in their respective forms of industrial organization, capital account liberalization had quite different effects in Korea and Taiwan. After the mid-1980s, inward foreign investments in Korea were more in the form of portfolio investment than of direct investment. In 1996, for example, the ratio of portfolio investment to inward foreign direct investment in Korea was 6.2 to 1, whereas the ratio was only 1.7 to 1 in Taiwan. The reason for this difference, Chen and Ku argue, is that Korea's industries were oligopolized by its chaebols, leaving little room for foreign investors to invest directly in Korean industries. As a result, foreign investors were led to portfolio rather than direct investments in Korea.[2] This form of industrial organization left Korea highly vulnerable to external shocks. As for structural transformation, Korea's approach proceeded with intrafirm adjustments in the chaebols. In contrast, structural transformation in Taiwan was made mainly through off-shore production through outward foreign direct

2. See also chapter 8, where Chow argues that foreign direct investment should be preferred to portfolio investment and that long-term loans should be preferred to short-term loans. As Chen and Ku show in their chapter, the Korean case was just the opposite.

investment. Again, the difference in organization of industrialization led to divergent strategies in structural transformation and its resultant effects on balances of trade accounts as well as other macroeconomic fundamentals between Korea and Taiwan.

The Reasons for Taiwan's Relative Success

In chapter 6 Jiann-Chyuan Wang offers his own explanation of Taiwan's escape from the worst effects of the Asian financial crisis. He shows that in spite of its healthy economic fundamentals, Taiwan could not remain immune from speculative attack against its currency. The intervention in the foreign exchange market by the Central Bank early on, between July and October 1997, caused a sharp rise in interest rates and a decline in stock prices. Combining the index of exchange rates and stock prices, Wang shows how Taiwan's economy suffered a decline of 41.2 percent between June 30 and the end of 1997. By comparison, the index hit 49.8 percent in Korea, 64.5 percent in Thailand, and 112.5 percent in Indonesia during the same period.

At the sectoral level, Taiwan's traditional industries such as plastics, textiles, machinery, and petrochemicals, whose products were headed for export to Southeast Asia, were hurt more than its information and electronics sectors, whose products were mostly headed for the developed economies. Only 8 percent of Taiwan's total sales of personal computers were to Southeast Asia, and two-thirds of such exports consisted of semifinished goods or re-exports. As a result, they were less affected by the financial crisis. But in the immediate short term after the financial crisis, Taiwan faced a strong challenge from Korean exports due to the sharp depreciation of the Korean won. Korea-made dynamic random access memory and liquid crystal displays, but not necessarily monitors, tended to have more of a negative impact on Taiwan's exports of similar products. However, the Korean information industry also relies more on imports of intermediate products and components from abroad than does that of Taiwan. Hence, over the longer term, currency depreciation in Korea appears to be a mixed blessing for its exports.

On the other hand, according to Wang the Taiwan-based information technology industry has established a global logistics framework by switching its strategy from original equipment manufacturing (OEM) to build-to-order (BTO) manufacturing so as to assume the responsibility for shipments, inventory control, financial leverage, and preparation of components and raw materials. Wang argues that the development of the information industry in Taiwan left only a limited area for its small- and medium-size enterprises (SMEs), except in the areas of integrated circuit (IC) design, software design, and information services. Consequently, the high-tech industry in Taiwan became more oligopolized and more competitive internationally.

Following his six-part explanation of why Taiwan escaped the worst effects of the regional financial debacle, Wang concludes by offering four "response strategies" for the island's firms: upgrading production technology and process management to diminish production costs; strengthening the efficient management of materials, components, and inventory needs; forming strategic alliances with world-class manufacturers; and diversifying its export destinations. As for the government of Taiwan, Wang suggests several policy recommendations: developing a more flexible yet disciplined mechanism for setting the exchange rate; developing a more healthy and smooth-running capital market; pursuing financial liberalization; preserving the division of labor between large enterprises and SMEs; strengthening the effects of spill-over from the electronics technologies to other industries; enforcing fair competition between foreign and domestic firms; and pursuing sustainable economic growth. Wang believes that in following such prescriptions Taiwan can reasonably anticipate continued steady growth, even in the wake of the financial crisis.

Taiwan's Future Role

In concluding the book's focus on Taiwan, in chapter 7 Shin-Horng Chen and Da-Nien Liu define Taiwan's role in the economic and financial future of the Asia-Pacific economies. Recognizing the extent of the "contagion effect" of the crisis, Chen and Liu argue that de facto economic integration already exists within the region. In fact, Taiwan has actively taken part in regional integration through foreign direct investment (FDI) in the countries of the Association of Southeast Asian Nations (ASEAN) and in China since the Plaza Accord. As a result, trade flows between Taiwan (as well as other foreign investors such as Japan) and recipient countries have led to a more vertical division of labor dominated by intraindustry trade. Hence, it is fair to argue that after the Plaza Agreement, intraindustry trade—which used to dominate the trade pattern among the economies of the Organization for Economic Cooperation and Development (OECD)—has become the norm among developed and developing Asian economies. For Taiwan as well as other newly industrialized economies, there is a two-way foreign investment flow: both outward FDI and inward FDI have occurred simultaneously, with different technological hierarchies in each direction.[3]

Thus, Chen and Liu propose, Taiwan has been serving as an intermediary or "semiperipheral" pivot between the industrial center (core) and peripheral (developing) countries in the region. In doing so Taiwan has passively avoided the so-called branch plant syndrome and has actively promoted its intermediary function by further integrating multinational corporations (MNCs) with its indigenous firms through continuously upgrading their local operations.

Chen and Liu describe Taiwan's "midterm economic development blueprint, as exemplified by the Asia-Pacific Regional Operations Center (APROC) plan." The APROC grand plan is to further the vertical division of labor within the region by attracting MNCs to Taiwan to establish regional operations centers. Under this scenario Taiwan would serve as an Asia-Pacific hub for manufacturing, for sea and air transport, and for the financial, telecommunications, and media sectors. Using the information industry as an example, Chen and Liu argue that Taiwan-based firms have assumed "a larger responsibility by taking part in supply-chain management, logistics operations, and after-sale services." They argue that further technological innovation and regional integration by Taiwan—especially its drive to be the principal (APROC)—would pave the way for necessary restructuring.

Under the APROC plan Taiwan would need to further liberalize trade, reduce entry and exit restrictions on personnel, provide freer flows of capital, and upgrade the legal environment for an information society. Needless to say, Taiwan still has a long way to go before it could realize this aspiration, especially if its proposed financial center is to achieve the status enjoyed by Hong Kong and Singapore. One can reasonably argue that Taiwan is not only passively trying to escape the Asian financial crisis, but also actively promoting liberalization and internationalization by pursuing its ambitious APROC drive. By serving as a node of the global production network, Taiwan appears to have played a significant role in enhancing the growth and stability in the Asia-Pacific region as well.

Lessons Learned

In Chow's concluding chapter he attempts to distill the lessons from each of the specific preceding chapters so as to provide some answers to the question

3. Chow (1997).

"What can be learned from the Asian financial crisis?" The chapter begins with six general factors that caused the "economic miracle" to turn into a "financial disaster": uneven development between financial and real sectors; reversed capital flows and misalignment of exchange rates; financial liberalization without sound banking systems and appropriate oversight; a unique trade pattern in the region that aggravated the contagious effects of the financial crisis; special features of the regional political economy, including crony capitalism in Indonesia and chaebols in Korea, that contributed to the crisis; and predatory speculation (a too-large pool of "hot money" in too-shallow financial markets) that aggravated the crisis.

Specific characteristics of Indonesia, Korea, and Thailand also played a role. In Indonesia crony capitalism led to high concentrations of economic power tied to political families. Foreign lenders extended their short-term loans to those powerful borrowers with the mistaken assumption that political connections would ensure bail-outs in cases of insolvency. Moreover, due to nearly fixed exchange rates in previous years, most Indonesian foreign debts were not hedged. A large proportion of banking credits were extended for real estate deals and other speculative activities. Highly leveraged Indonesian firms were vulnerable to external shocks.

The Korean crisis resulted from overinvestment rather than poor saving. The government's ambitious plans for the country's heavy and chemical industries led to overborrowing from abroad after Korea liberalized its short-term capital inflows. Financial liberalization led commercial banks to seek alternative investment opportunities and increase their foreign borrowing by taking advantage of differential interest rates. Poor monitoring meant that the banks could avoid accountability.

In Thailand financial liberalization enabled the Bangkok International Banking Facility (BIBF) to borrow foreign capital and lend to domestic commercial banks, which in turn lent to unproductive projects, especially in real estate. Hence, the bubble burst as economic recession occurred and export revenues declined. In short, crony capitalism in Indonesia, chaebols in Korea, and real estate speculators in Thailand led to heavy short-term foreign debts without appropriate hedges.

It is important to fault not liberalization per se, but rather its sequencing, coupled with an absence of oversight and accountability.[4] For example, Korea liberalized its current account and its capital account almost simultaneously

---

4. McKinnon (1991); see also Fleming (1962), Mundell (1967), and Shaw (1973).

after its admission to the OECD. Thailand liberalized its banking industry, but still tightly regulated its financial companies. Hence, there was a two-tier financial system after the Thai government liberalized its foreign capital flows. Moreover, financial liberalization in many of these afflicted economies was not accompanied by well-regulated supervision. Hence, excessive borrowing from abroad in boom times led to investments in overly ambitious and poorly monitored projects.

On the other hand, globalization of financial markets in the 1980s led to the untimely opening of domestic financial markets to predatory speculation. With fragile domestic financial sectors, several East Asian economies exposed themselves to speculative financial flows without appropriate hedging against the risk of sudden reversals. The Bank for International Settlements (BIS) reported that there was a significant reversal of financial flows in five East Asian countries (Indonesia, Korea, the Philippines, Malaysia, and Thailand) between 1996 and 1997—a shift from net capital inflows of U.S.$95 billion in 1996 to net capital outflows of U.S.$12 billion in 1997. Clearly the 1997–98 financial crisis was a time bomb waiting to detonate within the financial systems of the affected economies.

It is fair to argue that although liberalization must be a long-term policy objective, any such effort must be integrated with short-term macroeconomic stabilization measures. Moreover, even though globalization of financial markets in the world economy is an irresistible trend, the institution of some policy measures is necessary for developing countries to insulate themselves from the potential shocks of short-term capital flows, especially hedge funds and foreign portfolio investments. Internationalization of financial markets in developing countries cannot be pursued at the expense of short-term macroeconomic stabilization. To reap the benefits of market globalization, it is more appropriate for developing countries, especially countries with fragile financial sectors, to employ the principle of gradualism rather than pushing for globalization when their financial infrastructures are not yet ready for it. Moreover, financial liberalization must be accompanied by prudential supervision.

Lessons also come from Taiwan's relatively less troubled experience. Taiwan had few official foreign debts, with foreign bank claims less than 10 percent of GDP in 1997. By comparison, this figure stood at 22 percent in Korea, 39 percent in Indonesia, and 50 percent in Thailand. Taiwan maintained a surplus in its trade account, and it had more than U.S.$90 billion in foreign reserves when the crisis hit. Its foreign assets in consolidated financial institutions exceeded its foreign liabilities by a factor of seven at the end of 1997. In addition, foreign portfolio investments accounted for less than 3 percent of the total capitalization of Taiwan's stock market.

Nevertheless, Taiwan's experience illustrates that a fundamentally healthy economy can still be subject to speculative attacks because of the shallowness of its capital market. Although liberalization of merchandise trade could promote more efficient allocation of productive resources and is mutually beneficial to all trading partners, free capital movements, especially speculative short-term capital flows, need not necessarily benefit developing economies with immature financial sectors. This argument does not condemn the globalization of financial markets, but it suggests that financial integration between developed and developing countries should proceed by allowing developing economies adequate time to adjust their financial structures. Again, the gradualism principle applies.

The Asian financial crisis also demonstrates that fixed exchange rate systems, free capital mobility, and monetary autonomy are not readily compatible. Relying on a "peg" system, Thailand and Indonesia reduced their monetary autonomy. Moreover, experience from pegging exchange rates in Hong Kong and stabilizing exchange rates in Taiwan shows that most developing economies did not have adequate policy instruments to manage their monetary and exchange rates policies. Policies to achieve stabilization (in exchange rates, inflation rates, and growth of output) must be accompanied by adequate policy instruments.

In sum, several key lessons can be drawn regarding the liberalization of financial markets for developing economies:

—The domestic sector should be deregulated before the foreign sector.

—The current account should be liberalized before the capital account.

—Overinvestment in East Asia can lead those countries to borrow too much from abroad, just as undersaving did in Latin America.

—Financial markets should be liberalized only when liberalization is accompanied by appropriate supervision and public scrutiny.

—Private institutions must hedge against exchange risks on foreign-denominated loans and, when borrowing, do so with long-term loans when possible.

—Policymakers must give priority to foreign direct investment over foreign loans.

—Overall, liberalization of foreign capital inflows must be implemented under the principle of gradualism in accordance with domestic financial developments, and transparency, accountability, and credibility should be the watchwords for financial liberalization.

This volume was completed by specialists from both sides of the Pacific Ocean, and it demonstrates a common concern for ensuring the continued growth and stability of the Asia-Pacific region. Legacies of the 1997 Asian financial crisis and its aftermath probably will be felt well into the twenty-first century. However, works such as this will provide some of the much-needed stock of cumulative knowledge and reasoned policy lessons to help the Asia-Pacific region meet its vast potential in the new millennium.

References

Chow, Peter C. Y. 1997. "Technology Hierarchy, Globalization of Production Networks, and International Division of Labor among Pacific Basin Countries." Paper presented at the First International Business Management Conference. National Chinan University, Nantou, Taiwan, December 20.

Fleming, J. M. 1962. "Domestic Financial Policies under Fixed and Flexible Rate." IMF staff papers, November, 369–79.

McKinnon, Ronald I. 1991. *The Order of Liberalization*. Baltimore: Johns Hopkins University Press.

Mundell, R. A. 1967. *International Economics*. London: Macmillan.

Shaw, Edward S. 1973. *Financial Deepening in Economic Development*. New York: Oxford University Press.

World Bank. 1993. *The East Asian Miracle: Economic Growth and Public Policy*. New York: Oxford University Press.

Part Two

RESTRUCTURING, READJUSTMENTS, AND RECOVERIES

CHAPTER TWO

International Monetary Fund Conditionality and the Korean Economy in the Late 1990s

Tatsuo Yanagita

Examining the impact on the Korean economy of the conditionality of the International Monetary Fund (IMF), this chapter reaches three principal conclusions. First, the main factor causing the won crisis at the end of 1997 was the high ratio of short-term debts to total external debts: the ratio of short-term debts to the gross national product (GNP) was 56.8 percent at the end of 1996 compared with 33.4 percent in 1982, when Korea was also under IMF standby arrangements. Meanwhile, the ratio of external debts to GNP was 32.8 percent at the end of 1997 and 52.1 percent in 1998 compared with 53.6 percent in 1983. As Kim and Rhee point out, this high ratio of short-term external debts was in part attributable to the policies the government mistakenly made in the process of financial liberalization.[1] By making it mandatory to notify authorities of long-term loans, but not short-term ones, the government provided financial institutions with incentives to borrow for the short term.

I thank Mr. Seok-Kang Park for doing statistical work and for translating Korean into Japanese. I also thank Professor Sung-Hwi Lee of Seoul National University for helping to collect Korean documents and statistics. The research was undertaken with partial financial support from the Chung-Hua Institution for Economic Research in Taiwan and the Zengin Foundation for Studies on Economics and Finance in Japan.
    1. Kim and Rhee (1998).

Second, the radical policy swing in the early stage of the IMF arrangements in 1998 had a devastating effect on corporations with large, increasing debts. This is because the debt-equity ratios of large conglomerates amounted to around 400 percent in December 1997. The overnight money market call rate rose swiftly, from about 12 percent annually in November 1997 to 32 percent in January 1998, then decreased radically to 8.5 percent in September 1998. The IMF should have encouraged the rescheduling of short-term debts into long-term debts instead of advising the imposition of a high interest rate. This would have led to restored confidence among foreign investors and to the stability of the won.

Third, the overeagerness for financial liberalization demonstrated by the IMF arrangements of the early 1980s resulted in financial turmoil in the mid-1990s due to increasingly futile portfolio investments in corporations made through nonbank financial institutions. Following the liberalization these financial institutions developed quickly, but exhibited limited expertise in corporate financing. Moreover, Korea quickly turned into an economy oriented to direct financing without adequate institutional support. A financial sector in the midst of restructuring was in a premature stage of development, with weak corporate governance and market discipline, a lack of transparent accounting by independent external auditing, and inadequate disclosures of corporate financial positions.

In addition, complex informal relationships among monetary authorities, financial institutions, and big conglomerates were also problematic. Traditional regulations and protections for financial institutions, including nationalized commercial banks, failed to build up expertise in credit screening, project evaluation, and risk management. The IMF conditionality practices have been based on a market-supporting institutional framework, so it was necessary to supplement the traditional instruments of conditionality by focusing on the microeconomic and institutional aspects of reform of the Korean financial sector.

To provide more detailed support for these conclusions, the following section of this chapter presents an overview of the won crisis in recent years, and the next section examines the IMF conditionality arrangements in 1998. A closing section offers policy analysis and recommendations.

An Overview of the Currency Crisis

When the financial crisis hit Southeast Asian countries such as Thailand, Malaysia, and Indonesia, at first Korea seemed little affected. However, as international investors started to curtail their exposure to risky financial assets in East Asia, Korea, with a high level of short-term debt and relatively moderate international reserves, faced a sharp short-term capital outflow, resulting in foreign debt insolvency and withering foreign confidence in Korean markets. Although its macroeconomic fundamentals were relatively sound in comparison with those of other developing countries that had muddled through the crisis, Korea had structural problems related to the soundness of its financial institutions and the dominance of big conglomerates or chaebols. These structural problems stemmed from the government's growth-oriented intervention in the country's business and financial sectors and from a poor regulatory and supervisory system.

Looking back on the economic environment from the early 1990s to 1997, capital inflow to the five Asian countries (Indonesia, Korea, Malaysia, the Philippines, and Thailand) demonstrated a 95 percent increase, from U.S.$47.4 billion in 1994 to U.S.$92.8 billion in 1996. Direct investment or portfolio investment grew from U.S.$12.2 billion in 1994 to U.S.$19.1 billion in 1996. The inflow of capital to the five Asian countries had increased greatly each year, owing particularly to inflows from Japan. Then the increasing trend suddenly reversed, and the five Asian countries suffered a net private capital outflow amounting to U.S.$12.1 billion in 1997, whereas the net inflow had amounted to U.S.$93 billion in 1996. However, the sharpest decline was in inflows from commercial banks: the direction of borrowings from commercial banks reversed, from a net inflow of U.S.$55.5 billion in 1996 to a net outflow of U.S.$21.3 billion for the five Asian countries in 1997. In Korea alone, a net inflow of borrowings from commercial banks amounted to U.S.$13.1 billion between January and September 1997, but was reversed to a net outflow of U.S.$8.8 billion between October and November 1997.

As table 2-1 shows, the sharp decline in net borrowings by Korea can be attributed to a withdrawal of Japanese banks that refused to roll over maturing contracted loans. The amount of outstanding loans from Japan decreased from U.S.$23.7 billion to U.S.$20.3 billion, accounting for 13.7 percent of the total international lending to Korea at the end of December. Already facing their own crisis as the economy bubble burst in the early 1990s, Japanese banks began to collect maturing debts in the region. Once the Japanese banks, which

Table 2-1. Korea's Foreign Debt by Country, 1996 and 1997
Millions of U.S. dollars

Country	June 1996	December 1996	June 1997	December 1997
France	6,994	8,887	10,070	11,135
Germany	8,529	9,977	10,794	9,616
Japan	22,152	24,324	23,732	20,278
United States	9,582	9,355	9,964	9,533
Total	59,462	70,462	103,432	94,180

Source: Bank for International Settlements (1998).

were most familiar with the Korean economic situation as the largest Korean creditors, started to collect matured short-term debts, other countries' banks followed suit in short order, abruptly prompting the liquidity squeeze on the Korean foreign exchange. As a result, U.S.$34.2 billion in private capital flowed out of Korea in a few short months, including U.S.$9.2 billion collected by international banks and U.S.$25 billion of short-term capital.

Facing the difficulties of Korean banks in rolling over their short-term foreign liabilities, the Bank of Korea shifted its foreign exchange reserves to offshore branches, and the government announced a guarantee of foreign borrowing by Korean banks. In spite of this measure, external financing conditions for Korean banks deteriorated significantly in late October, and the won fell sharply. Monetary policy was tightened for a while, but was relaxed in light of the impact of higher interest rates on the highly leveraged corporate sector. By early December the won depreciated by over 20 percent against the U.S. dollar, and the usable foreign reserves declined to U.S.$6 billion from U.S.$22.5 billion at the end of October.

According to Kim and Rhee, the high ratio of short-term external debts to total debts was in part attributable to the policies the government had mistakenly made in the process of financial liberalization.[2] The government provided financial institutions with great incentives to borrow for the short term by making it mandatory for them to notify authorities of long-term foreign debts, whereas short-term loans, regarded as trade-related financing, were not so regulated. Therefore, banks and firms operated business on a long-term basis, with short-term capital borrowed abroad. This resulted in a significant discrepancy in the maturity structure. Also, the government expected that the

2. Kim and Rhee (1998).

Table 2-2. Total Korean Foreign Liabilities, 1996 and 1997

Billions of U.S. dollars

Liabilities	December 1996	September 1997	November 1997	December 1997
Foreign debts[a]	104.7	119.7	116.1	120.8
Long-term debts	43.7 (41.7)[b]	54.1 (45.2)	54.5 (47.0)	69.6 (57.6)
Short-term debts	61.0 (58.3)	65.6 (54.8)	61.6 (53.0)	51.2 (42.4)
Offshore borrowings[c]	56.0	50.9	40.8	33.6
Long-term debts	27.0 (30.4)	12.5 (24.6)	10.2 (25.0)	16.4 (48.8)
Short-term debts	39.0 (69.6)	38.4 (75.4)	30.6 (75.0)	17.2 (51.2)
Total external liabilities	160.7	170.6	156.9	154.4
Long-term debts	60.7 (37.8)	66.6 (39.0)	64.7 (41.2)	86.4 (55.7)
Short-term debts	100.0 (62.2)	104.0 (61.0)	92.2 (58.8)	68.4 (44.3)

Source: Financial Statement Analysis, 1997 and 1998, Bank of Korea.

a. Foreign debts are based on the criterion of the International Bank for Reconstruction and Development (IBRD).

b. The numbers in parentheses represent the weights of long-term or short-term debts.

c. Offshore borrowings include borrowings from offshore and overseas branches.

credit rating on bank loans of Korean companies would improve in the international financial market, so it induced financial institutions to transform long-term external debts into short-term debts (see table 2-2).

Economic Developments

The period between 1993 and 1995 was characterized by a smooth recovery from a moderate economic slowdown in 1992. The annual growth in the Korean economy in terms of real gross domestic product (GDP) was spurred from 5.8 percent in 1993 to 9 percent in 1995, and it slowed down moderately to 7.1 percent in 1996. The inflation rate in terms of consumer prices was stable. The unemployment rate was 2.4 percent in 1990 and 2 percent in 1996. The balance of payments deteriorated gradually in line with a mild economic boom, with a deficit of U.S.$8.5 billion in 1995. The deficit enlarged to U.S.$23 billion in 1996.

Until the first quarter of 1997 the economic environment had been satisfactory, with GDP growth rates of over 5 percent annually and unemployment rates below 2.8 percent. However, after experiencing a moderate economic slowdown in 1997, the Korean economy faced a serious recession in the first quarter of 1998. The annual growth rate in terms of real GDP was –3.9 percent in the first quarter and dropped quickly to –6.8 percent in the third quarter of 1998. Reflecting the seriousness of this economic recession, the unemployment rate rose sharply, to 6.5 percent in the first quarter of 1998 and even further, to 8.5 percent, in the first quarter of 1999.

In addition, a series of corporate and bank failures had aggravated the Korean economy since the beginning of 1997. After Hanbo Steel collapsed with U.S.$6 billion in debts in January 1997, big conglomerates such as Sammi, Jinro, and Kia went bankrupt. In response to these bankruptcies, it was revealed that the scale of nonperforming loans in the financial market was much larger than had originally been disclosed. By the end of September 1997, nonperforming loans were estimated to amount to nearly 30 trillion won and over 7 percent of the GDP. This situation further scared off foreign investors and lenders, including Japanese commercial banks.

The IMF Standby Arrangements

According to an IMF report entitled "IMF Supported Programs in Indonesia and Thailand: A Preliminary Assessment," the Korean government, faced with a currency crisis, asked for IMF financial support on November 21, 1997.[3] On December 4, 1997, the executive board of the IMF approved a three-year standby arrangement with Korea amounting to U.S.$21 billion. Financing amounting to U.S.$14 billion had been committed by the World Bank and the Asian Development Bank, and interested countries pledged to lend U.S.$22 billion, for a total package of U.S.$58.4 billion (see table 2-3). To enable greater market confidence, the IMF proposed macro-economic conditionality, aiming to bring about an improvement in the current account, build up foreign exchange reserves, and contain inflation by adopting a tightening monetary policy and some fiscal measures. Also, conditionality encompassed a range of structural reforms in the financial sector.

Upon approval of the conditionality arrangements, Korea drew U.S.$5.5 billion from the fund. Facing difficulties in rolling over short-term debts and exhausting usable international reserves, with the won depreciating rapidly, Korea reached a temporary agreement with private bank creditors on Decem-

---

3. Lane and others (1999).

Table 2-3. Official Foreign Financing Committed to Korea, 1998

Source	In SDRs (billions)	In dollars (billions)	Percent of annual GDP	Percent of quota[a]
Fund	15,500	21.1	5	1,938
Asian Development Bank and World Bank		14.2	3	
Other		23.1	5	
Total package		58.4	13	

Source: International Monetary Fund (1999).

a. The duration of the original arrangements was thirty-six months for Korea.

ber 24, 1997, and negotiations began on rescheduling short-term debts. The won depreciated against the dollar, going from 910 won to the dollar in September to 1,484 won to the dollar in December 1997. Then on December 30 Korea requested a rephrasing of purchases made under the standby agreement to permit an advancement of drawings. At the same time the structural reform agenda of the program was strengthened to accelerate restructuring of the financial sector and facilitate capital inflows into the domestic stock and bond markets. Interest rates had been raised significantly, and conditions for the provision of foreign currency liquidity support to banks had been tightened.

In late December, however, with the rollover of short-term debts down sharply and usable official reserves effectively depleted (notwithstanding the injection of about U.S.$10 billion from the IMF), negotiations with creditor banks became critical. Talks in Japan, the United States, and Europe led to voluntary cooperative understandings on the maintenance of interbank credit lines to Korea through the end of March 1998. At the same time discussions on a framework for voluntary restructuring of short-term debts were initiated. A detailed debt-monitoring system was set up to track the daily rollover rates. In early January the rollover rates rose significantly.

On January 28, 1998, the Korean authorities reached an agreement in principle with a committee of foreign banks on a voluntary restructuring of the short-term debts of thirty-three commercial and specialized banks (including their overseas branches), as well as certain merchant banks. The eligible debts, amounting to some U.S.$24 billion, covered interbank obligations and short-term loans maturing during 1998. According to the Bank for International Settlements data given in table 2-1, in June 1997 Japanese commercial banks lent U.S.$24 billion, accounting for 23 percent of total Korean foreign debts. German, French, and American commercial banks independently lent U.S.$10 billion. When the IMF's executive board approved the original standby arrangement with Korea on December 4, 1997, it was expected that the program, combined with the announcement of a large financing package, would turn market sentiment around. The debt-restructuring agreement was signed on March 31, 1998, with 134 creditor banks from thirty-two countries tendering loans and deposits amounting to U.S.$21.8 billion. The original obligations were exchanged for government-guaranteed debts of one-year maturity at 225 basis points over the London interbank offer rate (LIBOR) (17 percent of the total), two-year maturity at 250 basis points over LIBOR (45 percent of the total), and three-year maturity at 275 basis points over LIBOR (38 percent of the total). As a result of the debt restructuring, Korea's short-term debts declined from U.S.$61 billion at the end of March to U.S.$42 billion at the end of April 1998.

The Content of the Initial Arrangement

According to the letter of intent, the contents of the IMF support agreement between the Korean government and the Fund were as follows. First, macroeconomic policies adjusted to ease the burden of capital flight on the private sector were to be buttressed by tightened monetary policies. Second, structural reforms were to be made to build confidence and stop capital outflows. Third, to further restore foreign investors' confidence, the government promoted the restructuring of big conglomerates, as well as current and capital account liberalization. Therefore, the parts of the IMF conditionality package can be classified into three categories: macroeconomic policy, financial sector and corporate restructuring, and current and capital account liberalization.

MACROECONOMIC POLICY. The initial arrangement projected a GDP growth of 2.5 percent in 1998. Fiscal policy was ascribed a rather modest role in these programs at the time, because the need for external current account adjustment was seen as relatively small. Fiscal policy was therefore originally intended to provide only limited support for a modest current account adjustment, mainly by reversing an initial deterioration of fiscal positions and covering the prospective carrying costs of financial sector restructuring. The budget surplus was to be within about 2 percent of GDP to make room for the costs of restructuring in the financial industry. The fiscal measures to be taken to accomplish this included widening the bases for corporate and income taxes and value-added taxes, with reductions in government expenditure.

Monetary policy was assigned the role of countering downward pressure on exchange rates to contain the overshooting of the exchange rate beyond the degree of real exchange rate adjustment needed in light of underlying fundamentals. It was thought that, if unchecked, such overshooting could trigger depreciation-inflation spirals; also, excessive depreciations could elicit corresponding exchange rate movements in competitor countries, with detrimental effects on the system as a whole. Moreover, continued depreciation would impose substantial burdens on both the corporate and the banking sectors, which were already suffering from overexposure to liabilities in foreign currency.

The program was formulated by setting a ceiling on net domestic assets of the IBRD criterion. The former ceiling was presumed to provide an adequate limit on the growth of broad money. In order to watch developments in the monetary indicators, special attention was given to interest rates.

STRUCTURAL REFORM. Financial sector restructuring stood at the top of the structural reform agenda. The strategy of the program had two broad strands. First, the serious weakness in the balance sheets of financial institutions had to be addressed. Second, the system had to be reformed to minimize the likelihood of a recurrence. The government was to implement a comprehensive restructuring in the financial industry that introduced a clear and firm exit policy for financial institutions, strong market and supervisory discipline, and independence of the central bank. The operations of nine insolvent merchant banks were suspended; two large distressed commercial banks received capital injections from the government, and all commercial banks with inadequate capital were required to submit plans for recapitalization.

In addition, the arrangement envisioned the establishment of transparent and efficient ties among the government, banks, and businesses in order to upgrade their accounting, auditing, and disclosure standards. This required that corporate financial statements be publicized on a consolidated basis and certified by external auditors and that there be a phaseout of the cross guarantee system among conglomerates.

CURRENT AND CAPITAL ACCOUNT LIBERALIZATION. Under the arrangement trade would be liberalized by setting a timetable in line with World Trade Organization commitments to eliminate trade-related subsidies and the import diversification program, as well as to streamline and improve the transparency of import certification procedures. The capital account was to be liberalized by opening up the Korean money, bond, and equity markets to capital inflows and liberalizing foreign direct investment. Labor market reform was also demanded to facilitate the redeployment of labor. Finally, the publication and dissemination of key economic and financial data, including usable foreign reserves, were required.

Adjustment of the Arrangement

The first quarterly review of the standby arrangement, on February 17, 1998, took place against the background of an improving exchange market situation and growing signs of a pronounced decline in economic activity. The agreement with bank creditors had helped to improve financing conditions, the amount of usable reserves had increased, and the won had appreciated by nearly 20 percent by late December 1997. With domestic demand contracting, the revised program was based on lower (but still marginally positive) growth projections. The fiscal target for 1998 was lowered from a surplus of 0.2 percent of GDP in the original program (including bank restructuring costs) to a deficit of 0.8 percent of GDP. The monetary policy was expected to remain tight as long as the exchange market situation remained fragile. Although a number of steps had already been taken to implement the arrangement's comprehensive structural reform agenda, commitments in several areas, notably financial sector restructuring and capital account and trade liberalization, were further specified. In addition, based on a tripartite accord between business, labor, and the government, the agenda was broadened to include measures to strengthen the social safety net, increase labor market flexibility, promote corporate restructuring, and enhance corporate governance. Amid these developments, a new government took office in late February 1998.

A supplementary budget was prepared to stimulate a stagnant economy and to strengthen the social safety net. The current account surplus was expected to reach nearly U.S.$35 billion. The projections of annual economic growth were revised downward from –1 percent to –4 percent in the second quarterly review on May 29, 1998. The sharp decline in economic growth increased instability in the Korean economy, causing a sharp rise in the unemployment rate, from 2.3 percent in the second quarter of 1997 to 7 percent in June 1998. Regarding monetary policy, the growth rate of the money supply of M2 decelerated from 5.3 percent at the end of 1997 to 1.5 percent in June 1998, bringing a focus on maintaining exchange market stability.

As a result of these developments the won appreciated gradually against the U.S. dollar, going from 1,505 won to the dollar in January to 1,397 won to the dollar in June 1998. This appreciation enabled the Korean monetary authorities to further decrease interest rates. The call rate in the money market decreased sharply, from 22.47 percent to 16.32 percent annually. Inflation had slowed and was anticipated to be an average of 9 percent for the year. The current account surplus increased to U.S.$33 billion in comparison with the target of U.S.$21 billion. Korea successfully issued a global sovereign bond, with a significant amount of capital flowing into the domestic financial market, and the foreign reserves available exceeded U.S.$30 billion.

In the third quarterly review of the arrangement, on August 28, 1998, the conditionality of the macroeconomic policies was adjusted in order to counter the recession and to strengthen the structural reform agenda. The IMF projected a 5 percent contraction in GDP and a further deceleration in the inflation rate to 8 percent for 1998. In spite of errors in projecting these macroeconomic indicators, the current account surplus reached nearly U.S.$35 billion.[4] Regarding structural reforms, emphasis was placed on the rationalization and strengthening of the banking system as well as the restructuring of the chaebols. By the end of October 1998, U.S.$27.2 billion of the total package of U.S.$58.2 billion had been disbursed, including U.S.$18.2 billion from the IMF and U.S.$9 billion from the World Bank and the Asian Development Bank.

Evaluating the Policies of the IMF and the Korean Government

To be eligible for loans granted by the IMF as part of an IMF rescue program, a recipient country must meet a set of requirements based on the policy objectives proposed by the loan applicant. To receive IMF conditionality, a debtor government must comply with many aspects of macroeconomic policies. Therefore, to evaluate the effectiveness of the IMF rescue program for Korea, it is necessary to examine the IMF conditionality as well as the policy actions concurrently undertaken by the Korean government, especially with regard to big conglomerates with huge bank loans.

Macroeconomic Policies

Regarding monetary policy, although the IMF arrangement achieved its basic objectives by curbing the depreciation-inflation spiral, it also brought about a serious economic recession with a high rate of unemployment. The tightening monetary policy was the major cause of the economic recession. The IMF advises a relevant member country to maintain short-term interest rates at

4. Lane and others (1999).

a fairly high level until the exchange rate stabilizes, and it stresses that maintaining aggregate demand on a sustainable path calls for some control over the flows of domestic financing, and specifically over the rates of monetary and domestic credit expansion. It also stresses the importance of the link between domestic credit expansion and increases in monetary supply, as well as their relationship with aggregate expenditure and income. In other words, it highlights the fact that a discrepancy between the supply and demand for money results in an imbalance between expenditure and income.

In the Korean case the overnight call rate in the money market rose swiftly, from around 12 percent a year in November 1997 to 32 percent in January 1998. Then it decreased radically, to 8.5 percent in September 1998. This radical swing devastated corporations with large debts and increasing financial burdens. The debt-equity ratio amounted to around 400 percent in December 1997. Fund economists will argue against this evaluation by saying that the hike of the nominal call rate did not negatively affect real lending in the manufacturing sector because the real lending rate, calculated on a basis of a three-month moving average, was negative from December 1997 to February 1998. This argument is not valid, because nominal interest rates are essential to the financial position of corporations in the short term. Moreover, the construction industry had already felt the economic slowdown and had to face serious financial burdens at the end of 1997. Therefore, the tight money policy had a further contractionary effect on industries such as construction.[5] The IMF also claims that high interest rates stabilize the exchange rate through two principal

---

5. In addition, the tight money policy had a critical effect on financing for small- and medium-size corporations by increasing immediately through arbitrage the average rate of short-term loans without collateral in the informal money market in Korea. The average lending rate in those markets was 23.7 percent per annum in 1993 and about 25.2 percent from 1985 to 1993. According to *Chosen Nippo Newspaper* (June 1994), the Korean Development Institute estimated that the volume of transactions in the informal money market amounted to about 15 percent of GNP at that time. Fund economists have a tendency to formulate the target of interest rates, quoting interest rates in the informal money markets. This is because they believe the rates in the informal markets are close to the market clearing rates, regarding informal assets as close substitutes for assets in the formal financial markets. Therefore, restoration of a sound relationship between expenditure and income will entail keeping domestic credit expansion in line with the prospective path of desired money holdings in economy. These considerations are behind the emphasis placed on domestic credit expansion as a policy variable in the application of conditionality.

mechanisms. First, if the interest rate differential between domestic and international markets widens due to the high domestic interest rate, this will attract foreign capital and the exchange rate will appreciate. Second, high interest rates will increase savings and decrease consumption and investment, thereby improving the current account. However, this reasoning does not seem persuasive in the Korean case. This is because foreign investors acquire assets denominated in won by taking account of the expected rate of change in value of the won to the dollar. After the IMF arrangement was introduced the won showed huge fluctuations due to speculative currency transactions made by market participants with limited information who were uncertain about the future. In addition, foreign capital inflow slowed despite the high interest rates because the credit risk involved in the payment of principal was too high. Unless uncertainty is reduced, it is very difficult to attract foreign capital through high interest rates. The Korean case suggests that the gap between domestic and international interest rates is not in itself a sufficient condition for stabilization of the exchange rate through interest arbitrage.

In addition, seeking currency stability through high interest rates with the intention of curtailing consumption and boosting savings has its limits in a country like Korea, where savings rates are already very high. Indeed, there are serious empirical and theoretical controversies among economists on this question. For example, in *The East Asian Miracle* the World Bank acknowledged that artificially lowered interest rates (moderate financial repression) may actually have benign or positive effects on economic growth.[6]

Nevertheless, the IMF required the maintenance of high call rates by the Korean government. High call rates induced by the tight monetary policy raised the long- and short-term market interest rates through interest rate arbitrage. This resulted in a series of company bankruptcies, because a higher interest rate increased financing burdens when the debt-equity ratio was already high in Korea. Company bankruptcies then led to the insolvency of financial institutions and scared off foreign investors, decreasing the inflow of foreign capital. Such a tight-money market as the IMF mandated brought further financial disorder to the troubled economy in Korea.

Changing the exchange rate policy was another essential element of the IMF arrangement. The monetary authorities made a decision to float the won rather than readjusting the pegs to rates. Floating the won reduced investors' confidence in future exchange rates. In addition, given the excessive exposure of

6. World Bank (1993).

residents to exchange rate volatility, depreciation of the won had side effects that could destabilize the Korean economy. Therefore, monetary authorities could use monetary policy to defend the won by raising interest rates. As the foreign reserves needed to defend the won were depleted in Korea in usable terms, the authorities replenished them to a level adequate to defend a new peg. This pegging ran the risk of further reducing credibility. Unfortunately, this resulted in abandonment of the new peg. Another concern about repegging was that a rate that could have been defended against short-run market pressures might be much too depreciated to be appropriate to lock in for the medium term. In the present case, the won was depreciated considerably after the inception of the IMF arrangement and far overshot the level consistent with medium-term economic fundamentals, then rebounded in January 1998.

Monetary policy sought to curb the overshooting of nominal exchange rates and evade depreciation-inflation spirals. Without preannounced target rates, however, the rate seemed to be revised frequently in accordance with market conditions. The government's policy of keeping the value of the Korean won high and the miscalculation of capital cost by domestic banks and firms caused the rapid increment of foreign debts in the 1990s. When the current account deficit grew, and therefore the Korean won needed depreciating, the government did not adjust the overvalued currency, but instead financed the deficit with foreign capital inflow by keeping the value of the won high. The overvaluation of the currency led banks and firms to underestimate the cost of foreign capital. Even though such an overvaluation of the currency is temporary, commercial banks and big conglomerates kept expanding their new investments. Once they were heavily indebted to foreign capital, they preferred to adopt an appreciation policy rather than a depreciation policy in order to reduce the cost of servicing their foreign debts. This circular process of currency overvaluation and capital cost underestimation further increased the amount of foreign debts.

Regarding fiscal policy, the IMF prescription of budget cuts also had a critical defect. In the domain of fiscal policy such cuts bring to the forefront issues such as the efficiency and composition of public spending, the structure of the tax system, and the public sector pricing policy, all of which are critical for efficient resource allocation. Expansion of aggregate demand in the commodity markets frequently reflects imbalances in the fiscal accounts. The correction of disequilibria originating in public finance encompasses the fiscal dimension of macroeconomic management. This includes the development of policy measures to curtail fiscal spending or raise fiscal revenues to restore viability to public sector finances. The specific mix of measures chosen influences the general performance of the economy, which will vary depending on whether the strategy is based on measures to control outlays or on revenue-raising actions. The former will tend to restore balance to the economy by lowering the weight of the public sector in terms of aggregate demand. In contrast, raising revenue will likely entail a reduction in the share of private demand. The mix of fiscal measures will also influence the speed and certainty of the adjustment process. This is because expenditure reduction and revenue mobilization are not equally effective: a government's ability to control its outlays usually exceeds its ability to increase its receipts.

In Korea the budget had been almost balanced or had shown a slight surplus. The government needed to spend the budgeted amount to bolster social expenditures, including those for unemployment benefits, and to provide resources for business and financial sector restructuring. Therefore, the IMF's prescription of budget cuts, which was a standard way to deal with irresponsible governments running large deficits in their current accounts, was not appropriate for Korea, and in fact became a factor that aggravated the crisis further. Even the preliminary IMF assessment predicted that bank restructuring would cost 75 trillion won or 18 percent of GDP, including 65 trillion in government-guaranteed bonds. The interest cost to the budget in 1998 was estimated at 0.8 percent of GDP. The interest cost to the central government's budget was expected to rise to about 1.5 percent of GDP over the medium term.

Current and Capital Account Liberalization

In spite of excessive exposure to capital movements, Korea had taken important steps to liberalize its capital account prior to the crisis in support of the IMF. The Korean government has gradually implemented trade, capital, and foreign exchange liberalization measures since the early 1980s. However, right after the crisis the government started to float the exchange rate in the market. Korea planned to eliminate trade-related subsidies, restrictive import licensing, and an import diversification program. Capital liberalization enabled foreigners to hold up to 55 percent of the stocks of Korean corporations by the end of 1997, and complete liberalization was enacted at the end of 1998, allowing foreigners to hold 100 percent of the stocks of Korean corporations. In addition, in 1998 purchases of domestic corporate bonds and short-term financial assets by foreigners were allowed without limit, and limits on foreign borrowing by private corporations were abolished.

However, without adequate institutional developments to hedge portfolio investment risks due to currency fluctuations, the Korean economy was directly exposed to high risks in international currency transactions as the exchange rate was completely floated. Even if the stock and bond markets are liberalized, speculative attacks by international institutional investors may lead to destabilized asset prices. Financial markets have to be sufficiently developed to efficiently deal with uncertainty through the futures market, with new financial instruments introduced to cope with currency risk and improve risk management techniques.

Management of External Debts

The amount of real external debt is the total sum of foreign liabilities, including both the official figure and the figure for offshore borrowings of the private sector as well. Korean banks operate abroad and conduct transactions involving huge amounts of foreign currency. The problem was that nobody knew the exact amount of the total external liabilities because commercial banks and big conglomerates operated businesses with capital financing abroad. After the IMF bailout program began, the total external liabilities of Korea amounted to U.S.$170.6 billion, which was a sum 1.5 times larger than that of the country's official foreign debts.

Including local loans by the business sector from foreign banks, Korea's total liabilities were estimated to be over U.S.$190 billion as of September 1997, which was about 45 percent of GDP, the highest since Korea graduated from IMF surveillance at the beginning of the 1980s. The ratio of its external debts to GNP was 53.6 percent, and the ratio of its short-term debts to its external debts was about 33.4 percent in 1982 under the standby arrangements. Moreover, the government did not yet have a clear idea of the amount of offshore borrowings by the local bodies of Korean companies without the payment guarantees of the parent companies, nor of the off-the-record investments in derivatives made by financial institutions.

The inconsistent policy of foreign capital liberalization was directly linked to this expansion of offshore borrowings. Although the government took a very cautious and gradual approach to opening Korea's domestic markets to capital inflow, the restrictions on capital outflow were radically deregulated by admitting domestic commercial banks and big conglomerates to international financial markets. As a result, they borrowed funds in foreign currencies abroad without repatriating them, and the amounts of offshore borrowings mounted quickly. The vulnerability of the Korean economy rapidly increased as its short-term debts came to occupy an excessively large portion of its foreign debts. The ratio of Korea's short-term debts to its total foreign debts was fairly large. This ratio had stayed at the level of 40 to 45 percent before the 1997 financial crisis, but it suddenly increased and reached nearly 60 percent just before the crisis.

As noted earlier, Korean government policy provided financial institutions with incentives to borrow for the short term by making it mandatory that they notify authorities of long-term foreign debts, whereas short-term loans were regarded as trade-related financing and therefore were not especially regulated by the monetary authorities. As a result, banks and firms had been operating on a long-term basis, with short-term capital borrowed abroad, leading to significant discrepancies in the maturity structure of financing. Also, the government's guidance of financial institutions contributed to increases in the amount of short-term external debts. When Korea became a member of the Organization for Economic Cooperation and Development, the government, expecting that the credit rating on Korean loans would be lowered, encouraged financial institutions to transform long-term external debts into short-term debts at a lower interest rate.

The shorter the maturity, the larger the liquidity squeeze when credibility declines. This is precisely the situation in which Korea found itself in 1997. It was asserted that Korea could be protected from volatile capital flows because liquid asset markets were not open to foreigners. But once the country's credibility deteriorated, the short-term capital affected by foreign investors' lack of confidence in Korean markets turned into short-term external debts. In this way international liquidity was squeezed and rollovers of short-term external debts were refused in the private international markets.

Restructuring of Financial Markets

The overeager financial liberalization that was part of the IMF arrangements of the early 1980s resulted in financial turmoil in the mid-1990s due to increasingly futile portfolio investments in corporations made through non-bank financial institutions. Following the liberalization these financial institutions developed quickly, but exhibited limited expertise in corporate financing. Moreover, Korea quickly turned into an economy oriented to direct financing without adequate institutional support. A financial sector in the midst of restructuring was in a premature stage of development, with weak corporate governance and market discipline, a lack of transparent accounting by independent external auditing, and inadequate disclosures of corporate financial positions. In addition, complex informal relationships among monetary authorities, financial institutions, and big conglomerates were also problematic. Traditional regulations and protections for financial institutions, including nationalized commercial banks, failed to build up expertise in credit screening, project evaluation, and risk management. The IMF conditionality practices have been based on a market-supporting institutional framework, so it was necessary to supplement the traditional instruments of conditionality by focusing on the microeconomic and institutional aspects of reform, especially with regard to restructuring the Korean financial sector. The banks associated with the conglomerates in Korea had no incentive to monitor the credit position of a borrower's firm.[7]

Note also that after the 1960s the Korean government had intervened in the bank loan market and made use of financing in the form of policy loans for economic development. This had resulted in expectations that the government would never let big conglomerates fail. As the World Bank reported in *The East Asian Miracle,* the Korean government adopted a credit policy with mild financial repression:

> The predominant source of financial support for Heavy Chemical Industry was preferential policy loans directed to key industries. In 1977, for example, 45 percent of the total domestic credit of the banking system was engineered in direct support of the HCI sector. Implicit interest subsidies to the HCI sector in 1977 alone were an estimated 75 billion won or 0.4 percent of GNP (calculated by applying an interest differential of 3–4 percent vis-à-vis the interest rates for general bank loans).[8]

With limited possibility of bankruptcy, the big conglomerates were given strong incentives and kept expanding without prudential consideration of the associated returns and risks, and banks had little incentive to scrutinize the financial soundness of such borrowers. Also, in 1984 the total share of policy loans (those made in accordance with the preferential lending policy) was reduced to 14 percent, in line with the promotion of the banks' autonomy. The growth-oriented policy of the big conglomerates resulted in the vulnerability of their financial positions. Due to the profligate making of loans by banks, the

7. Nam (1996).
8. World Bank (1993, box 6.3).

financial positions of the thirty leading conglomerates deteriorated to the extent that their debt-equity ratios rose to over 400 percent by the end of 1997. These excessive credits to large businesses characterized the Korean economy as a loan economy. Also, the conglomerates invested a lot of money in assets markets, which are particularly susceptible to the business cycle. Consequently, the big conglomerates became more exposed to business fluctuations and external shocks.

During 1986 and 1987, for example, the share of the conglomerates' total assets invested in nonperforming loans reached almost 10 percent. Between 1985 and 1988, seventy-eight corporations were rationalized. Not until 1993 did the Korean government announce a medium-term plan to transfer policy loans—which still accounted for more than 40 percent of total domestic credit—to separate accounts and to handle their financing through the budget.

Regarding accounting, the financial statements of banks did not always reflect their status accurately, because the accounting standards set by bank regulators were adjusted every year. In order to improve the credibility of financial statements, the Banking Supervisory Authority now enforces accounting standards in accordance with international standards. The disclosure requirements in relation to banks' internal management have also been strengthened. Prudential regulation standards were introduced by incorporating the Basle Core Principles for Effective Banking Supervision in June 1998.[9]

Regarding exit policy, around twenty merchant banks had to cease their operations, and sixteen of these have since had their foreign exchange licenses revoked due to their inability to meet their current liabilities. Also, two securities companies on the brink of insolvency had their licenses revoked, one investment trust management company was dissolved after a run on deposits, and two additional securities companies were ordered to suspend their business. It was decided that nonbank financial institutions such as securities, insurance, and leasing companies that were facing insolvency in the process of bank restructuring should be liquidated forthwith. The remaining institutions, encouraged to raise additional capital from major shareholders, were to seek a management turnaround through their own efforts. If such attempts proved futile, they would in turn be forced to leave the market.

9. Bank for International Settlements (1997).

Conclusion

Integrating domestic capital markets into the world has increased the mutual interdependence of individual countries and increased their exposure to external events and disturbances. At the same time, although it is possible to do so in theory, it remains difficult to fully identify institutional defects of financial markets in practice, whether related to the IMF, governments, or private institutions. Opinions vary greatly, and defects are rarely recognized by all market participants in the world. Therefore, adequately coping with market defects and developing financial institutions that contribute to smooth global growth calls for willingness and eagerness to invest financial and human resources in researching means of financial development that can be regarded as international public goods. Although some progress has been made, the Korean experience certainly shows that we have not yet accumulated sufficient knowledge about how best to structure financial markets in developing economies.

References

Bank for International Settlements. 1997. "Core Principles for Effective Banking Supervision." Basle: BIS.

———. 1998. "The Maturity, Sectoral, and Nationality Distribution of International Bank Lending." Basle: BIS (January).

International Monetary Fund. 1997. "IMF Supported Programs in Indonesia and Thailand: A Preliminary Assessment." Washington: IMF (January).

———. 1999. "IMF-Supported Programs in Indonesia, Korea, and Thailand: A Preliminary Assessment." Washington: IMF.

Kim, In-June, and Yeongseop Rhee. 1998. "The Korean Currency Crisis and the IMF Program: An Insider's View." In *East Asian Development Model and Economic Crisis.* Seoul University.

Lane, Timothy, Atish R. Ghosh, Javier Hamann, and others. 1999. "IMF-Supported Programs in Indonesia, Korea, and Thailand: A Preliminary Assessment." Washington: International Monetary Fund.

Nam, Sang-Woo. 1996. "The Principal Transactions Bank System in Korea and a Search for a New Bank-Business Relationship." In *Financial Deregulation and Integration in East Asia,* edited by Takatoshi Ito and Anne O. Krueger. University of Chicago Press.

World Bank. 1993. *The East Asian Miracle: Economic Growth and Public Policy.* Oxford University Press.

CHAPTER THREE

Indonesia:
Long Road to Recovery

Steven Radelet

The Indonesian economy collapsed brutally in April 1998, shrinking by an estimated 14 percent. The speed and magnitude of the economic disintegration was stunning. The Indonesian economy had grown by an average of more than 7 percent a year between 1990 and 1996, and it grew by 5 percent in 1997. The turnaround of 19 percentage points in economic growth in one year is among the most dramatic economic collapses recorded since the Great Depression. Both foreign and domestic investors fled, and hundreds of corporations went bankrupt. The banking system ground to a halt, with very little new lending taking place and dozens of banks insolvent. Imports during the first eleven months of 1998 were 35 percent below their 1997 level (in terms of U.S. dollars), indicating the extent to which domestic demand plummeted. Thousands of Indonesians lost their jobs, and millions more faced a substantial reduction in their standard of living. There is no immediate prospect of a quick economic rebound. The government projected zero growth for fiscal year 1999–2000, but most private sector analysts predicted that the economy would contract in 1999 by an additional 3 to 4 percent. Moreover, in early 1998 the

I thank Karl Jackson, John Bresnan, Joe Stern, Soedradjad Djiwandono, and participants at the Chung-Hua Institution for Economic Research/Brookings conference held on April 5, 1999, for their comments on an earlier draft. Thanks, too, to Mumtaz Hussain for his superb research assistance and to Susan Baker and Peter Rosner for providing valuable background information. All opinions and errors are my own.

economic crisis quickly cascaded into a major political crisis, with long-time strongman President Suharto resigning in May. In the political vacuum left after his departure, social tensions rose and violence became commonplace.

This chapter, written before the parliamentary elections of June 1999, examines the collapse of the Indonesian economy and the most pressing economic problems inhibiting its recovery. It explores several weaknesses that emerged in the economy in the early 1990s, including a high level of dependence on short-term foreign borrowing, a weak banking system, a modestly overvalued exchange rate, and the seemingly unbridled growth of the business interests of the family and associates of President Suharto. These serious problems left the economy vulnerable to a significant slowdown. However, on their own they cannot explain the magnitude and speed of the Indonesian collapse. Mismanagement of the crisis by the Indonesian government, especially President Suharto, and by the International Monetary Fund (IMF) made the contraction much deeper than was necessary or inevitable. The last section of the chapter explores several of the most pressing problems facing policymakers as they try to end the contraction and return Indonesia to a path of economic growth.

A Brief Economic History

Indonesia recorded one of the fastest growth rates in the world between 1970 and 1996. The economy grew by 7.2 percent a year, propelling an annual increase of 5.1 percent in per capita income. As a result, real annual income for the average Indonesian was nearly *four times* higher in 1996 than it was in 1970. Moreover, when the Indonesian experience is compared to that of many countries, these gains were spread fairly equitably. For example, between 1976 and 1990 income per person in the poorest quintile of Indonesia's population grew by 5.8 percent per year, whereas the average income of the entire population grew by 4.9 percent a year.[1] Indonesia's rapid growth was translated into the largest reduction in poverty recorded anywhere in the world during the period. In 1970 more than 60 percent of Indonesia's population was below the official poverty line, but by 1996 the share living in poverty had fallen to 11 percent, according to official estimates. Although some analysts dispute the

---

1. Gallup, Radelet, and Warner (1998). Some analysts argue that the income of the richest 2 or 3 percent of the population grew faster than that of anyone else. Although this is entirely plausible (and in my own opinion likely), there are no data to support or refute this claim.

precise magnitude of these numbers, no one doubts that Indonesia recorded a remarkable drop in abject poverty during the past three decades. A range of other social indicators bears out this success. Life expectancy at birth increased from forty-nine years to sixty-five years, adult literacy rates jumped from 57 percent to 84 percent, and infant mortality rates fell from 114 per thousand to 49 per thousand.[2]

Four pillars supported Indonesia's rapid growth. First, during the 1970s the country primarily relied on its rich and diverse base of natural resources, including oil and gas, copper, tin, gold, rubber, and palm oil. Revenues from exports of these products financed widespread construction of roads and ports, an expansion of primary schools, and other infrastructure improvements. Although there was clearly extensive waste and abuse, Indonesia managed its resources far better than most resource-abundant developing economies during the 1970s and 1980s.

Second, starting in the early 1970s agricultural output grew steadily, supported by green revolution technologies that rapidly increased rice production on Java and some of the outer islands. The government offered remunerative and relatively stable prices to rice farmers, consciously preferring to offer farmers adequate returns rather than provide huge subsidies for consumers. It further supported agriculture with large investments in irrigation and other forms of agricultural infrastructure and by connecting villages to larger markets through construction of new roads.

Third, the government actively promoted a switch toward labor-intensive manufactured exports, especially beginning in the mid-1980s after the fall in world oil prices. Exports of textiles, clothing, footwear, toys, furniture, and other products soared, providing thousands of jobs and establishing a conduit for the introduction of new technologies. Barriers to foreign investment were rapidly (albeit not completely) dismantled during the late 1980s and early 1990s, at least in many sectors. Indonesian firms quickly became more integrated with globalized production networks.

Fourth, able economic managers adopted prudent macroeconomic policies that kept the budget basically in balance, inflation rates low, exports competitive, and the current account deficit at reasonable levels. Effective economic management helped Indonesia steer through the difficulties of the steep oil price hikes and declines in the 1970s and 1980s and kept the macroeconomy largely in balance right up to the onset of the crisis in mid-1997. The govern-

2. World Bank (1998a).

ment essentially proscribed domestic financing for the budget, a strategy that kept both expenditures and monetary growth under reasonable control. Between 1992 and 1996 inflation averaged 8 percent a year, the budget balance was slightly positive, and the current account deficit averaged 2.7 percent of the gross domestic product (GDP).

Emerging Vulnerabilities

Although the Indonesian economy was growing rapidly and most macroeconomic indicators were relatively healthy, there were several growing problems.[3] Four stand out: large capital inflows, a large portion of which was of a short-term nature; a slightly overvalued exchange rate and slowing export growth; a weak banking system; and the rapidly growing business interests of President Suharto and his family and close associates.

With regard to the first problem, between 1990 and 1996 Indonesia received capital inflows averaging about 4 percent of GDP. Although these inflows were not nearly as large as those received by Thailand (10 percent of GDP) and Malaysia (9 percent of GDP), they still amounted to a large amount of capital for the economy to absorb. Right up until the onset of the crisis, foreign creditors were eager to provide financing to Indonesia, especially through bank loans. By mid-1997 Indonesia's total debt outstanding to foreign commercial banks amounted to U.S.$59 billion. As shown in table 3-1, Indonesian banks owed about U.S.$12 billion of this amount, whereas Indonesian corporations owed about U.S.$40 billion (with the balance of U.S.$7 billion owed by the government). Although much of this financing was used for productive investment projects, a significant amount went to weaker projects, many of which were controlled by the Suharto family and their associates. Foreign lenders were more than happy to finance these projects, often without undertaking adequate risk analysis. In some cases creditors provided financing to poor projects because they believed the projects carried an implicit guarantee from the government. More important, however, most creditors simply believed that rapid growth would continue, so that even marginal projects would be able to pay off their loans.

The key to Indonesia's vulnerability was the maturity structure of the foreign borrowing rather than the total magnitude of these flows. Of the U.S.$59

3. For discussions of some of these issues in relation to the other countries affected by the crisis, see Radelet and Sachs (1998a, 1998b).

Table 3-1. Indonesian Debt Outstanding to Foreign Commercial Banks, 1997 and 1998

Billions of U.S. dollars

Period	Debt by sector					Foreign reserves (excluding gold)
	Total	Banks	Public	Nonbank private	Short-term debt	
June 1997	58.7	12.4	6.5	39.7	34.7	20.3
December 1997	58.4	11.7	6.9	39.7	35.4	16.6
June 1998	50.3	7.1	7.6	35.5	27.7	17.9

Period	Bank claims on Indonesia by country of origin					
	Total	Japan	United States	Germany	Other European	All others
June 1997	58.7	23.2	4.6	5.6	16.9	8.4
December 1997	58.4	22.0	4.9	6.2	17.1	7.9
June 1998	50.3	19.0	3.2	5.9	16.1	4.2

Sources: Debt data: Bank for International Settlements (1998); reserves: International Monetary Fund, *International Financial Statistics* (various issues).

billion owed to foreign banks in mid-1997, U.S.$35 billion was in the form of short-term debt that was due for payment within one year. In addition to this amount, Indonesian firms had taken out substantial lines of short-term credit in foreign currencies from Indonesian banks, adding to the short-term foreign currency exposure of Indonesian firms. By comparison, Indonesia's foreign exchange reserves in mid-1997 totaled about U.S.$20 billion, so the short-term debts owed to foreign commercial banks were about 1.75 times the size of Indonesia's total foreign exchange reserves.

Indonesian firms found short-term foreign currency loans appealing since they generally carried relatively low interest rates. Firms assumed they would be able to easily roll over the loans when they fell due, and in fact they did so for several years, until mid-1997. Indonesia's exchange rate system added to the appeal of short-term debt. In the mid-1980s Indonesia adopted a crawling peg, and the rupiah depreciated between 3 and 5 percent per year with little variation in the trend. The predictability of the exchange rate made short-term dollar loans seem much less risky, and therefore much more attractive. This predictability also undercut the incentives for firms to hedge against their exposure to exchange rate movements. According to one estimate, hedging added about 6 percentage points to the cost of borrowing.[4] Very few firms covered their exposure.

Indonesia's vulnerability was all the greater because its largest creditors were Japanese banks, which supplied about 40 percent of the total credit from foreign banks (Korean banks apparently were also large lenders, but the exact amounts are unavailable, since the Bank for International Settlements [BIS] tracks Korea as a borrower rather than as a creditor country).The underlying weaknesses of Japanese banks made them more likely to try to quickly pull their loans once the crisis started. Apparently this may have been just what happened. In mid-August 1997, as Thailand reached agreement with the IMF on its first program, Japanese banks agreed to keep U.S.$19 billion in trade and other credit facilities open for certain Thai commercial bank borrowers. Japanese banks did not want to be caught in a similar situation in other countries, so they apparently began to withdraw their credits from Indonesia, Malaysia, Korea, and other countries in the region, helping to spread the crisis.

Indonesia's slowly crawling peg contributed to the second problem: a modestly overvalued exchange rate and slowing export growth. As prices for many nontraded Indonesian goods and services grew in the early 1990s, the rupiah became increasingly overvalued.[5] This trend accelerated after the U.S. dollar began to appreciate against the Japanese yen in 1995, meaning that the rupiah was appreciating against the yen. Between 1990 and mid-1997 the rupiah appreciated approximately 22 percent in real terms.[6] Growth in Indonesia's non-oil exports slowed from an annual average of 26 percent in 1991 and 1992 to 14 percent between 1993 and 1995 and to just 10 percent in 1996 and 1997. The overvaluation and export slowdown, although smaller than in the other Asian countries that experienced crisis, clearly pointed toward the need for some moderate adjustments to reestablish the international competitiveness of Indonesian firms.

Indonesia's third problem was its financial system, especially its banks. Beginning in the late 1980s, Indonesia began a series of initiatives and reforms aimed at opening and expanding its financial sector. Privately owned banks were allowed to operate and compete directly with the large state-owned banks that had long controlled financial activities. The government substantially reduced (although it did not eliminate) the extent of state-directed lending, giving the

4. World Bank (1998b).
5. Radelet (1996).
6. Radelet and Sachs (1998a).

banks much more leeway in their lending decisions. Bank capitalization requirements were eased, and the number of banks more than doubled, to well
over 200 between 1988 and 1993. The government also moved to deregulate
equity, bond, insurance, and other financial activities, although these did not
expand as quickly as banking. These changes were encouraged and generally
applauded by the international community. Indeed, financial deregulation
brought many benefits to the economy by diminishing the role of the state in
allocating credit, providing Indonesians with many more options for financial
services, and reducing the costs of financial intermediation.

However, the government did not develop the supervisory and regulatory
capacity needed to keep up with the greatly expanded and more sophisticated
financial system. Some banks—especially state-owned banks—were undercapitalized or allowed to violate other prudential regulations without penalty.
Several large business groups opened their own banks, using bank deposits to
finance their own activities with little scrutiny. As a result, many banks had
substantial exposure to affiliated companies. In addition, the state-owned banks in
particular had large exposures to firms controlled by the Suhartos and their
friends, and few of these loans were fully paid off.

The problems in the banking system were relatively well known, and efforts
were made between 1993 and 1997 to clean them up. In fact, some progress
was made. Ironically, many banks were much weaker in 1993 and 1994 than
they were in 1997 at the onset of the crisis. The number of nonperforming loans
(NPLs) rose quickly in the early 1990s, especially following a major monetary
contraction in early 1991. But they declined in subsequent years as banks
regained profitability and were able to write off some bad loans. For example,
the share of NPLs in privately owned banks fell from 11 percent in 1992 to 5
percent in 1996 as a core of relatively well-run private banks began to develop.
The World Bank, in a report on Indonesia issued just before the onset of the
crisis, concluded that "the quality of commercial bank portfolios continued to
improve during 1996, albeit slowly."[7]

Although Indonesian banks borrowed offshore, they had accumulated far
less foreign debt by mid-1997 than banks in Thailand or Korea. Indonesian
banks owed about U.S.$12 billion to foreign banks in mid-1997, compared to
the U.S.$26 billion and U.S.$67 billion owed by Thai and Korean banks,
respectively. One reason for this pattern is that in 1991, as foreign borrowing
began to grow, the Indonesian government introduced limits on offshore bor-

7. World Bank (1997).

Table 3-2. Indonesian Stock and Land Values, 1990–97

	Stock price index		Capital value: Grade A office space in Jakarta
Period	Rupiah[a]	U.S.$[b]	(U.S.$/square meter)
End of 1990	418	100	3,019
End of 1991	247	57	2,788
End of 1992	274	61	2,327
End of 1993	589	127	2,402
End of 1994	470	97	2,358
End of 1995	514	102	2,179
End of 1996	637	123	2,250
End of Q2 97	725	136	2,267

Sources: DataStream and Jones Lang Wootten.

a. Jakarta Composite Price Index.

b. 1990 = 100.

rowing by commercial banks, the government, and state-owned enterprises. The government did not explicitly limit foreign borrowing by private companies, arguing that private sector borrowing decisions were best left to the market. Partly as a result, the vast majority of Indonesia's foreign borrowing in the early 1990s was by private firms. Ironically, what seemed a prudent measure at the time may have partly backfired: when the crisis hit, it was much more difficult to restructure debts owed by Indonesia's diffuse private sector firms than it was to deal with the more limited number of debtors (mostly banks) in Korea and Thailand.

The credit growth of Indonesian commercial banks was rapid, but not enormously so. The amount of credit extended to the private sector grew about 20 percent per year in the early 1990s. By mid-1997 the total stock of claims outstanding to the private sector by Indonesian banks was the equivalent of about 56 percent of GDP, compared to over 140 percent of GDP in Thailand, Malaysia, and Korea. Lending in Indonesia financed a diffuse set of activities. Some loans financed large utility projects (especially in electricity generation), heavy industries such as the petrochemicals industry, and consumer durables such as automobiles. Other loans went into property and real estate, especially in Jakarta, but there was not a property boom akin to that in Bangkok. As shown in table 3-2, property prices in Jakarta remained essentially unchanged (in terms of U.S. dollars) between 1992 and mid-1997. Still other loans financed the purchase of portfolio equities in the stock market. Again, however, the rise in stock prices was not abnormally large, registering a 7 percent average annual increase between 1990 and the end of 1996 and a 16 percent average increase in 1995 and 1996. By comparison, the yield on one-month central bank certificates averaged about 13 percent in 1995 and 1996. There was much less of a boom-bust cycle in asset markets preceding the crisis in Indonesia than there was in Thailand. In this regard, Krugman's description of the Asian crisis as predominately a boom-bust story may resonate for Thailand, but is far from a complete story in Indonesia.[8]

Indonesia's fourth major problem was the rapid expansion of the business interests of the family and close allies of President Suharto, especially his children. Of course corruption and cronyism had long been features of the Indonesian economy. Special economic favors were given to the military and a small circle of businessmen throughout the 1970s and 1980s. In the late 1980s and early 1990s, however, Suharto's children came of age and became involved in a growing range of businesses, including those involving shipping of oil and gas, production of petrochemicals, and clove marketing, as well as hotels, toll roads, and a plethora of others. The children seemed to be involved in almost every large business deal consummated in the mid-1990s. Foreign creditors were more than happy to lend them money, believing (with good reason) that the government was unlikely to allow their businesses to fail. Perhaps most important, Suharto seemed unwilling to rein in his children's businesses, even during difficult economic times. One of the hallmarks of Suharto's economic management in the past had been his ability and willingness to make difficult decisions and cut back on special favors to his cronies during economic downturns, but he seemed far less willing to do so when his children's business interests were at stake.

At a broader level, Indonesia's rapid economic development was not matched by similar political and institutional development. As President Suharto consolidated his power during the 1970s and 1980s, he tolerated no political opposition or discourse. Decisionmaking and power were extraordinarily centralized. The two opposition political parties were tightly controlled and offered only token opposition. Presidential elections were carefully orchestrated, with Suharto running unopposed in all seven of his election campaigns. Even after thirty years in office, he was never able to bring himself to groom a successor, and he failed to put into place any institutions that might ensure a smooth transition of power. His tight control extended to

8. Krugman (1998).

essentially all the country's most important legal, social, government, and business institutions.

In summary, Indonesia suffered from a growing number of problems in the mid-1990s, and adjustments and reforms were clearly required. As a result of these problems a withdrawal of financing, a reduction in productive investment, and a modest recession would not have been surprising, and perhaps would have been beneficial to the economy in the long run by helping to bring about needed adjustments. However, as significant as were these growing weaknesses, they do not, on their own, add up to an economic crisis of the magnitude that Indonesia experienced beginning in late 1997. Most of these problems were well known, and yet no one predicted a crisis in Indonesia. Even after the crisis started and observers had taken a closer look at the economy, few believed the situation would lead to a major contraction. For example, an IMF press release of November 5, 1997—several months after the crisis had started—predicted an economic growth of 3 percent for Indonesia in 1998. Sadly, it was not to be. To account for the full depth of Indonesia's collapse, one must look at how the Indonesian government and the IMF managed the crisis, and how, partly because of their mismanagement, the economic crisis quickly spun into a political crisis.

Crisis Management

Indonesia was widely praised in the early stages of the crisis for taking swift and appropriate action. The government widened the trading band on the rupiah, then let it float before it spent down its foreign exchange reserves in what would have been a futile and wasteful defense of the currency. It sharply raised interest rates in August, such that overnight interbank rates rose by a factor of six (for a brief period of time), from 15 percent at the end of June 1997 to as high as 98 percent on August 20. Interbank interest rates remained around three times their precrisis level in the months that followed, far higher than in the other countries that experienced crisis (see figure 3-1). The government postponed several large investment projects and quickly eased restrictions governing foreign direct investment. Most observers believed that Indonesia would be much less affected by the crisis than its neighbors.[9] The IMF described

9. On September 5, 1997, for example, following the government's easing of foreign investment rules, the *Asian Wall Street Journal* ran the following headline: "In Battle for Investors, This Is No Contest: Amid a Crisis, Indonesia Opens Up and Thrives as Malaysia Stumbles."

Figure 3-1. Exchange Rate and Interest Rates, July 1997 through March 1999

Rate (July 1, 1997 = 100)

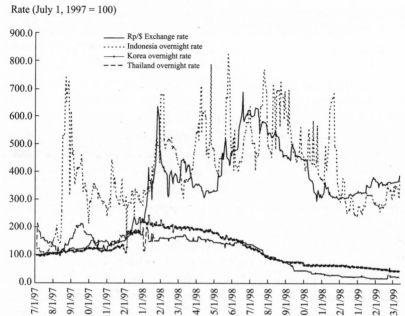

Source: Datastream Online.

Indonesia's initial response as "timely and broadly appropriate."[10] In mid-October 1997 the central bank's foreign exchange reserves amounted to U.S.$20 billion, about the same as they had been at the end of June. In other words, Indonesia did not make the same mistake Thailand had made—and Korea would later make—in using up its foreign exchange reserves.

Ultimately, however, the Indonesian crisis was badly mismanaged by both Suharto and the IMF. Suharto's unwillingness to enforce policies that might damage the business interests of his family and close associates, his inconsistency, and ultimately his confrontational approach undermined confidence and accelerated Indonesia's economic contraction. The IMF's lack of familiarity with the Indonesian economy and its key institutions and its poorly conceived economic restructuring program did the economy far more harm than good. Together they took a bad situation and made it much worse than it should have been.

10. "IMF Approves Stand-by Credit for Indonesia." IMF Press Release 97/50, November 5, 1997.

The first bad sign came before the IMF entered the scene, in early September. The government postponed 150 investment projects, only to announce several days later that fifteen of the biggest would be allowed to go forward. The fact that Suharto's close associates controlled all fifteen of these projects was an early indication that Suharto would resist reforms that directly affected his friends.

In mid-October the government called in the IMF, and the two parties reached agreement on Indonesia's first reform program on October 31. The government's decision to call in the IMF was curious: the central bank had not depleted its reserves, Indonesia's early handling of the crisis had been widely praised (other than the reversal of the fifteen investment projects), and a relatively strong group of economic managers was in place. One possible reason it did so was that these managers had some doubts as to whether Suharto would be willing to take action, and they brought in the IMF to provide support and pressure for what they assumed would be an appropriately designed reform program, accompanied by sufficient financing.

From the outset, however, the IMF program was badly designed to deal with Indonesia's basic economic problems—the loss of confidence of foreign creditors, rapid withdrawals of short-term credits, and a weak banking system. The IMF sent in a team of people unfamiliar with Indonesia and expected them to design a comprehensive economic restructuring program in about two weeks. Given this foundation, it is perhaps not surprising that things went so badly. The IMF program had three basic components: tighter fiscal and monetary policies, financial reforms based on bank closures, and a range of other structural reforms aimed at specific sectors.[11] The first two merit some elaboration.

Tighter Fiscal and Monetary Policies

According to the IMF's press release, the first priority of the program was to generate a fiscal surplus of 1 percent of GDP. Putting tight fiscal policies at the top of the agenda was odd, since excess demand was not at the root of Indonesia's problems and the capital withdrawals already well under way meant that the economy was already contracting significantly. The initial fiscal tightening simply added to the contraction, further undermining investors' confidence in the short-term economic outlook and adding to the capital flight that was under way. Several months later the IMF recognized this mistake and

11. "IMF Approves Stand-by Credit for Indonesia."

ndonesia (as it did in Thailand and Korea), but
done. The IMF also aimed to keep monetary
terbank lending rates, after their initial huge jump in
nd three times their precrisis level in September and
Oct͟   larger rise in interest rates than in either Thailand or
Korea, as s͟   gure 3-1), and they remained high after the IMF program
was introduced. ͟   and Stiglitz show that higher interest rates had little of
the salutatory effect on the exchange rate in Indonesia that those designing the
IMF program had hoped they would.[12] However, higher interest rates did
weaken the financial conditions of both corporations and banks.

Financial Reform through Bank Closures

As described earlier, there is little doubt that Indonesia's banking system was
weak, poorly supervised, and in need of substantial reforms. Many banks
needed to be closed. The important issues in October 1997 were which banks
to target, how to close or merge them, when to do it, and how to otherwise
restructure the financial system. The IMF program called for a sudden closure
of sixteen banks on November 1, 1997, in an attempt to send a strong signal to
foreign investors that the government was serious about reform. Unfortunately,
the closures were very hastily and poorly conceived and were not accompanied
by a comprehensive strategy to appropriately restructure the financial system
(for example, recapitalizing certain banks, restructuring the assets and liabilities of both the closed banks and those that remained open, protecting
depositors, and so on).

The bank closures backfired badly. In its preoccupation with sending a
signal to foreign investors the IMF ignored the fact that there was no deposit
insurance in place and failed to take into consideration how depositors in other
banks would react. The bank closures caused a series of bank runs (adding to
the withdrawal of bank deposits, which had been under way for several months)
that seriously undermined the rest of the banking system, including healthy
banks. The IMF later estimated that the closures sparked withdrawals of U.S.$2
billion from the banking system in November and December and caused a shift
in deposits from private banks to state-owned banks (which depositors believed
were safer). In addition, since it was not clear what would happen to the
creditors of the closed banks, creditors of other Indonesian banks became more

12. Furman and Stiglitz (1998).

anxious to withdraw their loans. Far from enge█████
exacerbated the ongoing liquidity squeeze in fina█████
more difficult for all banks to continue their norma█████
now widely recognized by both the World Bank a█████
closures were a mistake.[13]

The IMF program was equally misguided in its bank ███████████on plans. Before the crisis Bank Indonesia (BI) had required b█████ maintain a minimum capital adequacy ratio (CAR) of 8 percent (the minimum standard recommended by the BIS), and it had planned to increase the statutory minimum to 9 percent at the end of 1997. With the banking system clearly under a great deal of stress and bank capital quickly eroding because of the exchange rate collapse, the IMF initially allowed for no forbearance. It not only required that Indonesian banks maintain an 8 percent CAR, but actually explicitly required that BI maintain the requirement of increasing the CAR to 9 percent at the end of December 1997. This gave the banks just two months to recapitalize to well above their precrisis levels. Under the conditions prevailing in the market in Jakarta at the time, banks had little choice but to stop new lending, thus further adding to the economic contraction. Only after the banking system had seized up in January 1998 did the IMF finally consider temporary forbearance and allow BI to lower the CAR.

The bank closures were bad enough, but Suharto immediately made the situation worse. One of the closed banks was owned by his son, who publicly threatened legal action to keep his bank open. Within a few weeks he was allowed to open a new bank—using the same buildings and employees. This was taken as a clear sign that Suharto was not committed to making the difficult decisions necessary to turn things around.

The government had a very difficult time managing monetary policy in the aftermath of the closures. Bank Indonesia, clearly stunned by the bank runs and without a comprehensive financial restructuring strategy in place, began to issue large amounts of liquidity credits to keep troubled banks open. Between November 1997 and June 1998, BI issued approximately Rp 130 billion (around

13. Goldstein (1998) concludes that Indonesia's mistake was that it did not close enough banks at the outset of the program. This argument ignores the fundamental problems with the IMF's approach: it was done too hastily, there was no deposit insurance in place, and there was no strategy for dealing with the liabilities and assets (both good and bad) of either the closed banks or those that remained open. In this context, closing even more banks would have stopped the payments system (and the economy) even more abruptly and with more damage.

they su   illion) of liquidity credits. These credits added substantially to the
     ne of   ly and helped ignite inflation in early 1998. Moreover, although
son   e credits went to relatively decent banks with legitimate needs, a
significa   unt went to banks owned by Suharto's friends.

The IMF   r strongly criticized Indonesia for these large credits, with some justification, and frequently pointed to them as a sign that Indonesia was not willing to take strong action. However, to a very large degree the liquidity credits were a direct result of the IMF-mandated bank closures (and the lack of an adequate financial restructuring strategy in the IMF program). The IMF itself made the connection clear in its Memorandum of Economic and Financial Policies with Indonesia of January 15, 1998:

> Following the closure of 16 insolvent banks in November last year, customers concerned about the safety of private banks have been shifting sizeable amounts of deposits to state and foreign banks, while some have been withdrawing funds from the banking system entirely. [Para. 14.] These movements in deposits have greatly complicated the task of monetary policy, because they have led to a bifurcation of the banking system. By mid-November, a large number of banks were facing growing liquidity shortages, and were unable to obtain sufficient funds in the interbank market to cover this gap, even after paying interest rates ranging up to 75 percent. At the same time, another smaller group of banks [the state and foreign banks] were becoming increasingly liquid, and were trading among themselves at a relatively low JIBOR (Jakarta Interbank Offer Rate) of about 15 percent. As this segmentation continued to increase, while the stress on the banking system intensified, Bank Indonesia was compelled to act. It provided banks in distress with liquidity support, while withdrawing funds from banks with excess liquidity, thereby raising JIBOR to over 30 percent in early December, where it has since remained. [Para. 15.] Nevertheless, despite this increase in interest rates—to levels higher than in any other country in the region—the problems of the Rupiah have only intensified. [Para. 16.]

These events demonstrate precisely why abrupt bank closures are such a bad idea in the midst of a panic: such changes, when made quickly (and primarily to show the government's determination and resolve rather than as part of a well-designed strategy) are likely to be poorly designed and badly implemented and therefore will add to the confusion and panic rather than reestablish confidence. Given these problems, it is ironic that Indonesia was later roundly criticized for not fully implementing the IMF's prescriptions, since the government initially did exactly what the IMF demanded. The disastrous bank

closures created doubts about the efficacy of the IMF program, they
certainly added to the government's reluctance to follow the IMF'
later critical junctures.

An additional flaw in the original IMF program was that it p   d only a
very minimal amount of financing to ease Indonesia's enc   us liquidity
squeeze. The newspaper headlines proclaimed that the international community had pledged U.S.$40 billion in support, but in reality the amount was
much smaller. First, rather audaciously, the IMF counted U.S.$5 billion as
Indonesia's contribution to its own program! Second, U.S.$17 billion repre-
sented "second line of defense" pledges from a variety of governments. None
of this support materialized in the first year of the program. Third, and by far
most important, the IMF planned to make very little financing available to
Indonesia early in the program, when it was most needed. The IMF program
scheduled Indonesia to receive U.S.$3 billion in November 1997 and nothing
else for at least five months, with the next disbursement scheduled for March
1998. This was a woefully inadequate amount of financing to engender
confidence and stop Indonesia's panic. By comparison, Korea received over
U.S.$10 billion in financing and arranged a U.S.$22 billion debt rescheduling
in the first two months of its program, which immediately halted the financial
panic in that country. Note that the small amount of up-front financing in
Indonesia was not the result of the political turmoil that developed in 1998, nor
was it a penalty for noncompliance with the program. It was an explicit part of
the first IMF program of November 1997.

Following a brief rally after the signing of the agreement regarding the first
IMF program, the rupiah continued to depreciate and Indonesian stock prices
continued to fall, more or less in line with movements in Thailand, Malaysia,
and Korea. In early December the signing of the agreement relating to Korea's
first program with the IMF led to renewed flight from Asian currencies,
including the rupiah. The very next day, rumors that Suharto had fallen ill sent
shudders through the markets, and stocks and the currency plunged briefly
before rebounding somewhat the following week. Suharto's illness raised the
possibility that he would be unable to lead effectively during the crisis or that
he might suddenly die without a clear successor in place. This sudden reminder
of Suharto's advanced age and mortality, as well as the lack of political
institutions to ensure a smooth succession, made investors very nervous and
put new pressure on the financial markets. In retrospect, his illness also marked
the beginning of the political crisis that would explode with great ferocity in
early 1998.

The next big blow to Indonesia came in early January, when the international community severely criticized Indonesia's proposed new budget, which was based on a 32 percent nominal increase in spending. The criticisms sent the markets reeling, and the value of the rupiah immediately plunged from 6,000 rupiah to the dollar on January 2 to 10,100 rupiah to the dollar on January 8. It turned out, however, that the criticisms were misleading and had been made hastily without a full analysis of the budget. All of the increase in spending was simply due to the exchange rate movements (mainly due to debt service payments, aid-financed infrastructure spending, and a fuel subsidy). In real terms, the budget actually represented a decline in spending. Several days later Stanley Fischer, deputy managing director of the IMF, told CNN that the new budget was "not as bad as it was being portrayed." Two weeks later the IMF quietly approved a new budget with a 46 percent increase in spending, but the damage to market perceptions had been done. The incident made clear that an antagonistic relationship had developed between the international community and the Indonesian government. It was at about this time that the pattern of currency and stock price movements in Indonesia deviated very sharply from those in the other countries that experienced financial crisis, and Indonesia never recovered (see figure 3-2).

On January 15, 1998, Indonesia signed its second agreement with the IMF. The new program eased up slightly on fiscal policy and on the capital adequacy ratio required for banks, but otherwise kept the same basic strategy as the first program. The new program got off to a bad start during the official signing ceremony when Michel Camdessus, managing director of the IMF, leaned over Suharto, with arms folded, as Suharto signed the papers. This image offended many Indonesians and amplified the already strong anti-IMF sentiment among the general population.

When the details of the program were announced, the markets immediately reacted negatively, with the rupiah falling 11 percent in two days. One key reason was that the new program included almost no strategy for dealing with Indonesia's short-term foreign debt, which was at the heart of the market turmoil. This omission was all the more surprising given the success of the IMF and U.S. Treasury–backed rollover of Korea's short-term debt, which had been initiated just a few weeks before. The difference between the treatment of Indonesia's foreign debt and the treatment of foreign debt in Korea and Thailand is stunning. With the strong support of the U.S. Treasury, Korea was able to roll over U.S.$22.5 billion in short-term debt that was owed by Korean banks and fell due in the first quarter of 1998. The rollover marked the turning

Figure 3-2. Nominal Exchange Rate Index, July 1997 through March 1999

Rate (July 1, 1997 = 100)

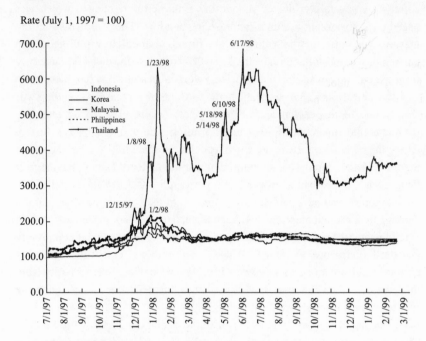

Source: Datastream Online.

point in the Korean financial crisis, as the currency immediately began to appreciate, stock prices rebounded, and shortly thereafter interest rates fell. In August 1997 Thailand received assurances (at the time it signed the agreement related to its first IMF program) from Japanese creditor banks that they would maintain credit lines of U.S.$19 billion for foreign banks resident in Thailand.[14] The Thai government also managed to delay or restructure about U.S.$4 billion in debts owed by the fifty-six finance companies suspended in the first IMF program.[15] In Indonesia, on the other hand, debt restructuring was not made a priority by the IMF until its third program in April 1998, at which point it was far too late. Some have argued that debt restructuring was put off in Indonesia because the fact that its debt was mainly corporate (rather than commercial bank) debt made the situation much more complicated, but that fact hardly justified ignoring the problem.

14. International Monetary Fund (1999a).
15. Institute of International Finance (1999).

In late January the government acted on its own and announced a "voluntary" suspension of private sector debt payments. At one level this announcement changed little, since very few corporate debt service payments were being made by this time. Nevertheless, the announcement—and the fact that it was not opposed by the IMF—seemed to calm the markets. At the same time, the government announced that it would guarantee all commercial bank liabilities, including those of both foreign and domestic creditors and all deposits. Although the guarantees raised a number of significant problems, the government had little choice given the disintegration of the banking system that was under way. These two announcements finally provided a modicum of stability to the markets, and the declines of the rupiah and the stock market stopped, at least temporarily.

By this time, however, Suharto had adopted a much more confrontational approach and made it clear that he was not going to fully adopt the program for which he had just signed the agreement. Even though there were good reasons to doubt the efficacy of the new program, his approach simply made market participants even more nervous, and the pressure on the rupiah continued. Suharto waffled and backtracked on several structural reforms in the program, such as dismantling the clove marketing board (controlled by his son), removing tax breaks that heavily protected production of a national car (also controlled by his son), and other issues.[16]

Most controversially, Suharto began to flirt publicly with the ill-advised idea of introducing a currency board in Indonesia.[17] He quickly latched on to the idea, despite widespread opposition both inside and outside the country. He did

16. The IMF program called for enactment of a long list of structural reforms throughout the Indonesian economy. Although many of these reforms were very beneficial to the economy in the long run (and had been pushed by reformists within the government for many years), they were of less importance to the immediate crisis than the bank and debt restructuring. Debate on these reforms distracted urgent attention from the key issues. See Feldstein (1998) for a discussion.

17. A currency board system was clearly not appropriate for Indonesia in early 1998. The relatively large share of export revenues that Indonesia earns from a range of natural resource–based commodities makes the economy vulnerable to rapid changes in its external terms of trade. Given its relatively large share of nontraded and semitraded goods, a rigidly fixed exchange rate system would mean that adverse external shocks would be translated into sharp increases in interest rates and economic contraction rather than into a smoother transition through exchange rate adjustment (which Indonesia frequently employed in the 1970s and 1980s). Most important, two key prerequisites for

so perhaps partially because he thought it might be the silver bullet that its advocates promised it would be, but more likely because he hoped it could be used as a negotiating foil with the IMF. He also recognized that if a currency board were put in place, even temporarily, it would allow his family and friends to convert their assets to dollars at a more favorable exchange rate. Controversy over the currency board apparently was a major factor in Suharto's decision to dismiss the highly respected governor of the central bank, which further undermined confidence. The currency board controversy made it clear to investors, both foreign and domestic, that Suharto and the IMF had fundamental disagreements as to the basic strategy for reform, that there were differences within the Indonesian government as to how to proceed, and that the international community was not going to provide Indonesia with adequate foreign financing.

Indonesia's contraction was deepened by two additional economic shocks. First, in 1997 the country was hit by a severe drought, which seriously undermined agricultural production just as the financial crisis was beginning to evolve. In particular, rice production fell sharply, leading to price increases that added significantly to overall inflationary trends. Weak farm production also meant that there were fewer employment opportunities for urban day workers who were laid off as the financial crisis began. During past economic downturns it had been common for unskilled urban workers to return to their family farms; this option was not attractive in late 1997.

Second, export prices fell sharply in 1997 and continued to be low throughout 1998. Weak oil prices, in particular, hurt both export earnings and budget revenue. Prior to the crisis, oil revenues accounted for approximately a quarter of Indonesia's export earnings and about the same share of its government budget revenues. The fall in oil prices cost Indonesia approximately U.S.$4 billion in export earnings in 1998. Prices also fell for a range of other export

---

a successful currency board were not in place in early 1998: adequate foreign exchange reserves and a functional banking system. Advocates of a currency board in Indonesia never made clear where they thought the needed foreign exchange reserves would come from, nor did they spell out a plan to reorganize the banking system in such a way that a currency board system could function effectively. Of course, had these prerequisites been satisfied, Indonesia's crisis would have been over. In the end, the currency board idea was fixated on the most obvious symptom of Indonesia's problems—volatility in the currency markets—and not on the underlying problems themselves—excess short-term debt and a weak banking system.

commodities, including plywood, copper, and rubber, leading to a loss of an additional U.S.$3 billion in lost export revenues.[18] The total losses, U.S.$7 billion, were the equivalent of about a seventh of total export earnings in 1997. To put this amount in some perspective, the total disbursements from the IMF during all of 1998 were U.S.$5.7 billion. In other words, IMF financing fell short of making up for lost export revenues from international price shocks, much less the massive withdrawal of private capital flows. The lost export exchange earnings clearly were an important factor in keeping downward pressure on the rupiah. This factor alone would have caused a substantial depreciation of the rupiah, even in the absence of the collapse of the banking system and the panic-driven withdrawal of foreign credits.

Although Suharto and the IMF both mismanaged the crisis, in the end Suharto must bear the brunt of the blame for Indonesia's debacle. For years he had ignored calls to strengthen the banking system and moderate the economic largesse given to his family and friends. When the crisis started he refused to make difficult choices and allowed his country's relationship with the international community to deteriorate beyond repair. Perhaps most important, his failure to allow the political system to mature and to groom an eventual successor set the stage for political disaster. His centralized control had probably helped Indonesia react quickly and firmly in past crises, but as Andrew MacIntyre has pointed out, "a political system of this sort also entails real economic risks, for if the leadership begins to behave in ways that are damaging to investor confidence there are no institutional checks or balances to constrain it."[19] Indonesia's institutional structure could not combat the expansion of the Suharto family's financial empire in the early 1990s and could do little as Suharto's relationship with the IMF eroded irreparably in early 1998.

From Economic Crisis to Political Upheaval

In January and February 1998, Indonesia's economic crisis began to quickly evolve into a major political crisis. In mid-January Suharto named B. J. Habibe as his running mate for the elections scheduled for March 1998. Market reaction was swift and harsh, since Habibe was seen as being closely associated with large and wasteful government spending projects rather

18. My thanks to Peter Rosner for supplying these estimates.
19. MacIntyre (1998).

than with economic reform. Shortly thereafter Suharto added to the uncertainty by firing the governor of the central bank. Doubts began to surface about his ability to grasp the gravity of the situation and provide the leadership that Indonesia needed. As the economic problems deepened, street protests and demonstrations became more commonplace and increasingly became directed at ethnic Chinese.

Suharto named a new cabinet in March following his reelection earlier in the month to a seventh straight term.[20] He removed many of his economic managers and filled the cabinet with close associates and cronies, including his daughter and the head of the Indonesian plywood cartel. The composition of the cabinet was interpreted both domestically and by foreign observers as a sign that Suharto was much less interested in economic reform than in consolidating the power of his family and close associates. Domestic opposition became more vocal, and student protests began to flare up. The situation became more chaotic in April and early May, with larger and more frequent protests and growing calls for Suharto's resignation. In early May Suharto raised fuel prices very sharply, and the situation exploded.[21] Several days of rioting and chaos culminated in Suharto's resignation on May 21, and Vice President B. J. Habibe took over as president of Indonesia.

Suharto's resignation created an enormous political vacuum, and several groups tried to fill the void. Social tensions increased dramatically, and episodes of violence spread throughout the archipelago. The new government had at best a weak mandate to govern, and key decisions were delayed for long periods of time. Parliamentary elections were scheduled for June 1999, with presidential elections to follow later in the year. As a result, at best, the current political uncertainty will remain for some time to come. Rules on the formation of political parties and electoral representation were changed, and the limits of political dialogue were tested. Over 100 political parties have appeared since

20. In Indonesia the president is elected indirectly by an assembly that, until 1998, was composed of 1,000 delegates, half of whom were the 500 members of the parliament. The other half were handpicked by the president, supposedly to represent various social groups and geographic regions. This body elected Suharto every five years by unanimous vote in each of his elections, starting in 1968.

21. The fuel price increases (although not their precise timing) were required under the IMF program. The program specified that the price increases had to take place sometime between April and July (possibly in stages), not necessarily all at once in early May, as Suharto called for.

Suharto left office, and 48 were approved to contest the parliamentary elections. It is far from clear who will be elected president and what form the government may take in the future. The struggle for power during the next year is certain to distract government officials and is likely to engender new street violence. Therefore, Indonesia's current task is doubly difficult compared to those of other Asian countries that experienced financial crisis. Political and social leaders must simultaneously rebuild the shattered economy and fundamentally redesign the entire political system. In any event, it will likely take years for political and economic certainty to return to Indonesia.

The Economic Situation in 1999

The Indonesian economy finally began to achieve a modicum of stability in the last half of 1998. After depreciating to less than 16,000 rupiah to the dollar in the aftermath of the May riots, the rupiah finally began to stabilize and appreciate in the latter half of 1998. For the six months between mid-September 1998 and mid-March 1998, the rupiah fluctuated within a (relatively) narrow band, between 7,000 and 9,000 rupiah to the dollar. The main stock index increased 43 percent in terms of rupiahs between September 1998 and March 1999, although it was still 47 percent below its precrisis level in terms of rupiahs and an astonishing 85 percent below in terms of U.S. dollars. Inflation, which reached as high as 80 percent on an annual basis in early 1998, dropped quickly in the latter part of the year. For the six months ending in February 1999, inflation was 20 percent on an annual basis. As the rupiah appreciated and inflation fell, interest rates finally began to decline, with the rate on Bank Indonesia's one-month paper dropping from 70 percent in early September 1998 to 37 percent in March 1999. Agricultural production rebounded following the disastrous 1997 drought, rice prices have fallen, and rice supplies have become adequate. In 1998 production boomed for certain agricultural cash crops, including rubber, cashews, cloves, coffee, and pepper.

Although the relative stability provided welcome relief, the economy may not have reached bottom. The economy is expected to continue to contract until at least the latter part of 1999, and perhaps until early 2000. New investment is negligible, as foreign creditors remain on the sidelines and domestic banks are unable to lend. Although there are many critical issues at this stage, five seem most important in terms of reinvigorating the economy.

Achieving Political Stability

In the absence of a greater degree of political stability and certainty, the economy will not rebound any time soon. Potential investors are simply unwilling to make significant commitments until they are more confident about the new government. Ethnic Chinese who fled after the riots of May 1998 are in no hurry to return, as the street violence continues. It is likely to be several years before confidence returns to anything close to the precrisis levels. Political uncertainty has also affected the government's ability to implement crucially needed reform measures. At one level the political reconstruction process is (necessarily) taking time and resources away from economic policymaking. In addition, however, weak authority makes it difficult for the government to push through key policy changes, and is therefore delaying recovery.

The dilemma, of course, is that the relationship between political stability and economic stability runs both ways. Just as political stability is required for an economic rebound, economic stability (and some growth) is needed to help speed the return of political calm. For many years Indonesia enjoyed the benefits of a mutually reinforcing positive relationship between political and economic stability. With the onset of the crisis the reinforcing nature of that relationship turned negative. A fundamental challenge for Indonesia is to break the negative cycle and turn the relationship around. Progress on the economic and political fronts is likely to move forward in small steps and will have to occur in tandem rather than in sequence, a process which will inevitably be both slow and halting.

Recapitalizing the Banking System

The banking system is essentially moribund, with most banks undercapitalized and illiquid and normal lending operations seriously curtailed. Nonperforming loans have reached the level of 60 to 75 percent by some estimates. Over 60 banks have been closed, and dozens of others are under the supervision or management of the Indonesian Bank Restructuring Agency (IBRA). IBRA focused its efforts in mid-1998 on beginning the process of recovering at least part of the Rp 130 billion in liquidity credits that Bank Indonesia had provided to ailing banks in late 1997 and early 1998. The owners of these banks have pledged U.S.$16 billion in assets to the government to cover the loans. The owners have four years to repay the loans, or they will lose the assets. Although this mechanism should help the government recover at least some of the credits, the method for disposing of the assets has been hotly disputed.

In September 1998 the government announced its basic strategy to recapitalize the banking system. Banks will be separated into three groups. First, any
bank with a capital adequacy ratio (CAR) of less than –25 percent will be
closed. Second, those banks with a CAR of more than 4 percent will be allowed
to operate normally and will be expected to increase their CAR to 8 percent
over the next several years. Third, banks with a CAR of between –25 percent
and 4 percent will be eligible to apply for government recapitalization plans.
Owners of banks in that category that meet certain eligibility requirements will
be expected to immediately provide 20 percent of the funds necessary to
increase their banks' CAR to 4 percent. The government will supply the
remaining 80 percent of the recapitalization funds. The owners of the banks
will have the option to repurchase the government's shares within three years
and will have the right of first refusal to buy the shares for five years. In
addition, these banks will be able to remove some of the nonperforming loans
from their books by swapping them for government bonds. Any amounts the
banks collect on these loans can be used to buy back the government's capital
share.

In early March 1999 the government closed an additional thirty-eight banks
and nationalized seven more banks. It announced that 73 of the remaining 128
private banks had met the minimum standard of a 4 percent CAR. Nine banks
were declared eligible for the government recapitalization scheme. The
government announced that it plans to issue Rp 300 trillion in bonds (about
U.S.$35 billion to U.S.$40 billion, equivalent to about 30 percent of GDP) to
recapitalize these banks, along with seven state banks, fourteen regional banks,
and eleven recently nationalized banks. Half of these bonds will carry a fixed
interest rate of 3 percent; the other half will carry a rate of 3 percentage points
above the rate of inflation. The budgetary costs for interest payments on these
bonds, if the total value remains within the current estimate, will amount to
about 3.5 percent of GDP. The IMF's estimates (as of late 1998) of the costs of
bank restructuring for Indonesia and other countries in the region are shown in
table 3-3. Many observers, however, believe the ultimate costs in Indonesia
will be higher than these estimates indicate.

These actions are major steps forward, and they should help put at least some
banks on more solid footing. But there is a long way to go, with the future of
many banks yet undecided. Even with the recapitalization, many banks remain
illiquid and have little incentive to begin lending. With one-month Bank
Indonesia certificates trading at around 37 percent in mid-March 1999, most
banks would prefer to put what few available funds they have in these instru-

Table 3-3. Estimated Costs of Bank Restructuring, 1998

Costs	Local currency cost[a]	U.S. dollar equivalent (billions of U.S. $)[b]	Percent of GDP
Interest			
Indonesia	40 trillion	5.4	3.5
Korea	8 trillion	6.4	2.0
Malaysia	3.5 billion	0.9	1.25
Philippines	11.9 billion	0.3	0.25–0.5
Thailand	143 billion	4.0	3.0
Total		17.0	
Total			
Indonesia	300 trillion	40	29
Korea	74.7 trillion	60	18
Malaysia	48.4 billion	13	18
Philippines	110 billion	3	4
Thailand	1583 billion	43	32
Total		159	

Source: International Monetary Fund, "World Economic Outlook: Interim Assessment" (December 1998).

a. IMF staff estimates as of November 30, 1998. The estimates include both budgetary and extrabudgetary costs and are intended to measure the up-front financing costs.

b. Converted at exchange rates on November 30, 1998.

ments rather than in new loans. As a result, banking activity is likely to remain slow. Moreover, these moves constitute what is essentially a temporary nationalization of the banking system. The seventy-three private banks that met the standard of having a 4 percent CAR have deposits that comprise only about 5 percent of bank deposits.[22] The remainder of the banks will be either fully or partially state owned, at least for several years. For example, four of the seven state banks that existed before the crisis will be merged into a single bank that alone will manage 30 percent of banking system deposits. Extricating the state from the banking sector will be a major challenge in the coming years.

Restructuring Corporate Debt

Although the short-term foreign debt owed by Indonesian firms was at the heart of the crisis, almost nothing was done about the issue (with the exception of the voluntary debt suspension discussed earlier) until June 1998. At the end

22. International Monetary Fund (1999b).

of June 1998 Indonesian firms owed about U.S.$36 billion to foreign banks, an amount that was down only slightly from the U.S.$40 billion owed just prior to the crisis (see table 3-1). Indonesia's short-term debt fell from U.S.$35 billion to U.S.$22 billion between mid-1997 and mid-1999.[23] Therefore, even two years after the crisis the debt burden remained very high, both because debtors were unable to pay the debts and because creditors were unwilling to reschedule them.

In June 1998 the government reached agreement (the "Frankfort Agreement") with a group of private creditors on restructuring Indonesian debt. This agreement had three major provisions. First, Indonesian commercial banks were expected to repay U.S.$6 billion in trade credit arrears, in return for which foreign banks would try to maintain trade credits at the (already depressed) April 1998 level (all the new trade credits would be guaranteed by Bank Indonesia). Second, about U.S.$9 billion in debts owed by Indonesian commercial banks that fell due before March 1999 would be exchanged for new loans that would mature in one to four years (also guaranteed by Bank Indonesia). These two provisions have been seen as generally successful, albeit at least six months too late.

The third portion of the agreement covered corporate debts. Indonesia agreed to establish the Indonesian Debt Restructuring Agency (INDRA) to facilitate repayment of an estimated U.S.$64 billion in corporate debt. INDRA acts as an intermediary between creditors and debtors and is designed to provide protection against further real depreciation of the rupiah (that is, a rate of depreciation exceeding the inflation rate) and to provide assurances that adequate foreign exchange will be available to make payments. The agreement provided little cash relief for debtors and little incentive for creditors to write down their loans. To further encourage restructuring the government announced the "Jakarta Initiative" in September 1998. The initiative offered guidelines on the formation of creditor committees, standstill arrangements, exchange of information, subordination of old loans to new credits, and other related issues. However, it did nothing to address the fundamental problem of burden sharing between debtors and creditors.

A major hurdle for Indonesian debt restructuring has been the reluctance of Japanese banks to offer any substantial debt relief or to write down Indonesian debt. This problem is all the more pressing since Japanese banks are by far the largest of Indonesia's creditors. Many Japanese banks were fairly weak to begin with before the crisis and had not made adequate provisions to write off

23. Bank for International Settlements (1998).

substantial amounts of Asian debts. A common complaint since the onset of the crisis has been that when other banks were willing to move forward with substantial debt relief, Japanese banks would not agree. They have continued to insist that borrowers make interest payments on time so that the loans will remain current in their books. Substantial progress in opening up the log jam of Indonesian debts may not be possible without more active participation and assistance by the Japanese government. More broadly, Indonesia's debt burden has become so large that the country is likely to require significant formal debt relief in the future from the foreign creditors that helped fuel the crisis.

Despite these problems, there was some halting progress in early 1999. According to the IMF, by mid-March 1999 some 125 firms had entered negotiations under the framework of the Jakarta Initiative to cover U.S.$17.5 billion in foreign debt and Rp 7.8 trillion in domestic debt. Agreements were reached with fifteen companies to cover about U.S.$2 billion in foreign debt and Rp 600 billion in domestic debt.[24] Although these agreements represent welcome progress, they cover just a tiny fraction of the amount outstanding.

Expanding Exports

One of Indonesia's main hopes for recovery was through an expansion of exports. The large depreciation of the rupiah substantially increased the international competitiveness of Indonesian firms and made Indonesia one of the lowest-cost producers in the world of many commodities and other products. Through the first three quarters of 1998 export performance was very strong, at least in terms of volumes. Export volumes were about 28 percent higher between September 1997 and September 1998 than a year earlier. Exports of furniture, chemicals, jewelry, pulp, and paper grew especially rapidly, and textile and garment exports also expanded. Indonesia's export performance (in terms of volume) compared very favorably with that of other Asian countries through late 1998 (see table 3-4).

More recent information, however, suggests that the strong volume performance deteriorated sharply after mid-1998, at least for manufactured exports. Following the May 1998 riots, apparently many foreign buyers became convinced that Indonesian firms could no longer be relied on for timely delivery of products, and they switched their orders to firms in other countries.[25] The

24. International Monetary Fund (1999b).
25. Thanks to Peter Rosner for these observations.

Table 3-4. Export Growth, 1997–98

Country	1997: Q3	1997: Q4	1998: Q1	1998: Q2	1998: Q3	1998: Q4
Values (in U.S. dollars)						
China	20.5	14.0	12.6	2.5	–2.0	–7.3
Hong Kong	2.5	7.4	–0.9	–3.2	–10.4	–13.7
Indonesia	9.6	2.4	0.9	–8.4	–9.4	–16.5
Korea	16.1	4.4	8.4	–1.9	–10.8	–6.2
Malaysia	2.6	–5.4	–10.8	–9.1	–10.0	. . .
Philippines	24.3	19.6	23.5	14.4	19.2[a]	11.5[a]
Singapore	3.2	–3.9	–6.6	–13.9	–14.8	. . .
Taiwan	17.1	7.1	–0.3	–7.5	–9.6	–12.9
Thailand	5.4	4.3	–1.8	–6.9	–6.2	–10.0
Volume						
China	. . .	. . .	. . .	. . .	22.1[b]	. . .
Hong Kong	4.4	9.6	1.4	–0.5	–7.1	. . .
Indonesia	33.5	33.0	32.8	19.1	27.6	. . .
Korea	35.3	23.2	32.6	20.6	11.4	. . .
Singapore	10.5	7.8	7.6	–2.0	–0.7	. . .
Taiwan	9.7	11.4	3.8	0.8	. . .	. . .
Thailand	11.7	16.3	14.1	12.8	5.7	. . .

Sources: Export values data are from the International Monetary Fund, *International Financial Statistics* (various issues). Taiwan's data are from the International Monetary Fund, "World Economic Outlook" (November 1998). Export volumes are from the IMF, "World Economic Outlook" (November 1998) except those for China, which are from news media reports.

a. Export values data for the third and fourth quarters of 1998 are from the National Statistics Office of the Philippines.

b. Percent change during the first ten months from the same period in 1997.

volume of manufactured exports began to decline sharply in the middle of 1998 and did not shown signs of recovery by the end of the year. In fact, the value of nonoil exports fell very sharply in early 1999 to about the same level as recorded in January 1995, four years earlier. Unfortunately, once foreign buyers switch their suppliers it is very hard to convince them to come back, especially in the case of Indonesia, since the political situation there remains unsettled. Here again, the elections and political succession in Indonesia loom large, as they provide an opportunity to begin to convince buyers that Indonesian firms can again become reliable suppliers to world markets.

In addition to these recent problems with export volumes, export prices plummeted for many products, especially commodities, as discussed earlier.

Most important, prices for petroleum products fell by about 50 percent during 1998. To a large extent, of course, the fall in world export prices is itself a result of the drop in demand in Asia. As a result of the price declines, and despite the strong growth in export volumes through the first half of the year, the U.S. dollar value of exports fell 9 percent in 1998. Prices were only slightly better for products excluding oil, with the dollar value of nonoil exports dropping 2 percent for the year.

Reducing the Budget Deficit

After years of prudent fiscal policy with essentially balanced budgets, Indonesia's budget deficit ballooned in 1998–99 to around 4 percent of GDP, and it is expected to reach 6 percent of GDP in 1999–2000. Domestic tax revenues collapsed with the fall in economic activity. In addition, revenues from exports of oil (which accounted for 23 percent of total revenues before the crisis) fell by about a third in U.S. dollar terms. These two forces put tremendous pressure on the budget. There was little room to maneuver on the expenditure side (which was not unusually large by international standards before the crisis, at 14 percent of GDP). Debt service payments from previous government borrowing are the largest expenditure category, and they could not be substantially reduced. Indonesia gained some relief by rescheduling some of its sovereign debts with the Paris and London Clubs in 1998, but there is little scope for further action on that front. Subsidies for certain consumer items (especially fuel) represent another large expenditure, but the government has little room to raise prices and reduce these subsidies without sparking renewed protests and violence. Moreover, because of the crisis there is a plethora of demands for funds for critical social welfare programs. On top of this, of course, is the cost of recapitalizing the banks. The result is a huge deficit, with little immediate relief in sight. Receipts from new privatizations are unlikely to be large enough to make much of a difference. Any further depreciation of the exchange rate would only make the deficit larger. By contrast, an appreciation of the exchange rate, which may come with political stability, would help ease strains on the budget.

Financing the deficit is the most immediate challenge. There is not enough liquidity in the economy to float a major domestic bond issue. Monetizing the budget risks sparking inflation, which, under the circumstances, could jump very quickly. That leaves foreign financing as the only viable option. The government has received significant commitments from foreign donors, but another U.S.$5 billion will be needed for the 1999–2000 fiscal year. Financing the budget will present a major challenge for several years into the future. At worst, the situation could lead to a sharp increase in inflation if the deficits cannot be financed. At best, inflation will remain in check, but the government's foreign debt burden will increase sharply.

Indonesia's political and economic challenges are enormous at this critical juncture of the nation's history. There are no quick fixes (such as pegging the exchange rate) that will solve these problems. Indonesia must rebuild confidence one step at a time through a combination of peaceful and fair political transition, economic policies that maintain stability and rebuild shattered banks and corporations, and support from the international community. At best, Indonesia's road to recovery will be long and arduous. The crisis has caused several years (perhaps as much as a decade) of lost economic growth. However, with some luck and skill the economic and political transitions required for recovery will help build the foundation for more sustainable long-run growth and development in the future.

References

Bank for International Settlements. 1998. "The Maturity, Sectoral, and Nationality Distribution of International Bank Lending." Basle: BIS (January, May, and November).

Feldstein, Martin. 1998. "Refocussing the IMF." *Foreign Affairs* 77(2) (March-April): 20–33.

Furman, Jason, and Joseph Stiglitz. 1998. "Economic Crises: Evidence and Insights from East Asia." *Brookings Papers on Economic Activity* 2: 1–114.

Gallup, John, Steven Radelet, and Andrew Warner. 1998. "Economic Growth and the Income of the Poor." Harvard Institute for International Development (November).

Goldstein, Morris. 1998. "The Asian Financial Crisis: Causes, Cures, and Systemic Implications." Policy Analyses in International Economics 55. Washington: Institute for International Economics (June).

Institute of International Finance. 1999. "Report of the Working Group on Financial Crises in Emerging Markets." Washington: IIF (January).

International Monetary Fund. 1999a. "IMF-Supported Programs in Indonesia, Korea, and Thailand: A Preliminary Assessment." Washington: IMF.

———. 1999b. "Indonesia: Supplementary Memorandum of Economic and Financial Policies." Washington: IMF (March 16, 1999).

Krugman, Paul. 1998. "What Happened to Asia?" Unpublished manuscript (January).

MacIntyre, Andrew. 1998. "Whither Indonesia? What America Needs to Know and Do." University of California, San Diego, School of International Relations and Pacific Studies (August).

Radelet, Steven. 1995. "Indonesian Foreign Debt: Heading for a Crisis or Financing Sustainable Growth?" *Bulletin of Indonesian Economic Studies* 31(3) (December): 39–72.

———. 1996. "Measuring the Real Exchange Rate and its Relationship to Exports: An Application to Indonesia." Harvard Institute for International Development Discussion Paper 529 (May).

Radelet, Steven, and Jeffrey Sachs. 1998a. "The Onset of the East Asian Currency Crisis." NBER Working Paper 6680 (April). Available from the research section of the HIID website: www.hiid.harvard.edu.

———. 1998b. "The East Asian Financial Crisis: Diagnosis, Remedies, Prospects." Brookings Papers on Economic Activity 1: 1–74.

World Bank. 1997. "Indonesia: Sustaining High Growth with Equity." Washington: World Bank, Country Department 3, East Asia and Pacific Region (May 30).

———. 1998a. *World Development Indicators.* Washington: World Bank.

———. 1998b. "Indonesia in Crisis: A Macroeconomic Update." Washington: World Bank (July 16).

CHAPTER FOUR

Thailand, the International Monetary Fund, and the Financial Crisis: First In, Fast Out?

Frank Flatters

This chapter reviews how Thailand coped with the Asian financial crisis and focuses on three areas of discussion in particular: domestic reactions to the conditions imposed by the International Monetary Fund (IMF); whether the reforms are likely to be maintained; and the short-term (one-year) and intermediate-term (three- to five-year) outlook for the country's economy.

The freeing of the Thai baht on July 2, 1997, is generally viewed as the trigger for the crisis that spread widely in the region and beyond. In August the Thai government called in the IMF for financial assistance and for help in designing measures to deal with the crisis. Before too long, and especially after a change of government in November of the same year, Thailand came to be seen as one of the IMF's star pupils. A more appropriate description would be "partner" rather than "pupil." The Royal Thai Government (RTG) has taken almost full ownership of the so-called IMF program. The IMF has shown great

I thank Popon Kangpenkae and Duangkamol Chotana for help with data and for very useful discussions while preparing this chapter. I am also grateful to Barry Bosworth and Russell Krelove for their comments on the penultimate draft. Special thanks to Ammar Siamwalla, not only for comments on the chapter, but also for many rewarding conversations about the political economy of the crisis in Thailand.

Table 4-1. GDP Growth Projections for Thailand for 1998 in Various Letters of Intent

LOI number	Date	1998 growth (percent)
1	August 14, 1997	6.5
2	November 25, 1997	0 to 1
3	February 24, 1998	–3 to –3.5
4	May 26, 1998	–4 to –5.5
5	August 25, 1998	–7
6	December 1, 1998	–7 to –8

Source: Author's own compilation from various letters of intent.

flexibility in acceding to Thai wishes and adapting the program to changing circumstances and to domestic political considerations.

As is now well known, the crisis turned out to be far deeper and more widespread than was predicted in mid-1997. In successive letters of intent (LOIs) that the RTG filed with the IMF, economic growth forecasts were revised relentlessly downward (see table 4-1). When the RTG stopped defending the baht in July 1997, it was generally thought to be overvalued by 10 to 15 percent, suggesting the need for a devaluation from the precrisis rate of 25 baht to the dollar to somewhere in the range of 28 to 31. By mid-July it had hit that level, and it continued to depreciate. It first hit 40 baht to the dollar in late October, and in mid-January 1998 it reached 56—a depreciation of 55 percent.

Early 1999 offered signs of stabilization. The baht recovered and re-mained in a range of 36 to 38 to the dollar for some time. Interest rates, which had soared in response to government attempts to lean against the wind in the foreign exchange market, fell substantially. The inflation rate, which, despite the substantial devaluation of the baht, had never gone very high (peaking at less than 10 percent in mid-1998), began to fall off. These and other indicators prompted some observers, and certainly government spokespersons and IMF officials, to suggest that recovery was in sight, with the RTG predicting positive growth for 1999. However, there are many reasons to believe that this prediction was optimistic. To look clearly into the future, however, it is necessary to review Thailand's policies and its relationship with the IMF in the period before and during the course of the crisis. Over this period there was a complex relationship between economic events, public expectations, domestic reactions to the program, and evolu-tion of the program itself.

The Background of the Crisis: A Case of Malign Neglect

The factors underlying the crisis are now fairly well understood. As characterized by Radelet and Sachs, it was a classic crisis of confidence brought about by several critical features of the Thai economy in 1996–97.[1] (For a slightly longer-term perspective, table 4-2 provides some key annual macroeconomic data for the period from 1993 to 1998.) These included the rapid buildup of private short-term foreign debt liabilities, a fixed-rate exchange system, a weak financial system, and an overheated "bubble" economy.

The problematic onset of short-term private debt liabilities was facilitated and encouraged by the establishment in 1993 of the Bangkok International Banking Facility (BIBF) for offshore banking. Unfortunately, despite some measures to limit such banking, the facility became a source of short-term foreign-denominated credits used to finance onshore loans, for which the ultimate security in many cases was baht-denominated revenue. This outcome was quite different from the original intent of the BIBF—to establish Thailand as a regional banking center and serve as an intermediary between offshore lenders and borrowers. Short-term debt liabilities rapidly outgrew the country's foreign exchange reserves, especially as the latter were decimated in the government's futile defense of the baht in early 1997 (discussed later).

The country's adherence to a fixed-rate exchange system was a second underlying problem. The rate had been fixed for so long relative to the dollar that many market participants ignored exchange rate risk.[2] Increased short-term capital mobility arising from the BIBF made the maintenance of the fixed rate increasingly problematic. This fact appeared to be lost on most market participants. By early 1997 calculations of the real effective exchange rate showed that the baht was overvalued by 10 to 15 percent.

Third, adherence to and enforcement of prudential rules had seemed irrelevant and unnecessary in the bubble economy of the previous decade. With annual growth rates of close to 10 percent for about a decade, it was difficult for bankers to make bad loans and thus to learn or appreciate the need to assess and manage risk. The spectacular collapse of the Bangkok Bank of Commerce between 1994 and 1996 as a result of mismanagement and fraud was a harbinger of things to come. The government's failure to appreciate the impor-

---

1. Radelet and Sachs (1998).

2. It was, in fact, fixed against a (secret) basket of several currencies. But the dollar had by far the greatest weight in this basket (probably in excess of 90 percent).

Table 4-2. Basic Macroeconomic Data for Thailand, 1993–98

Indicator	1993	1994	1995	1996	1997	1998
Percent real GDP growth	8.4	8.9	8.8	5.5	–0.4	–9.4
Percent manufacturing production growth	7.6	6.5	9.3	8.6	–0.6	–11.9
Percent export growth (in U.S. dollars)	11.6	22.2	24.7	–1.9	4.9	–6.9
Percent import growth (in U.S. dollars)	10.6	18.4	31.8	0.6	–15.7	–33.5
Current account (in billions of U.S. dollars)	–6.4	–8.1	–13.5	–14.7	–1.3	12.8
Capital account (in billions of U.S. dollars)	1.1	12.2	21.9	19.5	–8.7	–9.6
Net private capital (in billions of U.S. dollars)	10.3	12.0	20.8	18.2	–8.8	–15.6
Percent consumer price index growth (annual average)	3.3	5.1	5.8	5.8	5.6	8.1
Stock Exchange of Thailand index	1,682	1,360	1,281	832	373	356

Sources: Bank of Thailand, *Monthly Bulletin, Monthly Statistical Report,* and *Key Economic Indicators* (various issues).

tance of the systemic problems; its decision to bail out depositors, creditors, and shareholders of the failed bank; and its reluctance to prosecute those responsible sent dangerous signals to the financial community. Cavalier behavior by financial institutions and regulators continued in an increasingly open fashion until the outbreak of the crisis.

Finally, beginning in 1996, an overheating "bubble" was visible in declining export and import growth, the excess capacity of the real estate markets, especially in Bangkok, and the rapid decline of the Stock Exchange of Thailand (SET) index. For too long investments and expectations had been based on extrapolations of past performance rather than on realistic assessments of actual demand and supply in goods and asset markets.[3]

3. The overheating and the large short-term capital inflows that began in 1995 and 1996 can also be attributed to the government's reluctance to let its clearly undervalued exchange rate appreciate in that period. This is another instance of the government's ignoring good advice from the IMF.

With these problems looming, the Thai economy was in an increasingly fragile state in the year or so prior to the collapse of the baht. The state of the economy was matched by similar conditions in the financial sector and in its regulatory environment. The collapse of confidence that began in early 1997 resulted in an enormous and unprecedented reversal of capital flows, from a surplus of U.S.$19.5 billion in 1996 to a deficit of U.S.$8.7 billion in 1997. Almost all of this collapse was accounted for by a rapid decrease of private capital, which went from an inflow of U.S.$18.2 billion in 1996 to an outflow of U.S.$8.8 billion in 1997.

A key to Thailand's economic success in the 1980s and early 1990s had been her prudent macroeconomic management. This included extremely cautious fiscal policies (running a small surplus almost every year), a noninflationary monetary policy, and a fixed exchange rate that had been quickly adjusted on the few occasions necessary. These policies, which were consistently followed under a variety of elected and nonelected governments, were largely the responsibility of a highly qualified and dedicated technocracy at the highest levels of key economic ministries and institutions, most importantly the Bank of Thailand (BOT). This system broke down in the period preceding the current crisis. The failures in the BOT were especially spectacular.[4]

The IMF claimed that it had given many private warnings to the RTG about the country's macroeconomic imbalances and the need for policy adjustments. Had the RTG responded appropriately to this advice, it is argued, the crisis could have been avoided or at least made much less severe. Due to the privileged nature of the communications, however, neither the IMF nor the RTG released any details of these proceedings, making it difficult to make any judgments relative to this claim.[5]

However, the publication of an RTG-commissioned study of the precrisis role of the BOT (the Nukul Report) shed considerable light on the roles of the IMF and the BOT in the period leading up to the crisis.[6] The Nukul Report provides a fascinating case study, from the inside, of a terrible policy failure. The two principal blunders were the futile and costly defense of the baht during late 1996 and the first half of 1997 and the bleeding of the RTG's Financial

4. See Siamwalla (1997).

5. Should not the IMF have made its concerns public? The IMF responds that to have done so would have provoked the crisis that it was trying to avoid through its discreet communications with the RTG.

6. Prachuabmoh and others (1998).

Institutions Development Fund (FIDF) to prop up failing financial institutions while neglecting to take other actions to remedy the underlying problems.

The Futile Defense of the Baht

Capital outflows began in the second half of 1996 and intensified in December in response to evidence of ever-weakening fundamentals, especially declining export growth and difficulties of financial institutions. Waves of outflows continued in early 1997 as the economic data worsened and concerns about the real estate sector grew. The RTG used its foreign exchange reserves and forward swap interventions to fight off pressures on the baht. It periodically denied devaluation rumors and even made written commitments not to devalue the baht. These measures did not relieve the pressure on the baht. Foreign exchange reserves, which stood at almost U.S.$40 billion in the third quarter of 1996, had fallen to U.S.$38.1 billion at the end of February 1997. Furthermore, the government had incurred forward obligations amounting to U.S.$12.2 billion as well. In other words, net foreign exchange reserves had fallen from U.S.$40 billion to U.S.$26 billion.

The attack on the baht resumed in May, and the BOT continued its defense. On three different days, May 8, 13, and 14, the BOT used or committed U.S.$6.1 billion, U.S.$9.7 billion, and U.S.$10 billion, respectively, of foreign exchange reserves. Having almost exhausted its reserves, it then reverted to the desperate measure of forbidding Thai banks to lend baht in the offshore market. This was an effective temporary measure and imposed large losses on foreign speculators with short positions in baht. Since the baht defense was conducted largely through forward swap transactions, the country's true foreign exchange reserve position was not apparent from official figures. In fact, until late May 1997 even the minister of finance claimed to be unaware of the massive drain that had occurred. Even more amazing was the apparent absence of any serious discussion at high levels of government of the need to change or abandon the fixed exchange rate.

As early as December 1996 the IMF had urged the government to adjust its exchange rate system by lowering the weight of the U.S. dollar in the fixed-rate currency basket and widening the intervention bands. By late January 1997 it had become much more insistent, and in May it very specifically recommended an immediate devaluation of 10 to 15 percent, increased flexibility in the rate, and a number of other measures related to the government's overall macroeconomic stance and strengthening of the financial sector. The IMF's advice was delivered frequently over this period and in a number of forms, including letters from Managing Director Michel Camdessus and Deputy Managing Director Stanley Fischer to the Thai deputy prime minister and finance minister, as well as the prime minister; a visit and both verbal and written reports to Thai officials by an IMF mission under IMF article 4; secret visits by Camdessus and Fischer with senior government officials; and numerous telephone calls between Fischer and senior BOT officials. Nevertheless, further deterioration of economic news and the resignation of Finance Minister Amnuay in late June 1997 caused another speculative wave and brought about the inevitable collapse of the baht. By the end of June Thailand's net foreign exchange reserves stood at only U.S.$2.8 billion, about 7 percent of their value in late 1996.

The FIDF Bailout of Financial Institutions

The FIDF had been set up in 1985, under the guidance of the BOT, to "rehabilitate and improve financial institutions and to improve their stability." It was initially funded by levies on financial institutions and was used primarily as a source of short-term liquidity, usually in the form of temporary deposits, for banks and finance companies in short-term need. In principle, in the event that more serious assistance was needed, shareholders would have to bear the primary burden of any necessary adjustment, and the FIDF would hold the institutions' assets as collateral against any loans. As of August 1996 the FIDF had extended such assistance to only two institutions, in the total amount of Bt 9 billion. By the end of the year the number of recipients had risen to seven and the amount of assistance to Bt 27.5 billion. By February 1997 these numbers had grown to fifteen and Bt 53.8 billion, respectively.

Difficulties in the finance and banking sector escalated in the face of high interest rates, a rapidly declining stock market, and a deeply troubled property and real estate sector. The RTG was indecisive in developing a strategy to deal with these problems. In May 1997 ten companies were singled out for required recapitalization. By late June 1997 sixteen finance companies were suspended, whereas at the same time the government guaranteed both the security of all remaining banks and finance companies and the assets of all their creditors and depositors. In early August it announced the suspension of forty-two more companies. For the remainder of the year it continued to send confused and inconsistent signals about policies to clean up the growing mess. Suspensions originally set for thirty to forty-five days were dragged on for months until the

December 1997 announcement about the permanent closure of almost all of the companies.

Meanwhile, deposit runs and rising levels of nonperforming loans (NPLs) increased the financial sector's woes. The depreciation of the baht seriously aggravated the balance sheet problems of debtors with foreign-denominated loans, with predictable effects on the banks' and finance companies' NPLs. The FIDF continued to bail out every company that asked for assistance. The total financial commitments of the FIDF as a result of this exercise, with respect to loans to failed companies and guarantees to creditors and depositors, amounted to Bt 1.2 trillion to 1.5 trillion (between U.S.$26 billion and U.S.$45 billion, depending on the exchange rate used). The amount of this that will eventually be recoverable remains unknown, but it will certainly be far less than half. As in the case of the exchange rate regime, since at least December 1996 the IMF had been warning the RTG of the serious problems building up in the financial sector and the need for decisive action to deal with them. And as in the case of the exchange rate warnings, the government had failed to take action or to ask for IMF assistance.

Summary

The RTG's response to the growing crisis can most generously be described as one of sustained neglect. Malign would be a better adjective. The huge reversal of capital flows that occurred in 1996 and 1997 called for major economic adjustments. The RTG consistently failed to heed warnings from the market, from its own macroeconomic data, and from the IMF. The IMF's advice in late 1996 and the first half of 1997 was generally ignored. Its explicit offer in May 1997 to enter Thailand into a program to deal with the exchange rate and financial sector problems was not accepted, and the IMF was not called in until August. By then the government had squandered over U.S.$35 billion of foreign exchange reserves and the FIDF had built up liabilities estimated at Bt 1.3 trillion, or about U.S.$35 billion at the exchange rate of that time.

Could the crisis have been avoided with more timely and appropriate actions by Thai authorities? This question is difficult to answer, since some of the roots of the crisis were systemic difficulties with the domestic financial system, the Thai economy, and the global economic system. Could the costs of the crisis have been reduced by more timely and appropriate action? There is no doubt that some of the major costs could been reduced. A more orderly approach also would have reduced many of the subsequent secondary effects.

The First Year of the IMF Program

How effective were the IMF policy prescriptions?[7] The initial policy program that was developed with the IMF had two focal points: management of the exchange rate and restoration of financial market stability. As the crisis deepened, further programs were developed to improve the social safety nets and to provide special assistance to various sectors and those engaging in various activities. The majority of these other measures, however, were developed in collaboration with the Asian Development Bank (ADB), the World Bank, and bilateral donors. The first letter of intent (LOI) filed with the IMF was signed in August 1997. Six more were signed through March 1999.

Throughout the first half of 1997 the IMF urged a continuation of a pegged exchange rate, but with a widened band and less weight given to the U.S. dollar. The fear was that a floating rate would easily swing out of control, with dire consequences for inflation, the financial system, and the rest of the macroeconomy. By the end of June, however, and without the knowledge of the IMF, Thailand had almost completely exhausted its foreign exchange reserves, so there was no alternative to floating the baht.

Nevertheless, a central goal of both the RTG and the IMF was to use fiscal and monetary levers to lean against the wind and try to stop the baht from declining precipitously. On the fiscal side it was recognized that the FIDF obligations would require additional commitments, and these were estimated at 1 percent of GDP. To accommodate these commitments and at the same time achieve a balanced budget, a fiscal surplus was planned on all other items in the amount of 1 percent of GDP. This was to be achieved through a combination of expenditure cuts and tax increases (primarily an increase in the rate of the value-added tax from 7 percent to 10 percent). The capital costs of the bailouts would be covered by privatization of state enterprises, which was seen as a desirable goal in its own right. The key to the macroeconomic (read exchange rate) stabilization program, however, was to be tight money and high interest rates. The initial letters of intent filed with the IMF trumpeted the government's pride in its strict fiscal and monetary discipline. By this standard, the monetary and fiscal policies were quite successful. An immediate symptom was the continued rise in interest rates.

---

7. For more discussion of the first year of the IMF program, see also Siamwalla and Sopchokchai (1998).

The IMF has steadfastly declared, in retrospect, that it recognized that the Thai crisis was quite different from previous balance of payments crises in Latin America and elsewhere.[8] Whereas the latter had been directly linked to profligate government spending and lack of monetary control, the Thai crisis arose from a buildup of short-term private debts. Although the Thai government was certainly not blameless for the damage that followed, it could not be accused of monetary or fiscal profligacy in the lead-up to the crisis. Despite this crucial difference between the crises in Thailand and Latin America, the IMF's macroeconomic policy prescriptions for Thailand were hard to distinguish from those offered in Latin America. Furthermore, in the public pronouncements of senior IMF officials in the early days of the crisis it was difficult to detect an appreciation of the differences between the crises in Thailand and Latin America.[9] This failure to treat the two areas differently eventually became a major source of contention in public discussions and evaluations of the IMF program.

Restoration of financial market stability was the other top policy priority. Measures implemented or planned included tightening of the NPL reporting and provisioning rules and of the deadlines for and measures to encourage recapitalization of banks and finance companies to acceptable prudential levels. The general idea was to bring performance and the regulatory framework of the financial sector up to international standards.

The NPL reporting requirements were tightened quite quickly. Phasing in of higher capital adequacy requirements was done much more slowly, with new standards to be met only by the year 2000. As mentioned earlier, there were confusing and conflicting signals over criteria for finance companies to remain in operation or to be permitted to reopen once closed. Part of the problem, arising from lax financial sector supervision and reporting requirements, was a lack of reliable and up-to-date information on the performance of banks and finance companies. Nevertheless, by December 1997 the government had completed its review and made final decisions as to the closures of the fifty-eight suspended finance companies (all but two were closed).

A major problem in achieving market-based ways to recapitalize banks and restructure corporate debts was the absence of a legal and institutional frame-

8. Lane and others (1999).

9. One possible explanation is simply that the IMF's Asia personnel were largely ignorant of the details of what had happened in Latin America and hence were inclined to follow blindly the policies that had seemed appropriate there.

work for bankruptcy and foreclosure. Under the existing laws and regulations, debtors had the power to delay and forestall proceedings almost indefinitely, especially with regard to foreclosure, rendering this tool completely ineffective for creditors.[10] NPLs could continue to grow, and banks and other creditors had no power to resolve them. Illiquid and insolvent debtors had every incentive to stall negotiations and refuse to make concessions to their creditors. Many debtors who did not face serious liquidity or solvency problems began to make their debts "strategically nonperforming."

These problems were not fully appreciated in the early days of the IMF program. It was not until the second LOI was filed (in November 1997) that the RTG committed itself to revisions of the bankruptcy law by March 31, 1998. It was later still before it tried to implement a new foreclosure law by October 31, 1998. As will be seen later, neither of these commitments—nor others related to the legal framework for the investment and financial sectors—was properly met.

Initial Economic Effects and Political Reactions

The first LOI was issued by the Chavalit government, which had been so reluctant to take the IMF's advice through the first half of the year. In November, however, the ruling coalition lost the confidence of Parliament and there was a peaceful and orderly change of government. Unlike their predecessors, the leading party in the new government, the Democrats, had a reputation for being relatively clean and corruption-free. Several widely respected and experienced economic advisors were appointed to key cabinet posts. The new government signed the second LOI with the IMF and pledged not only to honor all of the commitments of the previous government, but also "to take a number of additional measures to strengthen the policy package and reinforce public confidence in the program."[11] With this commitment Thailand became a full and enthusiastic partner of the IMF. In light of the discredited policies of the Chavalit government prior to the crisis, it would be fair to say that the new

10. By simply refusing to appear for hearings and engaging in other similar tactics, debtors could easily postpone proceedings for five to ten years. By making one interest payment they could restart the clock at any time. In such circumstances the expected return to a creditor from pursuing foreclosure would almost never justify the costs and uncertainties involved. Making the asset market adjustments required by the enormous shock that had hit the Thai economy would take forever.

11. Second LOI, first paragraph. See Government of Thailand (1997).

government had quite strong and general public support in its determination to work with the IMF in developing a recovery program.

Unfortunately, the economic effects of the program were not what had been hoped. Contagion spread in the region. Despite high and rising interest rates and the government's adherence to strict monetary and fiscal discipline, the value of the baht continued to fall, reaching 40 to the dollar for the first time at the end of October en route to a level of 56 to the dollar in mid-January 1998. Rising interest rates and the collapsing baht played havoc with debtors' balance sheets and pushed NPL rates ever higher. The negative wealth effects of the depreciation and the collapse of asset markets, together with the failure of credit markets due to the financial turmoil, depressed domestic demand. The export slump continued, as did the even more severe contraction of imports, as the current account adjusted to the huge drop in net capital outflows. GDP started to decline in the second half of 1997 and continued to do so through 1998, constantly outpacing the (also declining) official projections.

The social implications were serious.[12] Labor market adjustment took several forms. The number of persons unemployed tripled from 1996 until the end of 1998. There were major reductions both in hours worked and in nominal wages.[13] Although the initial impacts on the labor force were largely in urban areas, the effects were also transmitted to the countryside through both return migration of urban workers and reduced remittances. On the other hand, agriculture benefited from depreciation-induced increases in the domestic currency prices of tradable goods. Fortunately, CPI inflation has been remarkably low despite the large baht depreciation.

Thailand does not have a well-developed formal social safety net. There is no unemployment insurance. Many basic social benefits, such as health care, are tied to employment, and until very recently they ceased when employment with a firm ended. The main "social insurance" systems have been the ex-

12. For a summary review of the social impacts of the crisis and some comparisons of the impacts in Thailand with those in neighboring countries, see Flatters, Kittiprapas, and Sussangkarn (1999).

13. The incidence of significant decreases in wages and hours worked is widely acknowledged. Wage reductions of 20 to 30 percent have been common in many sectors. However, poor labor market data make it difficult to make reliable quantitative estimates of the overall incidence or magnitude of these decreases. See Kakwani (1998) for some preliminary evidence of the importance of wage decreases and of underemployment in the adjustment of labor markets to the crisis.

tended family and the informal labor market. These have been severely tested in the crisis. Arguably the most important government contribution to social insurance has been the specification in Thai labor law of severance penalties, which make it costly for firms to lay off workers. This is the main explanation for the high proportion of labor market adjustment that has occurred through reduced wages and hours rather than unemployment. This market adjustment has ensured a certain amount of income spreading that could not have been accomplished under the formal social security system.

There had been initial forecasts of a speedy V-shaped recovery. By early 1998, however, it was clear that the recession would be deeper and would last longer than predicted. Manufacturing production continued to decline, as did exports, imports, and investment. Nevertheless, except for some gradual relaxation of fiscal targets, primarily on the revenue side, there was no fundamental change in policy direction. Relaxed revenue projections signified not a conscious effort to stimulate the economy, but rather a reluctant acceptance of the workings of automatic stabilizers in the tax system. Meanwhile, the collapse of the baht, high interest rates, and the declining real sector continued to create major problems in the financial sector. The NPL rates rose, and banks and the remaining finance companies accumulated substantial losses. Although some institutions were hit much harder than others, none were immune.

As economic conditions deteriorated, popular discontent began to develop, and it manifested itself in a variety of ways. Stories proliferated about insurmountable problems caused by the credit crunch. Business persons complained about lack of access to and/or the extremely high cost of bank credit. The complete collapse of the baht made the cost of foreign loans unbearable, thus feeding the NPL problems in the financial sector.

Summary

With the change of government in November, Thailand became a full and enthusiastic partner of the IMF. Having freed the baht, the initial focus of macroeconomic policies was to try to stop it from falling precipitously. The government planned a fiscal surplus and tight money, with rising interest rates. However, the baht tumbled until mid-January, and the real and financial sectors of the economy continued to deteriorate. Although final decisions were made about the future of the fifty-eight suspended finance companies, little progress was made on the deteriorating profit, the NPL and capitalization problems of the remaining banks and finance companies, or the restructuring of the huge numbers of defaulted or delinquent corporate debts. The real sector was reeling from the combined effects of high interest rates and crippling debt burdens. By mid-1998 public support for the government programs began to deteriorate. It was becoming clear that a fresh look and new policy initiatives were urgently required. But the choices would not be easy.

The First Anniversary of the Program: Time to Change Course

Mid-1998 marked a watershed in the evolution of Thailand's IMF program. The absence of the hoped-for rapid recovery and the growing disarray in the real and financial sectors forced a reevaluation of the program and the development of new approaches.

Macroeconomic Policies

By July 1998 there was widespread and increasingly vocal public pressure on the government to reverse its strict monetary and fiscal stance, which was seen as a major contributor to the alarming contraction of the real sector and the growth of NPLs. In response to and in general sympathy with this view, the government began to implement a major relaxation of the macroeconomic policy regime.[14] Monetary policy was switched from targeting the exchange rate to targeting money growth, with a view to producing sharp reductions in interest rates and significant increases in bank lending. The fiscal deficit would be increased. The overall goal was to assist the real sector through lower interest rates and to stimulate domestic demand. Lower interest rates were also seen as a means of easing loan payment burdens on debtors. The new policy thrust was announced in the fifth LOI (filed in August 1998).

The most important new fiscal initiative was setting up funds for job creation, local public works, and other socially beneficial community activities.

14. The fiscal deficit targets had been gradually easing over the successive letters of intent. The target in the first LOI had been a surplus of 1 percent of GDP. In the fourth, fifth, and sixth LOIs the target was reduced successively to −2.5 percent, −3.5 percent, and −5 percent of GDP, respectively, excluding the costs of financial sector assistance. Until the fifth LOI monetary targets had been expressed primarily in terms of the interest rates needed to try to maintain exchange rate stability. The fifth LOI changed the emphasis toward substantially easing interest rates and liquidity in order to stimulate domestic demand.

Among the most important was a U.S.$300 million social investment projects (SIP) fund. The fund was financed with loans from the ADB. To avoid problems of bureaucratic and political interference and to ensure that the funds were actually used for genuinely useful community purposes, U.S.$120 million of these funds would be allocated directly to community-based nongovernmental organizations. Special committees were set up outside of normal bureaucratic channels to evaluate proposals and award the funds. The first round of applications and approvals was set for September 1997, with further decisions to be made on a monthly basis after that.

These initiatives marked a major change of focus of Thailand's fiscal and monetary policies, and it was the RTG rather than the IMF that led the way. In an internal assessment of its crisis programs in Indonesia, Korea, and Thailand, the IMF stood quite firmly behind its initial focus on tight monetary and fiscal policies to help the foreign exchange markets lean against the wind.[15] Its only concession was to admit that it might have been appropriate for the RTG to ease up a bit earlier than it actually did. Many critics of the Thai-IMF program suggest that, in light of the huge negative aggregate demand shocks at the outset of the crisis, tight monetary and fiscal policies were wrong-headed from the beginning. A major weakness of the analysis underlying the IMF strategy certainly was its failure to predict the regional contagion that was to follow.

The Financial Sector

The government was faced with three interrelated problems with regard to the financial sector. First, how was it to deal with the assets and liabilities of the closed financial institutions, for which the government, through the FIDF, was generally the largest creditor? The Financial Sector Rehabilitation Agency (FRA) was assigned the task of disposing of the assets of the failed institutions through a series of auctions beginning in mid-1998. The burden of the guarantees on the deposits and credits of the failed firms was assumed by the FIDF. In the absence of adequate bankruptcy, foreclosure, and other commercial laws, however, there remained many thorny issues to be dealt with in carrying out these tasks.

Second, at what pace and with what sanctions and incentives was the government to enforce new and stricter prudential standards for the remaining banks and finance companies? How was it going to facilitate the huge bank

15. Lane and others (1999).

recapitalizations that were obviously required? On these issues there was considerable ambiguity, not in the least because of the public and political stature of the principals of a number of the major banks and therefore the government's reluctance to impose harsh measures on them.

Third, how could the government assist in reducing and facilitating restructuring of the enormous numbers of bad debts in the financial system? The less speedy and efficient the debt restructuring process, the greater the problems facing the banks in meeting tightened prudential standards. The absence of an adequate legal framework and the need to develop new rules and standards governing the obligations and rights of debtors and creditors in the midst of a protracted crisis remains one of the most difficult challenges facing the government. To define such rules and standards beforehand, in a "normal" situation, is very different from trying to do so at a time when enormous numbers of debts are actually in dispute and agents on the opposite sides of existing contracts have very clear, direct, and conflicting interests in the outcome.

Interwoven with these issues were strong and conflicting political pressures that buffeted the government. Debtors feared tougher foreclosure and bankruptcy laws, whereas bankers and other creditors wanted them to have more teeth. Bankers wanted assistance with recapitalization without significant capital write-downs. Domestic and international creditors certainly wanted to ensure the honoring of prior government guarantees on their loans to banks and finance companies. Meanwhile the government did not want to see the huge fiscal costs of its bailout policies spin further out of control.

Bank Recapitalization

Early in the application of the IMF program, the RTG announced a tightening of the NPL standards (loans would be deemed nonperforming once interest payments were delinquent for three months rather than for six months as previously), stricter requirements for provisioning against bad loans, and an increase in capital adequacy ratios to international standards. The new NPL reporting standard was implemented almost immediately, but the other two requirements were to be phased in gradually until the end of the year 2000. By mid-1998 the average NPL rate in the financial system was 33 percent and still growing (see table 4-3). As NPLs and operating losses piled up, the capital adequacy of the banks steadily diminished. The losses accumulated alone were already sufficient to wipe out the equity of a number of institutions even before provisioning for bad loans was implemented. The government was under-

Table 4-3. Nonperforming Loan Rates, Second Half of 1998
Percent

Type of institution	June	August	October	December
Private banks (8)	30.2	33.9	39.5	42.2
State banks	47.2	50.3	58.3	62.5
Foreign banks	5.5	6.6	8.1	10.0
Subtotal	31.0	34.4	40.5	43.9
Finance companies (35)	52.6	58.0	63.4	70.0
Total	32.7	36.2	43.3	45.9

Source: Bank of Thailand.

standably anxious not to force more bank or finance company closures, but on the other hand it wished to force them to take some drastic measures to increase their capital. In most cases this would require that existing shareholders take substantial losses. In the absence of adequate incentives, positive or negative, the banks were unwilling to do this. The fact that several of the major banks' major shareholders were well connected and influential made the government reluctant to be very heavy-handed. An additional concern of the government was that the banks were unwilling to issue new loans for fear of further aggravating their NPL problems.

A compromise policy package issued in mid-August 1998 contained some carrots and sticks to encourage recapitalization and increased lending. The banks were offered, on a noncompulsory basis, the opportunity to receive government bonds that would be treated as tier 1 or tier 2 capital and could be paid back at some later date when the banks were able to recapitalize from other sources. In return for the tier 1 capital, however, the banks needed to implement the new loan provisioning rules immediately and match any government capital contributions with capital to be raised by themselves. This would require significant write-downs of their own capital. The government also reserved the right to change senior bank management personnel. For the tier 2 support they would have to increase lending and debt restructuring at a rate proportionate to the amount of new funding taken. This was seen by bank management and major shareholders as potentially costly and very risky.

Other options considered or proposed included variations of the "Chilean model" whereby the government would take over the NPLs and inject its own capital into the banks and financial institutions. These proposals were rejected for two reasons. First, the government was justifiably concerned about the adverse consequences of asymmetries in information and management capabilities between the government and private lenders and borrowers. Second, there was growing political pressure for the government to switch its attention "from safety nets for the rich to safety nets for the poor." It was feared that bank rescues of the Chilean type would be viewed as further bailouts of the rich and privileged. This would be especially true if the government did not force big "haircuts" on the bank shareholders, something it was very reluctant to do. Interestingly enough, the government set aside a total of only Bt 300 billion for this capital support. This was only a small fraction of the total needed to meet the new capital adequacy standards. Estimates at the time suggested that the total recapitalization requirements ranged from Bt 600 billion to Bt 1.4 trillion.

Corporate Debt Restructuring

The NPL problem arose primarily because of the impact of the crisis on the income flows and balance sheets of borrowers. After a long period of almost double-digit growth, Thailand had limited experience in debt restructuring. In the wake of the crisis it was clear that there were fundamental flaws in the framework of Thailand's economic and commercial laws and their implementation, as well as serious flaws with corporate governance. Without major improvements on these fronts, the prospects for speedy and efficient debt restructuring were very slim. The main problems related to weaknesses of creditors relative to debtors with respect to foreclosure, great reliance on personal guarantees in addition to or instead of collateral, the incurring of large amounts of debt with minimal or no prudential or fiduciary standards, informational problems in tracing contractual guarantees and collateral, and insufficient protection of corporate assets and minority shareholders. There also appeared to be a growing incidence of "strategic NPLs"; debtors were taking advantage of the disarray of the financial system and weaknesses in basic economic and commercial laws to simply refuse to make payments on their debts.

New initiatives in the early to middle part of 1998 were of two types: a commitment to conduct a major overhaul of a number of basic economic laws related to bankruptcy, foreclosure, property rights, and restrictions on foreign investors and the development of informal, voluntary processes, assisted by a variety of tax and other incentives, to encourage arbitration without recourse to bankruptcy and foreclosure. According to the fifth LOI, eleven new economic laws and related regulations were to be implemented by the end of October 1998. The eleven laws can be grouped into three categories: provisions for liberalizing the Alien Business Law and the property ownership laws for foreigners, a bill to facilitate the privatization of state enterprises, and amendments to the bankruptcy and foreclosure laws and procedures.

Most important and most controversial were the bankruptcy and foreclosure laws. A new bankruptcy law had been passed earlier in 1998, but it was diluted during the legislative process to the point of ineffectiveness. The main goal of the laws was to speed up debt restructuring by increasing the power of creditors relative to defaulting debtors. The new laws had several objectives, including introducing a new bankruptcy court for competent, transparent, and speedy execution of the new laws; redressing the imbalance of power of debtors over creditors with respect to foreclosure and in negotiating and enforcing debt restructuring agreements; relieving the courts of the burden of "small" cases of bankruptcy and foreclosure; and reducing and clarifying the role of personal guarantees, which have traditionally played a big part in loan agreements in Thailand. As will be seen later, these laws have become a source of enormous contention that it is taking a long time to resolve.

The second part of the new debt restructuring strategy was to develop a parallel, more informal, and less litigious means for reaching debt restructuring agreements. To this end the RTG developed the "Bangkok approach," which was modeled after procedures used in the United Kingdom by the Bank of England. A Corporate Debt Restructuring Advisory Committee (CDRAC) was set up, and a number of tax and other legal incentives were provided to encourage major corporate debtors to come to market-based debt workout agreements with their creditors. The BOT played a major role in monitoring and supervising the process. A total of about 350 major corporate debtors, with debts totaling over Bt 750 million, were selected for inclusion in this program.

Financial Sector Rehabilitation Agency Sales

By mid-1998 the FRA had already auctioned a number of the physical assets taken over as a result of the finance company closures. It was now preparing the groundwork for auctioning the more difficult financial assets over the remainder of 1998 and the first part of 1999. A number of legal measures had to be taken to clear obstacles to asset transfers. The value of leases, hire-purchase agreements, business loans, and other such assets, however, would depend very much on the progress on the basic economic laws, as would the willingness of foreigners to participate in the auctions. The success of the FRA auctions would determine the size of the burdens on the public sector resulting from the massive FIDF bailouts in 1996 and especially in 1997.

Early Results of the Midcourse Correction

What results could be seen from the midcourse correction in terms of macroeconomic policies, bank recapitalization, economic laws, corporate debt restructuring, and FRA auctions? First, the easing of monetary and fiscal policies had the predicted effect on interest rates, as both lending and deposit rates fell rapidly and substantially, continuing until the present. It is important to note, however, that deposit rates have fallen much more than lending rates. This fact reflects the high costs of nonperforming loans and the perceived risks in issuing new loans. Bank lending did not increase significantly; it has been virtually constant in nominal terms since March 1998 (excluding BIBF credits). The government attempted without success to apply moral suasion to the banks to increase lending.

Nevertheless, the new measures led to a resurgence of stock market investment and a significant "bubblet" in the SET index in the fourth quarter of 1998. Slightly more surprising was a further strengthening of the baht, which the BOT actually attempted to restrain. Falling interest rates and improvements in the baht and the SET index encouraged policymakers and others who were predicting that the Thai economy was bottoming out and that recovery was on the horizon. However, most of the real economic indicators—exports, imports, manufacturing output, investment, bank lending, and employment—had not shown any signs of reversal by the end of 1998.

The government's new spending programs were implemented very slowly. Of the $120 million SIP fund set up in August 1998, only $1 million of expenditures had been approved by February 1999. This represented about 110 small projects out of over 5,000 for which proposals had been submitted. Although the insistence on transparency and accountability had much to recommend itself on grounds of good governance, it proved costly in terms of delayed program implementation.

Second, with regard to bank recapitalization there was little progress throughout the remainder of 1998. Not a single bank accepted the government's tier 1 or tier 2 recapitalization offers. Although two banks recapitalized by submitting to foreign takeovers and one other had found a foreign investor (and all of these events had occurred before the government made its offer package available in mid-August), the remainder of the banks continued to avoid the government's recapitalization programs. Several banks took advantage of a combination of gullible depositors and loose definitions of capital to raise new quasi-equity by converting deposits to Stapled Limited Interest Preferred Shares (SLIPS) and Capital Augmented Preferred Shares (CAPS). These are both instruments that dress up combinations of subordinated debt and preferred shares to qualify as tier 1 or tier 2 capital, enabling the banks to raise capital without diluting original shareholders' equity. In sum, the August package had not succeeded in facilitating recapitalization as of 1999. The total amount of recapitalization required is difficult to estimate, but estimates in spring 1999 of the banks' and finance companies' additional capital requirements ranged from Bt 700 million to over Bt 1 trillion ($19 to $27 billion).

Meanwhile, the number of NPLs continued to rise (see table 4-3), and by early 1999 the NPL rate had risen to a systemwide average of almost 50 percent, where it remained for the rest of the year. Although interest rates were falling, there was very little new bank lending. This was due to both demand and supply factors. Borrowers saw very few profitable investment opportunities, and lenders, who were maintaining a growing differential between lending and borrowing rates, were very risk-averse in assessing new loans. They did not want to risk further increases in NPL rates.

Recognizing the lack of success of its mid-August 1998 banking package, the government tried to apply more pressure. It used moral suasion on the banks to reduce interest rates and increase lending. Although rates continued to fall, there was no noticeable impact on lending. The government required all financial institutions to submit detailed recapitalization plans in January 1999. Unfortunately, the plans were required only for the period up to June 1999, at which time the stricter loan loss provisioning requirements would apply, but they would apply to only 60 percent of the value of NPLs.

Third, as noted above, the government committed itself to bringing eleven new basic economic and commercial laws into effect by October 31, 1998. This deadline was not met. The issue was diplomatically skirted in the sixth LOI. Enactment of the new laws was delayed initially by problems in preparing them and presenting them to Parliament, and then by political battles between the government and various vested interests. Rural debtors, especially poor farmers in the northeast part of the country, were justifiably alarmed at the prospects of being forced into personal bankruptcy (with very harsh consequences under the current law) on the basis of personal guarantees on loans for land or equipment purchases. A much more important barrier, however, was the opposition of a group of very wealthy debtors, a number of whom are influential members of the Thai Senate. This group used its power both to mount a major public campaign against the new laws and to delay their passage by Parliament. The campaign included appeals to nationalistic fears of sellouts to foreigners and to populist sentiments related to the unfairness of small and powerless debtors' being forced by rich (foreign) creditors into punitive personal bankruptcy. In order to preserve an image of broad popular support for the new laws, the government has felt it necessary to meet some of the opposition demands. In particular, it offered concessions with respect to minimum debt limits for application of the bankruptcy and foreclosure laws, relaxation of liabilities with respect to personal guarantees, and reduction of the number of years for which sanctions will apply with respect to personal bankruptcies.[16]

Only the Thai Senate has the legal power to delay new laws. Any changes proposed by the Senate must be approved by the Lower House. If the government disagrees with such changes, it must discuss them in a joint House-Senate committee (which can meet for up to 180 days), but can ultimately pass whatever version of the laws it wishes. Following a major public showdown in mid-March 1999, the Senate passed most of the new economic and commercial laws. The Senate's amendments appeared, by and large, to be acceptable to the government and did not threaten the laws' basic principles and objectives. By late 1999 all the laws had finally been passed by the Senate and Parliament. The time taken to debate these laws caused confusion and uncertainty for all actors involved in resolving the country's key financial sector problems. It delayed and imposed high costs on the debt restructuring process and on the resolution of the NPL and bank recapitalization problems. With the passage of these and other laws, implementation issues will certainly arise as well.

Fourth, progress with corporate debt restructuring has been painfully slow, and even by late 1999 the proportion of the debts that had been successfully restructured had been much smaller than hoped. As of mid-November 1999, fewer than 15 percent (by value) of the loans under the CDRAC process had been restructured. Another 31 percent have failed to be resolved in this manner

---

16. On the other hand, the government was not willing to yield on proposals such as one put forward in the Senate to postpone implementation of new bankruptcy laws for two years ("until the crisis is over") and others to exempt residential property from foreclosure law and to exempt from the bankruptcy law any debts for which collateral had been offered and agreed to, at the time of commitment, to cover the value of the loan.

and face legal action under the new bankruptcy laws. More worrisome is the fact that many of the restructuring deals that have been completed have been more of the nature of a rescheduling of debts than of a more complete restructuring. Neither the banks nor the major corporate debtors have made the major adjustments and submitted to the "haircuts" necessary for a major restructuring. There are reports that a number of supposedly restructured debts had returned to nonperforming status by mid-1999. As many as 20 percent of "restructured" debts are reported to have returned to nonperforming status by early 2000. The process may be postponing rather than solving some of the most serious debt problems facing the banks and the corporate sector.

Finally, progress also slowed on the FRA auctions of the assets of failed banks and finance companies. The December 1998 auction of business loans sold less than 50 percent of the assets on offer, and they were sold at prices that were much lower than the amounts received at earlier auctions of physical assets. The average sale returned only about 25 percent of the face value of the assets sold. Moreover, a large share of the sales were achieved only after the government made some controversial changes in the auction procedures. The December 1998 auctions were controversial as well because of conflict-of-interest concerns. Chief among these was widely reported preauction collusion between bidders and the defaulted debtors whose loans were being auctioned. This collusion was a way for debtors to bypass regulations against participating in the auctions of their own debts and for bidders to make a tidy profit without assuming any risk.[17]

In the presence of such well-known arrangements, other potential bidders were extremely wary of participating for fear of the "winner's curse" effect. There were also reports of collusion among bidders, and concerns were expressed about the propriety of allowing one of the FRA's chief foreign advisors to bid at the auction. Another important reason for the failure of this auction and for the slow progress on this front in general was the delay in passing and implementing the new economic laws noted earlier. The auction in late March 1999 achieved an average recovery rate of less than 20 percent of the face value

---

17. The FRA initially rejected many bids on the grounds that the prices offered were too low. In a number of these cases it then negotiated a new offer (after the auction, and solely with the company that had made each failed bid) that included a condition that all preauction contracts with debtors be dissolved for at least six months. The new price in each such situation also included a profit-sharing condition between the bidder and the FRA.

of the assets sold. A large portion of the assets, especially those of the lowest quality, were purchased by the government's Asset Management Corporation. By late 1999 most of the assets had been auctioned, with recovery rates continuing to decline as more risky assets were put up for sale.

Summary

In mid-1998, a year after Thailand's entry into the IMF program, there was a significant midcourse correction in the country's recovery strategy. Its fiscal and monetary policies were loosened, and the government launched new measures to speed up debt restructuring and bank recapitalization. By early 1999 there were some encouraging signs, especially in the form of lower interest rates and an appreciated and more stable baht. However, macro-economic fundamentals (sectoral output data, exports, imports, and employment) did not show signs of improvement well into 1999. The government fell far behind its schedule for improving the framework for debt restructuring. New economic laws were seriously delayed. Banks were not moving to make use of the government's recapitalization program, and were instead withdrawing from the market in order to avoid further risks and to avoid or delay diluting shareholders' equity. As a result of the apparent ineffectiveness of the government's program and increasing numbers of scandals reported in various ministries, the government's support and credibility were diminishing. Although the government comfortably survived no-confidence votes in February and December 1999, issues raised in the debates did not improve its reputation. Strong pressures are being brought to bear by special interests that stand to lose from economic reforms. More important, increasing numbers of more objective observers are increasingly questioning some of the foundations of the government's crisis recovery strategy.

Thailand's Short-Term Prospects

Where does all this leave Thailand for the immediate future? The government predicted full economic recovery by the middle of 1999. It was hoped that exports might lead the recovery. However, the strong baht, the depreciation of other Asian currencies, falling regional demand, and the declining prices of many basic industrial exports (20 percent in dollar terms for electronics over the past year or so according to industry sources) all make export recovery a slower and more difficult prospect. Furthermore, the high import content of manufactured exports means that export growth has a relatively small impact on overall economic activity.

Investment performance from 1997 through 1999 was very poor. Is this performance likely to improve in the near future? By the end of 1999 the manufacturing sector's capacity utilization was barely over 60 percent. In the face of such massive excess capacity, significant new investment is highly unlikely. Furthermore, even if there were investors interested in developing new projects, financing might be a major problem. The banking sector, crippled by massive undercapitalization and very high NPL rates, remains reluctant to make any new loans.

By late 1999 there were weak signs that consumption might be bottoming out. This could be due to the effects of SET increases in late 1998 and in the second half of 1999 or of consumer needs to replenish stocks of certain items whose purchases had been postponed during the early stages of the crisis. But layoffs and uncertainties about hours, wages, and overtime still dominated the labor market well into the second year of the crisis. As we shall see later, there have been significant new stresses on rural incomes. These income uncertainties make a speedy recovery of consumption unlikely.

Monetary and Fiscal Issues

The fifth and sixth LOIs highlighted a relaxation of the fiscal and monetary targets, as well as predictions of lower interest rates. These changes did not have the effects on the real economy that had been hoped for. Why? In a flexible exchange rate environment, monetary actions generally have a much greater impact than fiscal policies. Unfortunately, current monetary policies were not likely to be very effective at stimulating aggregate demand for (at least) two reasons.

First, as measured by growth in monetary aggregates, the policies were not very expansionary. Except for the month of November 1998, when it grew at 5.7 percent, the annual rate of growth of the monetary base was no more than 1.5 percent for the year following August 1998. Although this is better than the negative growth that was prevalent before August, it was not very expansionary. M1 growth showed a similar pattern. Other monetary aggregates have been growing at higher rates, and that growth, together with the government's substantial withdrawal from the markets, has been the reason for declining interest rates. The prime rate (or minimum lending rate) fell from about

15.5 percent in July 1998 to about 9.5 percent in mid-1999, and deposit rates fell even more.

However, lower interest rates have not yet had a significant expansionary effect on bank lending on their own. There are several reasons for this: lending rates have been much slower to adjust than deposit rates; undercapitalization of banks, low collateral values, and high NPLs are inducing highly risk-averse lending behavior; and, as mentioned earlier, there remains little demand for new loans as a result of the scarcity of profitable investment opportunities. These issues are closely related to problems associated with both the debt restructuring process and bank recapitalization.

In the current Thai environment (where there is a floating exchange rate with few controls on capital flows), fiscal policies will generally be much less effective than monetary policies in stimulating aggregate demand. The standard explanation is that fiscal expansion puts upward pressure on interest rates. This has two types of offsetting negative effects on aggregate demand. First, it has the direct effect of crowding out interest-sensitive private expenditures. Second, it puts upward pressure on the exchange rate, which decreases demand for domestically produced tradable goods. This fact explains the IMF finding that tight fiscal policies had only a small negative impact on aggregate demand in the early stages of the IMF program in Thailand.[18] The main effect of fiscal stimulus under these conditions will be to alter the composition of aggregate demand between the public and private sectors. However, in the current circumstances in Thailand, with few alternative investment opportunities and with interest rates arguably relatively insensitive to changes in money supply, fiscal expansion might be more effective than would be expected in normal circumstances. To the extent that a relaxation of the country's fiscal stance does affect aggregate demand, the quantitative effect will depend on the size of the deficit.

Until August 1998 the fiscal deficit had been almost entirely passive as the result of declining government revenues from the recession. After the filing of the fifth and sixth LOIs, the government attempted to implement new spending programs to provide a more direct stimulus to demand as well as to provide income relief in poor and especially needy communities. As we have seen earlier, disbursements have been very slow.

In early 1999 the government announced a new set of expenditure programs in a total amount of about Bt 53 billion (U.S.$1.45 billion), financed by loans

18. See Lane and others (1999).

from the World Bank (U.S.$600 million), Japan's Ex-Im Bank (U.S.$600 million), and Japan's Overseas Economic Cooperation Fund (OECF) (about U.S.$250 million). Only the last of these was offered on concessional terms. The focus of these loans was largely on employment generation and community improvement projects in areas such as health and education. In addition, some expenditures were earmarked for industrial promotion and administrative reform. The government indicated that speedy expenditure of these funds was its top priority. Government ministries were expected to have proposals ready for approval before the end of March, and all funds were to be expended by the end of the fiscal year (September 1999). These new expenditures, accounting for almost 1 percent of GDP, were all treated as off-budget expenditures. In other words, they were in addition to those that made up the fiscal deficit of 5 percent of GDP that was targeted in the sixth LOI.

Justifiable concerns were expressed as to how this massive new expenditure plan could possibly be accomplished in a productive and accountable manner. The fact that over a third of the funds were to be allocated to the Interior Ministry, widely noted in the past for the politicized nature of its expenditure allocations, added weight to these concerns. Nevertheless, viewed simply as part of a pump-priming exercise, these programs were likely to be much more successful than the previous SIP program. Speedier disbursements may or may not lead to more useful results. But old-style political and bureaucratic pork might be more effective at pumping money into stimulation of demand than is transparent and accountable community-based spending.

Additional Japanese OECF funds are likely to be made available to support major infrastructure projects, including roads, dams, transport systems, and the new Bangkok airport. Neither the exact amount nor details on projects that will be supported under this loan are known. However, the government expressed a strong willingness to use whatever funds are made available and to do so as quickly as possible.

After earlier insisting on improvements in the accountability, transparency, and productivity of public spending, it is remarkable how willing international donors and agencies seemed to be to sign on to "blank check" programs such as these to provide short-term stimulus to the Thai economy. Some local observers noted that, in light of the large amounts of excess domestic liquidity and the lack of interest in new private investments, Thailand might be much further ahead to finance new stimulus packages locally. Bringing in large amounts of foreign funds would put further upward pressure on the baht, which would make recovery of domestic export- and import-competing industries even more difficult.

The government also announced further fiscal stimulus measures on the revenue side, primarily in the form of a reduction in the rate of the value-added tax (VAT) from 10 to 7 percent and some reductions in income taxes.[19] The revenue stimulus provided by these measures was projected to be slightly larger than the expenditure increases funded by the World Bank and Japanese loans—that is, more than 1 percent of GDP.

Rural Incomes

During the first year and a half of the crisis, traditionally poor rural areas performed relatively well. This was due to a combination of good crop yields and substantially higher baht prices as a result of the depreciation of the baht and increases in the dollar prices of some key products. It was especially fortunate in light of the role of the villages in providing a social safety net for laid-off urban workers. However, it appears that the outlook for the immediate future will be substantially different. Most important, the recovery of the baht and falling dollar prices have resulted in substantially lower domestic crop prices.

Decreases in rural incomes in 1999, and possibly beyond, were unavoidable. These have put a drag on the recovery. The stimulative impact of a 5 percent (of GDP) government deficit are barely sufficient to offset the fall in rural incomes. Declining rural incomes not only affected aggregate demand, but also had negative implications for the informal social safety net provided by the villages, posing further threats to social and political stability.

Passage and Implementation of Legislation

Long delays in drafting and passing new basic economic laws have been an enormous and costly hindrance to the adjustment of the Thai asset markets required by the crisis. Delays certainly impede short-term recovery prospects. The next issue that must be dealt with will be the effectiveness of their implementation. For example, a variety of concerns have been expressed about the competence of Thai courts to deal with bankruptcy and foreclosure cases in a timely, fair, and efficient manner. It is for this reason that the laws provide for

19. This reduction in the VAT reversed the increase in the VAT announced in the first LOI.

a special new bankruptcy court and that crash training programs are being put into place for court officials. In any case, it will still be some time before these new laws and programs are put to the test.[20] Therefore, the effectiveness of the new laws will be a greater factor in the long run than they will be in shaping short-term recovery. Their main short-term impact will be in terms of the confidence-building (or -diminishing) effects of changing public perceptions of the government's progress in dealing with major issues through legislation.

Bank Recapitalization

The bank recapitalization problem remains problematic. The government remains unable to decide whether to be tough or easy on the remaining banks. Under the original IMF program, an Asset Management Corporation had been set up, with the intention that it would somehow take over the bad debts in the banking system. As described earlier, the Democrats decided to leave the NPLs with the banks. The problem became far worse than had been imagined when this decision was made. In early 1999 the government came under increasing criticism for simultaneously leaving the NPLs in the banks, enforcing stricter NPL reporting and provisioning rules, and imposing higher capital adequacy standards. The critics argued that these were impossible burdens and that it was far more important to simply get the credit system operating again than to try to meet these impossible international standards. Whatever the merits of these suggestions, the government's indecision left the bank recapitalization problem unsolved. This is possibly the most important item on the government's short-term policy agenda.

Political Stability

In October 1998 the government increased its slim ruling majority by bringing a major opposition party into the coalition. This was necessary to ensure passage of the new economic laws. The government now appears to be relatively stable, and it survived parliamentary no-confidence debates in February and December 1999. However, the no-confidence debates and a number of scandals within the government have tarnished its credibility. The personal reputation of Finance Minister Tarrin has certainly suffered. The government

20. A new obstacle has recently emerged in the form of a suit by a group of influential senators to contest the constitutionality of the new laws.

will have to call an election in 2000, and it is counting heavily on an early economic recovery before it has to go to the electorate. The greater the delay in the recovery, the greater will be the pressures on the government and the less success is it likely to have in the polls. The "old-style" opposition parties still have considerable support outside of Bangkok, and this will increase with continued recession and with likely economic problems in rural areas. A well-known wealthy businessman and former cabinet member has started a new political party that could be a threat to the Democrats in urban areas. Continued economic difficulties will increase the medium-term political uncertainties. The next election could be a major test of the effectiveness of the new constitution in reforming Thailand's old-style "money politics."

External Risks

Thailand has undertaken many measures to prepare the domestic economy for recovery. However, there remain a number of potentially dangerous external threats related to demand for Thai products in world markets, supply and cost of foreign capital, and competition for Thai-produced goods. The most important danger is the precariousness of the Japanese economy. Failure of the Japanese recovery measures would have serious implications for external demand for Thai goods and for the availability of supply capital and loans to support the Thai recovery. In China further banking and financial difficulties could lead to serious economic problems and a devaluation of the yuan, which could have a devastating effect on the competitiveness of Thai exports. Any weakness in the U.S. economy—triggered by a stock market correction, for instance—would affect demand for exports and the supply of capital everywhere. The collapse in Brazil did not have much effect on demand or capital supplies, but it increased competition and lowered prices even further for some key Thai exports, such as electronics.

Summary

Thailand's short-term recovery remains problematic. Despite falling interest rates and inflation and a stabilizing baht, recovery driven by exports, investment, or domestic demand will be very difficult. New fiscal measures might have some effect, but implementing them would require a major break from recent patterns and failures. There remain serious threats of difficulties in rural areas and of domestic political instability. There are potential external threats in the form of falling demand and increased competition for Thai exports.

By the second half of 1999 there were signals of recovery in several key variables. Import and export growth had resumed, along with manufacturing production. Although its growth was still negative, investment performance was becoming less weak. Nevertheless, financial sector weaknesses are still unresolved.

Barring major new external disturbances, the recovery is likely to continue, and short-term growth will probably exceed forecasts made in early 2000. But overall performance is still uncertain, as are longer-term prospects.

Longer-Term Prospects

Looking ahead, Thailand's prospects for the longer-term recovery of its growth and competitiveness depend on a number of factors. Three of the most important are related to the long-term costs of major shocks and policy errors, institutional and governance frameworks, and long-term competitiveness.

Long-Term Costs

The initial shocks that hit the Thai economy in 1996–97 and some of the policies that followed imposed very large costs on the economy. These costs will be borne over an extended period of time and will be a burden on longer-term recovery. The huge reversal of capital flows in 1997 deprived Thailand of the services of substantial amounts of capital. Some of this is made up for by official loans from a number of sources, which will be discussed further later. The amounts lost through the huge drain on foreign exchange reserves from the failed defense of the baht has been gradually recovered. The cost is not, of course, the total amount of reserves, but is related rather to the difference between their value when they were sold and when they are reacquired.

The costs of financial restructuring will be very large. When Thailand first entered the IMF program, it was estimated that the interest costs of debts incurred with respect to FIDF bailouts would amount to roughly 1 percent of GDP for a number of years and that the capital costs could be met from the proceeds of privatization of state enterprises. The costs have escalated considerably since then, and the state enterprise privatization program is no longer viewed as a means of financing them. Recent government and IMF estimates of the annual interest costs alone are about 4 percent of GDP. To meet the capital costs incurred by the FIDF, it was announced that substantial new bond issues will be required, in addition to the Bt 500 billion already authorized. Under various rescue packages from the IMF, the World Bank, the ADB, and bilateral donors, the RTG has taken on and is in the process of assuming large new debt burdens. Although some of these have been taken on concessional terms, most have not. The ultimate burden of these loans will depend in large part on how productively the funds are employed. Lack of transparency and accountability and reckless speed in planning and executing new expenditure programs raise serious questions about their likely long-term benefits to the Thai economy.

Finally, the skeletons of large numbers of partially completed construction projects—condominiums, office towers, residential complexes, and transport infrastructure—litter Thailand, and especially Bangkok. Many of these are deteriorating rapidly from exposure to the elements. Not only do these represent unfortunate sunk costs; many of them will now require demolition, a costly and sometimes dangerous activity. These are additional costs that will have to be borne, carved out of Thailand's future growth.

Institutional and Governance Frameworks

In Thailand, as in other countries in the region, financial crisis has exposed weaknesses and put great strains on institutional and governance structures, threatening future development possibilities. On the other hand, constructive responses to these pressures can yield great dividends for the future. In some respects Thailand has been extremely fortunate in this regard. Already one of the most open regimes in the region, at the time the crisis struck Thailand was in the final stages of a major and popular constitutional reform. The purpose was to consolidate democratic institutions and to eliminate the basis for at least the most egregious aspects of the country's old-style money politics regime. At possibly her most vulnerable time in the early days of the crisis Thailand experienced a peaceful, speedy, and fully legitimate change of government. As well as fully embracing the economic reforms initiated under IMF guidance, the new government took full responsibility for completing the constitutional reforms. Regardless of the short-term difficulties for implementing the government's reform program, there was a full and open debate about the key features of the new basic economic laws. This debate has certainly enhanced the legitimacy of both the political processes and the new legislative framework.

The government has made and continues to make major changes in the rules and regulations facing the financial sector. It has amended old laws and introduced new ones governing basic economic institutions. It is in the process of opening the economy to greater competition, domestic and foreign. Successful continuation of this process will create a much more sound and productive financial sector and a system of corporate governance that will enhance investment, productivity, and the interests of Thai workers and consumers. However, none of these prospects are guaranteed. On the negative side, there is no assurance that the constitutional reforms will succeed in eliminating money politics. There are many forces in the governing coalition and in the opposition that have had long experience with the old system and will try to exploit it in future elections. The declining popularity of reformist elements in the government could restore these forces to power.

It is too early to know how effectively the legal reforms in the financial and corporate sectors will be implemented. The government is far from resolving the complex problems of bank recapitalization and debt restructuring. There is still some danger, for instance, that slip-ups in implementation, in part or in whole under pressure from vested interests, could derail recovery and cause long-term damage to Thailand's debt culture, resulting in increasing nonpayment of debts, even among healthy borrowers. The process of reforming deep-seated practices of corporate governance has just begun. It is far too early to predict whether this will proceed in the best interests of Thailand's long-term development.

The economic stress caused by the crisis has given rise to major social tensions. These will increase with delays in the recovery. Protracted debates and confrontations over basic issues of creditor and debtor rights have been at least temporarily resolved by the passage of basic economic laws. However, the differences could still linger and not only cause difficulties in implementation of the new laws, but in the process also tear further at the country's social fabric.

Basic Problems of Long-Term Competitiveness

Even before the crisis, Thailand faced serious problems with long-run competitiveness.[21] Although overall growth in productivity was moderate, most of it was in agriculture or arose from interindustry shifts. There was little indication of growth of technological capabilities or of movements "up the ladder of

21. This section draws on Flatters (1999).

comparative advantage."[22] Among the widely recognized barriers to growth in competitiveness were very low levels and quality of education, serious deficiencies in infrastructure development and environmental management, and a policy regime at the microeconomic level that was too much geared to creating and preserving rents rather than fostering market competition.[23] Monopolies in basic services (such as telecommunications) and protection of upstream industries (steel and petrochemicals) were among the most obvious and egregious examples of misguided protectionism.[24] Although prudent macro-economic policies had always been regarded as a strength in Thailand, the financial and macroeconomic mismanagement that led to the crisis has called the strength of those policies into question as well. Political and bureaucratic corruption has been another continuing source of concern.

Although the crisis has drawn attention to some of these issues and provoked some policy improvements, many of the problems have been left "on hold," and some have become worse. One immediate effect of the crisis was a reduction in school enrollments, which will lower future education levels. Although the government has attempted to exempt major export industries from the costs of upstream protection, it has done little to attack the protection problem directly. The crisis seems to have fed the long-standing inclination to solve any adjustment or competitiveness problem in the real sector by creating a special government fund to throw public money at it. Unfortunately the IMF, other international agencies, and bilateral donors seem far too willing to accept and promote such policies. There has been considerable talk and some action in dealing with corruption in various ministries, and yet there has been little progress in systematic public service reform and introduction of realistic wage and incentive systems. Resolution of these problems is essential to the restoration and sustainability of Thailand's long-term growth and competitiveness.

22. See Tinakorn and Sussangkarn (1996).

23. For an early review of these challenges to Thailand's competitiveness, see Ak-rasanee, Dapice, and Flatters (1991).

24. The government's unwillingness to include pricing of irrigation water or to move agricultural prices to a more market-oriented regime as part of a U.S.$600 million ADB-funded agricultural loan program is a worrisome sign of a continuation of a subsidy-dominated sectoral policy regime. The same inclinations are revealed in a recent refusal to eliminate state subsidies from a new credit program for small to medium-size enterprises.

Conclusion

The short-term and longer-term prognosis for the Thai recovery are dealt with in the previous two sections. Although Thailand was the first of the countries in the region to enter the crisis, its process of recovery has not been fast. Its longer-term prospects depend on some major issues whose resolution is not yet known. Relative to other countries in the region, Thailand still has the potential to be a strong performer for the longer term.

Of critical importance is the relationship between domestic reactions to the IMF program, on the one hand, and prospects for long-term sustainability of the reforms, on the other. Domestic reactions have evolved with the program and with economic events. In tracing their path it is sometimes useful and important to distinguish among various groups in Thailand, in particular the government, various vested interests, critical observers, and the electorate.

The most important reaction to the IMF immediately before the crisis was the government's apparent unwillingness to listen to warnings about the weaknesses of the exchange rate regime and the financial system. Failure to heed these warnings has imposed large costs on the Thai economy. Although the government finally asked the IMF for assistance, it did so out of sheer necessity. Following the change of government in November 1997, Thailand became a full and willing partner of the IMF. The new government bought fully into the IMF program initiated under its predecessors, and it is fair to say that most of the public gave at least grudging acceptance to the program, if only because of the clear failures of the policies of the previous government and the general discrediting of that government.

As the economy fell deeper into recession in the first part of 1998, the voices of discontent became louder and were raised more frequently. The collapsing baht and escalating interest rates put increased pressure on the real sector, and the true weakness of the financial system became more apparent. By mid-1998 many critical observers were advocating a major change of policy direction. It was in response to these pressures, more than anything else, that the government made a major correction in the course of its macroeconomic program. At the same time, vested interests in the financial sector made it difficult for the government to be equally decisive in establishing its financial sector reform programs. As a result it chose a number of soft, voluntary options. It ran into similar problems with its program of legal and regulatory reform for debt restructuring and, as a result, important deadlines were missed. This created considerable social tension as vested interests representing the opposite sides of delinquent loan agreements fought over laws related to the balance of powers between debtors and creditors.

It appears that the battles over these basic economic laws are ending and that the integrity of this part of the program will be preserved. However, there remain major implementation issues that it will take some time to sort out. Moreover, the government is still struggling with its unwillingness to confront major vested interests in the banking sector over principles of bank recapitalization. Most important, delays in banking reform and debt restructuring have imposed large costs and have been a major barrier to economic recovery.

The longer the recession lasts (and some critics are now warning of the dangers of a W-shaped recovery), the greater will be the manifestations of social tension due to the real economic distress faced by many people. For some time the government, the IMF, and other international agencies responded to this distress with less and less well-considered social assistance and restructuring programs. The initial program principles of transparency, accountability, and market-based incentives to lead Thailand to short-term recovery and long-term sustainable growth were increasingly ignored. In the rush to defuse the social tension and prepare for upcoming elections, the government continues to back away from some important hard decisions. The principles of the reforms are being threatened, and the end result could still be the replacement of the current government by one similar to the one that got Thailand into this mess in the first place.

What can be said, then, about the sustainability of Thailand's reform program? It is clear from what has been said already that "the reform program" is an elusive and fast-moving target. A desirable feature of any crisis management program, of course, is flexibility and the ability to adapt to new information and changing circumstances. By this standard, Thailand and the IMF are not deficient. However, underlying the reforms are a number of important principles of economic management. It is still too early to say whether Thailand will continue to agree on and abide by these principles. It is not clear, either, how much the IMF will be willing to bend its own principles in order to continue its special relationship with and bask in the reflected glory of one of its star pupils.

Thailand is at a critical point in its constitutional, political, social, and economic development. This was true even before the crisis. There is no doubt that she is well placed to make major steps forward on all these fronts and become an even greater and more successful participant in Asia's development. Arguably, the economic crisis gave Thailand the opportunity (and the need) to push forward with its reforms even more quickly than otherwise. However, there are limits to the resilience of the social, political, and economic fabric. It remains to be seen whether the country's response to the crisis strengthens this fabric or tears it apart.

References

Akrasanee, Narongchai, David Dapice, and Frank Flatters. 1991. *Thailand's Export-Led Growth: Retrospect and Prospects.* Thailand Development Research Institute Policy Study. Bangkok: TDRI.

Flatters, Frank. 1999. "Thailand." *The Asia Competitiveness Report 1999.* Geneva: World Economic Forum.

Flatters, Frank, Sauwalak Kittiprapas, and Chalongphob Sussangkarn. 1999. "Comparative Social Impacts of the Asian Economic Crisis in Indonesia, Malaysia, the Philippines, and Thailand: A Preliminary Report." *TDRI Quarterly Review* (March).

Government of Thailand. 1997. "Letter of Intent to International Monetary Fund" (Second LOI; November 25). www.imf.org/external/np/loi/112597.HTM.

Kakwani, Nanak. 1998. *Impact of the Economic Crisis on Employment, Unemployment and Real Income* Bangkok: National Economic and Social Development Board, September.

Lane, Timothy, and others. 1999. *IMF-Supported Programs in Indonesia, Korea, and Thailand: A Preliminary Assessment.* Washington: International Monetary Fund (January).

Prachuabmoh, Nukul, and others. 1998. *Analysis and Evaluation of Facts Behind Thailand's Economic Crisis* (Nukul Report). Bangkok: Nation Multimedia Group (March).

Radelet, Steven, and Jeffrey Sachs. 1998. *The East Asian Financial Crisis: Diagnosis, Remedies, Prospects.* Harvard Institute for International Development (April).

Siamwalla, Ammar. 1997. *Can a Developing Democracy Manage Its Macroeconomy? The Case of Thailand.* J. Douglas Gibson Lecture, Queen's University, Canada (October).

Siamwalla, Ammar, and Orapin Sopchokchai. 1998. "Responding to the Thai Economic Crisis." Paper prepared for the United Nations Development Program, Bangkok.

Tinakorn, Pranee, and Chalongphob Sussangkarn. 1996. *Productivity Growth in Thailand.* Thailand Development Research Institute Research Monograph 15. Bangkok: TDRI.

Part Three

TAIWAN WEATHERING
THE STORM

CHAPTER FIVE

Differing Approaches, Differing Outcomes: Industrial Priorities, Financial Markets, and the Crisis in Korea and Taiwan

Tain-Jy Chen and Ying-Hua Ku

B oth Korea and Taiwan have been touted as economic miracles, with emphasis placed on the impressive pace of their economic growth, their rapid capital accumulation, and strong export orientation. Most scholars agree that rapid capital accumulation contributes to rapid economic growth, although there are concerns that the marginal contribution of capital may diminish over time, making capital-pushed growth unsustainable.[1] On the other hand, there is little agreement among scholars as to whether export orientation effectively contributes to economic growth. Although both Korea and Taiwan have promoted their export industries, they have also protected their import substitution industries.

However, studies comparing the economic success of Korea and Taiwan to that of other East Asian economies has focused on the1960s and 1970s.[2] Typically, because of their similarities Korea and Taiwan are treated as parallel cases, reinforcing each other in terms of the merits of export orientation or government intervention in economic development.[3] Only a handful of scholars have contrasted these two economies.[4] The Asian financial crisis

---

1. Krugman (1994); Rodrik (1998).
2. For instance, see World Bank (1993).
3. Amsden (1989); Krueger (1990); Rodrik (1995).
4. For example, Lau (1986).

attests to the value of the latter approach. Because Korea fell victim to the crisis and Taiwan managed to weather the storm relatively well, important differences in their approach to economic development became apparent. This chapter explores some of these differences.

On the surface both countries had achieved similar rates of growth in gross national product (GNP) in the 1980s and 1990s until the financial crisis of 1997. Even the chronic inflation that had plagued the Korean economy in the 1970s was successfully suppressed in the 1980s, eliminating the single negative economic woe that had made some view Korea's achievement as inferior to Taiwan's. However, the financial crisis soon overshadowed all the glowing economic figures that Korea had put in the record book. What went wrong in Korea that did not go wrong in Taiwan?

In this chapter we argue that the Korean financial crisis has its roots in the drive for development of the heavy and chemical industries (HCIs) in the 1970s. Although Taiwan was treading the same path of government-directed development at about the same time, it abandoned the policy altogether in the 1980s. The Korean government also tried to abandon HCI initiatives, but the institutions built during the initial HCI drive were never removed. This structural rigidity directed the Korean economy toward a developmental path that was biased toward capital-intensive technologies. It also locked in financial resources with a group of conglomerates that came to dominate the economy in the 1970s, despite the government's later efforts to liberalize the financial markets. Under such structural rigidity financial liberalization did not substantially improve allocative efficiency, and the power of business conglomerates to leverage their capital remained strong. Such a capital-biased developmental path had to be supported by a proportion of capital formation so large that it went beyond the capacity of even Korean savers, whose savings rate was among the highest in the world. The result was a chronic trade deficit that resulted in burgeoning foreign debts. It was such heavy foreign debt and highly leveraged business firms that bred the Korean financial crisis.

This chapter supports these arguments by first reviewing the HCIs' development drive in Korea and Taiwan, emphasizing the differences in policy and consequences. Next the chapter discusses financial market liberalization and explains why structural rigidity prevents liberalization from achieving allocative efficiency, and then it addresses how industrial structure shapes the course of economic development. Concluding remarks suggest policy findings of interest to analysts of development economics, especially with regard to East Asian economies such as Taiwan and Korea.

The Development of Heavy and Chemical Industries in Korea and Taiwan

The HCI development drive in Korea began in 1973 and was implemented until 1979.[5] In August 1973 the Economic Planning Board designated the steel, nonferrous metal, shipbuilding, machinery, electronics, and petrochemical industries as "strategic" sectors that would be eligible for promotion through various fiscal incentives.[6] This initiative represented a dramatic shift away from the export promotion policy regime that had been in place before then. Unlike the export promotion regime, in which incentives were based on performance, the promotion of HCI was sector specific. In fact, since the government restricted entry to these strategic sectors and allocated financial resources selectively to individual entrants, incentives were often firm specific with product stipulation.

Export Growth versus Import Substitution

Although the HCI development drive was import substituting in nature, Korean policymakers made it clear from the beginning that the eventual goal of the drive was to make these industries the mainstay of Korean exports. In other words, the HCI drive was a vehicle by which to transform the country's export structure. As stated in the Third Economic Development Plan, the share of HCI in Korean exports was to increase from 19.1 percent in 1971 to 60 percent in 1981.[7] HCIs were treated as infant export industries. This handling of the HCI drive in Korea stands in sharp contrast with Taiwan's version of the HCI drive; Taiwan's ambition was largely confined to import substitution, that is, servicing the domestic market. At most, HCIs were promoted in order to strengthen the competitiveness of downstream labor-intensive products that formed the mainstay of Taiwan's exports. This difference in goals led to differences in capacity investment. During Korea's HCI drive the industries were aggressive in terms of capacity buildup with the aim of establishing "world-class" operations. In contrast, in Taiwan the industries were relatively conservative in capacity buildup, aiming only at fulfilling domestic demand.

Both Korea and Taiwan, however, understood the importance of scale economies in HCIs. Both restricted domestic entry to eliminate "excessive" com-

---

5. Kim (1990).
6. Ishizaki (1996).
7. Kim (1990).

petition in favor of scale expansion by individual firms. For example, in the petrochemical industry Taiwan restricted entry through the allocation of upstream raw materials monopolized by the state-owned China Petroleum Corporation. This allocation of raw materials not only restricted entry, but also limited the capacity of entrants. In Korea the government adopted a "one item, one company" policy whereby licensing control was imposed on each product category in order to restrict entry. The Korean government further dictated the production capacity of entrants through the allocation of credit.

Both countries embarked on the development of HCIs with the help of state enterprises. After state enterprises jump started these industries, private firms took the major role in the subsequent expansion of HCIs in Korea, whereas state and semistate companies continued to dominate the industry in Taiwan. In Korea large conglomerates known as chaebols were the key force behind the country's HCI development drive. This drive enhanced the economic power of chaebols so much that thereafter they almost exclusively charted the course of Korea's economic development. In 1973 the value added by the top ten chaebols accounted for only 5.1 percent of Korea's GNP. This share increased to 10.9 percent in 1979 and to 13.0 percent in 1983.[8] That was because during the HCI drive financial resources were diverted into strategic sectors that the chaebols dominated.

In Taiwan conglomerates played a minimal role in the parallel HCI drive. As a result of that drive in the 1970s, the share of state enterprises increased in terms of capital formation and in terms of total value added by the whole economy, reversing the trend of the 1960s. The significance of small and medium-size firms did not consequently diminish, however.

Although both Korea's chaebols and Taiwan's state and semistate enterprises were equally inefficient, Taiwan's state and semistate enterprises were probably under more pressure from inefficiency to adjust, or at least their inefficiency was made more transparent to the public. That was because Taiwan's independent operators of the HCIs, whether they were state owned or not, drew their revenue from downstream exporters. If their costs were substantially higher than international norms, downstream buyers would lose their international competitiveness. Under these circumstances HCI producers were under pressure to lower prices in order to save the struggling downstream industries, particularly if these producers were state enterprises, since they were supposed to serve the "public interest."

8. Hattori (1996, p. 332).

Conversely, if domestic prices were lower than international norms and downstream exports were at an advantage in international competition, the government could restrict the export of such materials to ensure a sufficient domestic supply, preventing HCI producers from engaging in price arbitrage. Although the downstream users were predominantly small and medium-size firms that had little political clout, they collectively controlled Taiwan's economic fate through their control of exports. Despite its HCI drive, the Taiwanese government remained committed to its export-driven developmental path, and HCIs were cultivated only for import substitution, not for replacing traditional exports. This basic policy stance forced HCIs to play a role subordinate to that of traditional exports.

In contrast, Korean chaebols indulged in cross-subsidies between their divergent business units, meaning that any inefficiency could be prolonged for some time. Even if enterprises were found to be uncompetitive, however, the government might still have had to support them with favorable loans or equity investment in the hope that they would grow out of it, as in the case of the Daewoo Shipyard in the aftermath of the Second Oil Crisis.[9]

Differences in Financing

The most significant difference between Taiwan's and Korea's approach to the HCI drive, however, was in the area of financing. In Korea the government diverted financial resources to the targeted industries during the drive. First the government guided the allocation of bank loans by designating a certain portion of bank loans as policy loans, which were to be allocated according to policy. It is estimated that during the Korean HCI drive about a third of related bank loans were classified as policy loans. Strategic industries were favored over traditional industries (light manufacturing) in the appropriation of policy loans. As a result of policy preferences, the share of bank credit allocated to the six priority sectors doubled, from approximately a third in 1973–74 to about 60 percent in 1975–77.[10]

In addition to encouraging bank loans, the Korean government established the National Investment Fund (NIF) in 1974 to aid the development of strategic industries. The NIF provided long-term loans to businesses in the strategic industries at preferential interest rates for the purchase of domestic machinery,

9. Hwang (1997).
10. Kim (1990).

construction of domestic heavy machinery plants, purchase of domestically made ships, and finance of exports.[11] The NIF lent as much as two-thirds of its funds to HCI projects.[12] As the HCI drive moved along, the share of NIF loans to total bank loans increased, from 2.2 percent in 1974 to 10.8 percent in 1979.[13]

The allocation of foreign loans also contributed significant financial support to HCIs. For example, between 1972 and 1976 the manufacturing sector claimed 66.1 percent of the total amount of foreign commercial loans to Korea. Of this amount 64.1 percent went to HCIs.[14] Favorable bank loan allocation was aided by low interest rates, as domestic bank lending rates were suppressed by interest rate ceilings. Low nominal interest rates, coupled with high inflation rates during the 1970s, made Korea's real interest rates negative most of the time.[15]

In sharp contrast to the way things were done in Korea, preferential credit allocation was not a significant impetus in Taiwan's HCI drive. As in Korea, most banks in Taiwan were state owned, but there is no evidence that loan allocation in Taiwan was diverted to the strategic industries during the HCI drive. State enterprises that led the HCI drive received budget appropriations as well as credit support from banking institutions, but there was no systematic industry bias as there was in Korea. Interest rate subsidies had been in existence since the 1960s, and the main beneficiaries had been export businesses. The only noticeable special fund set up by the Taiwanese government during the HCI drive was the Industry Development Loan Fund, which was aimed at financing the purchase of domestically made machinery (Korea had a similar incentive scheme). The amount of the fund was limited, however. Despite the HCI drive, Taiwan maintained a policy of high interest rates throughout the 1970s. This policy, together with moderate inflation rates, kept real interest rates reasonably high. There was no interest rate subsidy for HCIs comparable to that in Korea, however.

Enjoying ample domestic savings and a relatively conservative attitude toward capacity expansion, Taiwan was able to build its import-substituting industries largely with domestic funds. In contrast, Korea relied heavily on

11. Koo (1984).
12. Kim (1990).
13. Koo (1984, table 10).
14. Cho (1996, p. 223).
15. Scitovsky (1986).

foreign loans to build up its HCIs. Korea's domestic savings rate stood at 22.2 percent in 1973 and 28.8 percent in 1979. Although these savings were respectable in a country with a per capita income still less than U.S.$1,000, they were insufficient to finance the country's aggressive HCI expenditures. Dependence on external financing was inevitable, and the Korean government favored borrowing over equity investment. Starting in 1974, the government tightened its control over foreign ownership in locally incorporated companies and raised the export performance requirement for foreign-owned enterprises. As a result, foreign direct investment fell sharply in 1974 and remained at a low level until the early 1980s, when the policy was reversed.[16]

Restriction of foreign direct investments, coupled with interest subsidy, encouraged Korea's domestic enterprises to borrow abroad. Its total foreign debt increased from U.S.$2.25 billion at the end of 1970 to U.S.$27.2 billion by the end of 1980. As a ratio to GNP, foreign debt increased from a moderate 28.7 percent in 1970 to a stunning 44.6 percent in 1980.[17] A particularly rapid increase was seen in the years 1978–80, when the second oil crisis reduced Korea's export earnings and the ensuing heightened interest rates in international financial markets increased the costs of debt services; foreign debt increased from U.S.$14.9 billion in 1978 to U.S.$27.2 billion in 1980. It is fair to say that the HCI drive of the 1970s was an early cause of Korea's deep-rooted indebtedness, from which it never managed to escape. By the end of 1997, the country's foreign debt had reached U.S.$121 billion.[18]

Trade Policies

In both countries the HCI drive represented a reversal of the trade liberalization course that was undertaken during the export expansion drive of the 1960s. This change of course in Korea was so far reaching that traditional export industries were severely damaged. To protect the newly installed HCIs, the original export incentive of tariff exemption on imported raw materials to be processed for export was eliminated in 1971. In its place the government introduced, in 1975, a "limited tariff drawback" system similar to Taiwan's. At the same time a "prior import recommendation" list was established whereby certain materials were permitted to be imported for export processing if the

16. Koo (1984).
17. Kim (1990, table 16).
18. Park and Rhee (1998).

price advantage of the imported items over domestic substitutes exceeded a minimum level. Compared with the policy in the export promotion era, when a comprehensive tariff exemption was allowed, this scheme widened the divergence of the effective rate of protection between HCIs and light manufacturing industries.[19] Moreover, in order to finance the HCIs with tax concessions and public funds, the Korean government was forced to scale down its fiscal and financial support for light manufacturing industries. For example, a 50 percent reduction of corporate and income taxes on export earnings, a fiscal incentive instituted during the export promotion era to encourage exports, was abolished in 1973. The interest rate differential between ordinary loans and export loans was also reduced steadily throughout the 1970s, reaching zero in 1982.[20]

In comparison, the reverse of the trade liberalization course was taken to a lesser degree in Taiwan. Although the pursuit of HCI entailed the imposition of import licensing controls on relevant products, imports had never been totally shut out during Taiwan's HCI drive. Moreover, the tariff drawback system instituted for export promotion was kept intact during the course of the HCI drive. Tax concessions on export earnings also remained in place. Interest subsidies on export credits remained effective until 1989. This was possible because the crowding-out effect of promoting strategic industries was less evident in Taiwan than in Korea.

As a result of policy-directed resources diversion, the light manufacturing industries declined relative to HCIs in Korea. HCI exports as a share of total exports increased from a mere 12.8 percent in 1970 to 38.3 percent in 1980, exceeding Taiwan's level by a large margin.[21] The capacity expansion of HCI exports enlarged rather than narrowed the balance of trade deficit, however. The rapid expansion of production capacity without commensurate productivity growth also led to a low level of capacity utilization. The second oil crisis and the assassination of President Park Chung Hee in 1979 sent Korean HCIs into a deep recession. Starting in 1980, the Korean government took action to restructure the financial institutions and the stricken HCIs, including forced mergers and capacity reduction. But, as is discussed later, the effort fell short of reconstituting the financial and industry structure as a whole.

19. Kim (1990).
20. Kwack (1984).
21. Cho (1996, p. 224).

Financial Market Liberalization

The Korean government took bold measures to liberalize its credit system in the aftermath of the HCI drive. Starting in 1982, the banking sector was liberalized step by step, and market forces were allowed to play a more important role in determining interest rates, which had until then been subject to government-imposed ceilings. As a first step toward liberalization of the banking sector, the government privatized four nationwide commercial banks between 1980 and 1983. It also relaxed requirements for establishing nonbank financial intermediates (NBFIs). To prevent business conglomerates from controlling the newly privatized banks, the government imposed strict ownership restrictions on commercial banks, allowing each shareholder to own no more than 8 percent of the equity share. But no such restrictions were imposed on NBFIs. Before long, many NBFIs had been effectively taken over by chaebols. Also in 1982, bank interest rates were unified, eliminating interest subsidies for policy loans.[22] In 1984 the Korean government lifted the ceiling on interbank call rates. This was followed by the decontrol of yields on convertible bonds and debentures with bank guarantees, as well as interest rates on CDs. Interest rate liberalization culminated in a complete decontrol of bank lending rates in 1988.[23]

In the 1970s interest ceilings, together with high inflation rates, were said to provide interest subsidies to favored borrowers. As interest ceilings were gradually removed and inflation was contained in the 1980s (the GNP deflator has been below 10 percent since 1982), the amount of interest subsidies has been drastically reduced. But the government's influence over the flow of funds had not diminished in the 1980s. Park estimates that policy loans accounted for 40.6 percent of all bank loans in 1974–79 in the wake of the HCI drive and remained at a high level of 34.6 percent in 1985–89 after interest rate deregulation and the privatization of commercial banks.[24] Policy loans included export credit, national development funds, housing loans, and a host of government-directed programs. Leipziger and Petri argue that the Korean government's refusal to keep its hands off the credit allocation process was driven by the need to control the behavior of chaebols through controlling credit availability.[25]

22. Sakong (1993, p. 73).
23. Park (1994, p. 150).
24. Park (1994, p. 156).
25. Leipziger and Petri (1997, p. 601).

Table 5-1. Korean Loans by Depository Money Banks, 1981–96
Billions of won

Year	Total	Manufacturing sector	Ratio	Heavy chemical industries	Ratio
1981	15,716.0	8,606.0	54.76	4,145.0	26.37
1982	19,169.1	9,636.0	50.27	4,792.7	25.00
1983	24,150.3	10,999.7	45.55	5,510.0	22.82
1984	27,978.9	12,295.3	43.94	6,240.1	22.30
1985	33,810.7	14,643.5	43.31	7,712.4	22.81
1986	39,098.6	17,912.5	45.81	9,670.4	24.73
1987	43,095.8	19,547.5	45.36	10,779.3	25.01
1988	48,805.4	21,586.5	44.23	12,038.1	24.67
1989	62,547.8	25,918.4	41.44	14,358.1	22.96
1990	74,028.6	31,072.9	41.97	17,734.3	23.96
1991	89,415.6	39,897.8	44.62	23,128.7	25.87
1992	102,797.0	45,048.3	43.82	26,619.9	25.90
1993	115,137.4	49,921.5	43.36	29,791.5	25.87
1994	135,850.3	57,127.7	42.05	35,061.7	25.81
1995	152,477.7	62,389.7	40.92	38,381.9	25.17
1996	177,184.1	69,473.9	39.21	42,829.6	24.17

Source: Bank of Korea, *Monthly Statistical Bulletin* (various issues).

Bias toward the Manufacturing Sector

The allocation of bank funds in Korea shows a strong bias toward the manufacturing sector and HCIs. Table 5-1 lists the proportions of bank loans extended to the manufacturing sector in general and to HCIs in particular. It indicates that immediately after the HCI drive, in 1981, 54.76 percent of bank loans were extended to the manufacturing sector, of which 26.37 percent were captured by HCIs. The abolition of HCI policy and financial deregulation brought the proportion of bank loans to the manufacturing sector down to 45.55 percent in 1983, but this proportion did not decline much further afterward despite a rapidly shrinking manufacturing share of the gross domestic product (GDP). In 1995, for example, the manufacturing sector in Korea still absorbed 40.92 percent of bank loans, whereas manufacturing output accounted for only 29.93 percent of GDP. Even more striking is the proportion of bank loans extended to HCIs. This proportion was 26.37 percent in 1981, and it declined only marginally, to 25.17 percent, in 1995, in spite of decade-long deregulations. These figures

Table 5-2. Korean Loans and Discounts by Nonbank Financial Intermediates, 1985–96

Billions of won

Year	Total	Manufacturing sector	Ratio	Heavy chemical industries	Ratio
1985	16,863.4	8,168.6	48.44	5,119.1	30.36
1986	20,454.4	9,282.5	45.38	5,864.9	28.67
1987	25,505.7	11,878.7	46.57	7,698.2	30.18
1988	30,319.9	13,988.2	46.14	8,947.2	29.51
1989	40,080.8	18,481.4	46.11	11,840.5	29.54
1990	51,172.6	24,017.2	46.93	15,354.0	30.00
1991	63,194.3	32,666.2	51.11	21,145.7	33.08
1992	80,345.0	42,228.3	52.56	27,959.1	34.80
1993	98,809.1	47,114.0	47.68	31,236.5	31.61
1994	131,231.8	56,671.2	43.18	37,141.5	28.30
1995	162,844.0	65,870.7	40.45	43,223.7	26.54
1996	198,258.7	80,437.4	40.57	54,818.5	27.65

Source: Bank of Korea, *Monthly Statistical Bulletin* (various issues).

show a clear bias in bank lending toward the manufacturing sector in Korea, and particularly toward HCIs.

NBFIs were less constrained in terms of ownership structure and interest rate setting than were commercial banks, and they were consequently more inclined toward relational lending. Although inaugurated only in the early 1980s, NBFIs had outcompeted commercial banks in the loan market because they were less heavily regulated than banks. As can be seen from table 5-2, the total loans of NBFIs quickly caught up with those of commercial banks and have surpassed the latter in recent years. However, the sectoral composition of NBFI lending is similar to that of commercial banks, except that the proportion of lending to HCIs was even larger. In 1995 NBFIs extended 40.45 percent of their total loans to the manufacturing sector, of which 26.54 percent went to HCIs.

It is hard to argue that the lending bias toward the manufacturing sector in general and toward HCIs in particular has been government directed, because NBFIs have been largely free from government control. Rather, it is the intrinsic structure of the Korean economy built around chaebols that explains the bias in the loan portfolio. Comparing Korean loans to Taiwanese loans illuminates this point. Table 5-3 shows the sectoral distribution of bank lending

Table 5-3. Taiwanese Loans and Discounts at Domestic Banks, 1980–96

Millions of New Taiwan dollars

Year	Total	Manufacturing sector	Ratio	Heavy chemical industries	Ratio
1980	693,599	338,977	48.87	199,139	28.71
1981	760,369	360,178	47.37	209,988	27.62
1982	903,567	398,187	44.07	229,739	25.43
1983	1,033,218	423,166	40.96	240,412	23.27
1984	1,146,106	444,706	38.80	245,396	21.41
1985	1,221,410	429,758	35.19	222,027	18.18
1986	1,354,803	421,747	31.13	124,279	9.17
1987	1,592,959	447,984	28.12	120,961	7.59
1988	2,215,397	571,869	25.81	303,629	13.71
1989	2,857,725	680,003	23.80	385,221	13.48
1990	3,141,678	729,031	23.21	439,231	13.98
1991	3,881,184	907,856	23.39	564,700	14.55
1992	4,916,138	1,096,918	22.31	. . .	. . .
1993	5,652,069	1,186,983	21.00	. . .	. . .
1994	6,727,491	1,289,441	19.17	. . .	. . .
1995	7,383,950	1,435,636	19.44	. . .	. . .
1996	7,861,661	1,399,614	17.80	. . .	. . .

Source: Central Bank of China, *Financial Statistics Monthly* (various issues).

in Taiwan. It can be seen that in 1981 the manufacturing sector took 47.37 percent of bank loans, whereas HCIs (defined similarly as in Korea) accounted for 27.62 percent. These proportions are comparable to those of Korea in the same period. However, the proportion of bank loans to both the manufacturing sector and HCIs declined sharply over time in Taiwan. In 1995 only 19.44 percent of bank loans went to the manufacturing sector.

Although the proportion of bank loans extended to HCIs was not observed in 1995, the proportion recorded in 1991 had fallen to only 14.55 percent. Compared to Korea, both the household and the service sectors took a much larger share of bank loans in Taiwan. At times, the Korean government restricted the credit share of chaebols, but chaebols remained privileged borrowers. In 1987, for example, the thirty largest chaebols claimed 24.43 percent of bank loans, and 39.70 percent of NBFI loans.[26] In 1991, chaebols' share of bank loans fell

26. Park and Kim (1994, p. 210).

to 16.8 percent, but of NBFI loans rose to 45 percent.[27] These statistics support the argument that chaebols had greater influence over the lending of NBFIs than of commercial banks, as government interventions into commercial banks were more prevalent.

Dependence on Debt Instruments

When interest rates were suppressed and credits were rationed, large business conglomerates were induced to maximize their assets and growth rather than to strive for immediate profitability.[28] The result was overinvestment and overcapacity. Dependency on loans and on other instruments of debt rather than on equity shares for funding also made Korean firms highly leveraged. Though a high leverage ratio is widely recognized as a problem in business governance, the Korean government failed to take persistent measures to eradicate the problem. Table 5-4 shows two indicators of the financial leverage of Korean and Taiwanese private manufacturing firms. For the Korean firms the ratio of loans to total assets was 44.59 percent in 1990, and the ratio of debt to equity 285.52 percent. These ratios were on the rise during the 1990s. A highly leveraged firm will remain solvent only through rapid growth, which, in turn, has to be supported by new capital investment. In order to protect their loans, Korean banks were forced to extend credit to borrowers who were nearly insolvent at the time.[29] This set in motion a vicious cycle. Also listed in table 5-4 is the ratio of loans to total assets and the ratio of debt to equity for Taiwanese firms. Both ratios were significantly lower than those of their Korean counterparts.

Through financial liberalization Korean firms were able to make more extensive use of other debt instruments such as commercial papers and corporate bonds to substitute for bank loans. This indeed was done in the early 1980s, but an ongoing recession at the time aggravated the chaebols' financial straits and undermined their ability to issue debt instruments. The stock market has also provided good access to capital in recent years in Korea. It has been argued that the underdevelopment of the stock market has hampered Korean firms' access to equity, which partially explains their high leverages.[30] Substan-

---

27. Sakong (1993, p. 63).
28. Cho (1996, p. 226).
29. Adelman and Nak (1998).
30. Kim (1990).

Table 5-4. Financial Structure of Private Manufacturing Firms in Korea and Taiwan, 1991–96

Percent

	Korea		Taiwan	
Year	Loan ratio[a]	Debt-equity ratio[b]	Loan ratio[a]	Debt-equity ratio[b]
1990	44.59	285.52	33.95	111.31
1991	44.51	306.68	34.64	115.22
1992	47.18	318.73	35.19	119.89
1993	46.75	394.88	33.74	118.95
1994	44.54	302.52	33.15	118.35
1995	44.76	286.75	33.20	126.62
1996	47.66	317.11	28.18	111.04

Sources: Korean data: Yeh and Wu (1998, table 2); Taiwanese data: calculated by authors from Central Bank of China, *Survey Report on the Status of Public and Private Enterprises* (various issues).

a. The loan ratio is the ratio of loans to total assets.

b. The debt-equity ratio is the ratio of debt to equity (own capital). Debt equals loans plus commercial papers, bills, and bonds issued by the enterprises.

tial improvements have been made in the Korean stock market since 1986, however. Using a worldwide scale of zero to ten to measure the maturity of stock markets and taking into account indicators such as market capitalization as a proportion of GNP and the turnover ratio, Pistor and Wellons rated the Korean stock market at 4.8 in 1980 and at 8.8 in 1995.[31] Indeed, the Taiwanese stock market was accorded exactly the same score in 1995, although its rating was slightly higher than Korea's in 1980 (at 5.6). Both stock exchanges went through a bull market in 1986–89 following the Plaza Accord. Nevertheless, Taiwanese firms drew a much larger proportion of funds from the stock market than Korean firms. In 1989 Taiwan's nonfinancial sector drew 23.0 percent of external funds from the stock market compared to only 18.3 percent drawn by their Korean counterparts.[32] During the stock market boom Korean chaebols obtained more funds by issuing shares, if only reluctantly, but these funds were used to substitute for corporate bonds rather than to reduce bank loans. In fact, chaebols increased their share of borrowings from banks and NBIFs during the bull market to take advantage of the low lending rates prevailing at the time. In

31. Pistor and Wellons (1997).

32. Park (1994, p. 177); Shea (1994, p. 279).

contrast, nonchaebol firms used share issuance to retire corporate bonds as well as to reduce borrowings.[33] The only explanation of this phenomenon is that chaebols were favored more by lending institutions than by investors in the capital market since it is in the interest of lending institutions to help chaebols maintain rapid growth.

Some scholars argued that Korean business conglomerates continued to be favored by lending institutions despite high leverages because of the government's presumed support of such corporations in the event of loan defaults. This practice results in a moral hazard problem.[34] It is true that during financial crises the Korean government has repeatedly bailed out troubled companies, such as in 1969–70, 1972, 1979–81, and 1984–88 and, more recently, in 1994.[35] The government came to the rescue of troubled companies in each crisis because it was worried that the bankruptcy of badly managed firms would lead to bankruptcy in major banks, which would ultimately ruin Korea's international credit worthiness because the country was burdened by large external debts, most of which were guaranteed by commercial banks.[36]

Government Bailouts

The typical approach of the Korean government to restructuring troubled firms is to first identify a takeover firm or group. After scrutinizing the value of an insolvent firm's assets and liabilities, the conditions for the takeover are agreed on between the takeover firm or group and the main lending bank of the troubled firm. The government then seals the takeover package with tax subsidies and by rescheduling the debt, which includes reducing the principals, forgoing or deferring interest payments, and providing fresh credit. The bank, in turn, is subsidized by the central bank (the Bank of Korea) to compensate it for some of its losses from the loan restructuring.[37]

Once it became evident that the government would be likely to bail out troubled firms, these firms began to borrow heavily from many sources at any interest rate simply to remain in business, awaiting the government's rescue. This distress borrowing subsequently burdened the financial institutions that

33. Kong (1998).
34. Krugman (1998).
35. Cho (1996, p. 228).
36. Park and Kim (1994, p. 212).
37. Park and Kim (1994, p. 12).

were involved in the rescue packages.[38] The result was a disproportionately high ratio of bad loans in Korean lending institutions, dating from 1980. In 1984 nonperforming loans accounted for 10.85 percent of the total loans extended by nationwide commercial banks; the ratio stood as high as 5.86 percent in 1989 after a series of rescue operations initiated by the Korean government for beleaguered shipping and overseas construction companies. The takeover firms, which were in most cases chaebols, enhanced their own market power after restructuring, but were still hampered by financial weakness.[39] The approach taken in the standard rescue package protects ill-advised financial institutions as well as relentless borrowers. Krugman has argued that such implicit government guarantees lead to severe moral hazard problems, with financial institutions engaging in excessively risky lending to overleveraged corporations.[40] Baily and Zitzewitz have disputed Krugman's claim and have argued that the moral hazard problem is not the primary cause of Korea's financial institutions' overlending to corporations, citing many instances in which financial institutions making such loans were also equity investors.[41]

Baily and Zitzewitz appear to have the better argument. Financial institutions in Korea, banks and NBFIs alike, preferred to lend to manufacturing firms in general, and chaebols in particular, either because they failed to explore alternative borrowers such as service firms and individuals or because they lacked the skills to evaluate the service-related projects or consumer loans. Therefore, this practice was more a problem of underdevelopment of financial institutions than of moral hazard.

38. Park (1994, p. 162).
39. In comparison, the Taiwanese government rarely bailed out foundering private corporations even though it was equally interventionist in the financial market. Taiwan experienced a financial crisis in 1984 that was sparked by debt problems in one of its largest business groups—Cathay. The Cathay group owned one of the largest credit cooperatives in the country, along with a diverse list of manufacturing companies ranging from the plastics to the home appliances sectors. The Taiwanese government arranged for a state-owned bank to take over the credit cooperative, but allowed all nonfinancial affiliates of the group to go bankrupt. As a result of this bankruptcy, the number of nonperforming loans rose to 6.93 percent of total bank loans in 1985, a historic high, though it soon declined to below 3 percent in 1989 after the failure of insolvent businesses and the write-off of bad loans. See Yang (1994, p. 313).
40. Krugman (1998).
41. Baily and Zitzewitz (1999).

Liberalizing Investment

Diversification of bank loans in Taiwan was precipitated by competition from foreign banks that started to aggressively penetrate Taiwan's untapped consumer loan market in the early 1980s. A parallel effect of foreign competition did not seem to exist in Korea. Korea and Taiwan both embarked upon capital account liberalization in the 1980s, but the effects were distinctive. In the case of Korea, foreign direct investment was liberalized in 1984. Later a closed-ended Korea Fund was launched in New York, and the Korea Euro Fund was subsequently introduced into the European market to provide a means for indirect investment by foreigners in the Korean stock market. In 1985 Korean firms were allowed to issue convertible bonds (CBs) and bonds with warrants in international financial markets. Starting in 1987, Korea's large security companies were allowed to participate in syndicates underwriting foreign securities. Beginning in 1992, foreigners were allowed to directly purchase Korean equities, though their holdings were subject to a predetermined ceiling of 10 percent.[42] Capital account liberalization was accelerated after 1994 as Korea prepared to join the Organization for Economic Cooperation and Development.

The timing and sequencing of capital account liberalization in Taiwan was quite similar to that in Korea. However, the effects of capital account liberalization on capital flows were quite different in the two countries. For the purposes of comparison, table 5-5 lists the inflows and outflows of international capital in Korea and Taiwan. It is acknowledged that the Korean policy stance toward foreign direct investment (FDI) had been conservative until the middle of the 1980s.[43] When the policy stance was reversed in the mid-1980s in favor of FDI, foreign investment in Korea started to increase, though the total amount of investment was still generally lower than that in Taiwan.

Meanwhile, however, with capital account liberalization going at a similar pace, the amount of foreign portfolio investment in Korea was much larger than that in Taiwan. In 1996, for example, portfolio investment was 6.2 times greater than direct investment in Korea, whereas the ratio was only 1.7 in Taiwan. An explanation of this difference lies in the fact that Korea's domestic market was monopolized by chaebols and its exports were likewise dominated by the same groups with integrated production. This leaves little room for foreign direct investment either to explore the domestic market or to comple-

42. Park (1994, pp. 152–53).
43. Kim (1998).

Table 5-5. International Capital Flows into Korea and Taiwan, 1980–96
Millions of U.S. dollars

	Korea			Taiwan		
Year	Inward direct investment	Inward portfolio investment	Outward investment	Inward direct investment	Inward portfolio investment	Outward direct investment
1980	96	46	...	161	45	42
1981	105	104	...	151	85	60
1982	69	15	127	104	145	32
1983	69	188	126	149	41	19
1984	110	333	37	201	50	72
1985	234	982	34	340	46	79
1986	435	301	110	327	75	65
1987	601	−113[a]	183	715	9	705
1988	871	−461[a]	151	959	541	4,121
1989	758	29	305	1,604	65	6,950
1990	715	899	820	1,30	69	5,249
1991	1,116	3,155	1,357	1,271	786	2,054
1992	551	5,761	1,048	879	1,149	1,967
1993	516	11,022	1,056	917	2,399	2,611
1994	758	7,276	2,075	1,375	2,902	2,640
1995	1,240	8,915	3,120	1,559	2,729	2,983
1996	1,953	12,092	3,934	1,864	3,256	3,843

Sources: Korea: Bank of Korea, *Monthly Statistical Bulletin;* Taiwan: Central Bank of China, *Balance of Payments.*
a. A negative figure indicates a reduction in portfolio assets held by foreigners.

ment Korea's export industries. Foreign investors seeking a share of Korea's impressive returns from rapid economic growth had to enter the market with portfolio investments. In comparison, Taiwan's investment climate was traditionally open to direct investment, with small firm-based production networks providing opportunities for complementary production activities for multinationals.

Even more significant was the borrowing of short-term capital by Korean financial institutions from overseas sources for relending at home in order to take advantage of interest rate differentials that started to widen in the 1990s. This practice resulted in a rapid accumulation of short-term liabilities that precipitated the financial crisis.[44] In contrast, foreign borrowing by commercial banks in Taiwan was limited partly because of government restrictions and

44. Adelman and Nak (1998).

partly because of smaller interest differentials between Taiwan and the world's major financial centers. Failure to take account of the exchange rate risks in interest arbitrage indicates that Korean financial institutions were not attuned to risky global financial operations. The same may be said about Taiwan's financial institutions, but luckily Korea's Taiwanese counterparts were under less pressure, and given less room, to borrow from abroad.

Industrial Organization

One thing that distinguishes Korea and Taiwan in terms of industrial organization is the predominance of large conglomerates in Korea and the prevalence of small firms in Taiwan. The financial liberalization and trade liberalization that have been undertaken by both countries since 1980 did not significantly change these salient features of the two economies. This, in turn, had important consequences related to the Asian financial crisis.

Capital Intensity

Table 5-6 illustrates the concentration of the economic power of chaebols in Korea and that of small firms in Taiwan in mining and manufacturing from 1976 through 1996. In Korea the thirty largest chaebols accounted for 32.0 percent of the total shipments in mining and manufacturing in 1977. This share increased to 39.7 percent in 1981 and then decreased after the end of the HCI drive, but still remained as high as 35.0 percent in 1990. The chaebols' share of fixed assets was comparable to that of these shipments, but their share of employment was substantially smaller. In 1990 the thirty largest chaebols accounted for 32.2 percent of Korea's fixed assets in mining and manufacturing, but their share of employment was merely 16.0 percent. This indicates that chaebols are much more capital intensive than other industries.

Likewise, the prevalence of small firms in Taiwan's economy proved resilient to financial and trade liberalization. Firms with fewer than 100 employees accounted for 27.0 percent of shipments in mining and manufacturing in 1976. This share rose steadily to 41.1 percent in 1996. These firms' share of employment and fixed assets also increased over time, and, not surprisingly, their share of employment was much larger than that of fixed assets. In 1996 small firms provided 60.5 percent of mining and manufacturing employment in Taiwan. It should be noted that the proportion of shipments and fixed assets accounted for

Table 5-6. Concentration of Chaebols in Korea and Small Firms in Taiwan in Mining and Manufacturing, Selected Years
Percent

	Korea's thirty largest chaebols			Taiwan's small firms (employment less than 100)		
Year	Shipment	Employment	Fixed assets	Shipment	Employment	Fixed assets
1976/77[a]	32.0	20.5	...	27.0	37.8	16.7
1981	39.7	19.8	36.7	...	...	...
1986	37.7	17.2	39.1	33.2	47.3	22.4
1990/91[b]	35.0	16.0	32.2	37.9	56.0	33.5
1996	...	...	...	41.1	60.5	33.2

Sources: Korea: Jwa (1997); Taiwan: Schive and Hu (1999).
a. The data for Taiwan are from 1976, for Korea from 1977.
b. The data for Taiwan are from 1991, for Korea from 1990.

by the largest enterprises, say those employing 500 persons or more, also slightly increased in Taiwan from 1986 to 1996, but only at the expense of mid-size enterprises (those employing between 100 and 500 persons) rather than small firms.

In both Korea and Taiwan the structure of industrial organization seemed to be robust with respect to changing market conditions and government interventions. Nevertheless, in Korea chaebols are considered excessively diversified and lacking in specialization. Jwa estimates that each of the top five chaebols owned an average of forty-two subsidiaries and four financial institutions in 1993–94.[45] Compared to firms of advanced countries, Korean chaebols have been shown to lean toward technology-unrelated diversification as opposed to technology-related diversification, which is common practice among large Western corporations.[46] This indicates that the diversification of Korean chaebols is based more on their ability to access financial resources than on their technological excellence. To curb the propensity of chaebols to over-diversify and overextend, the Korean government has taken initiatives to promote business specialization and ownership diffusion, such as restricting entry, restricting ownership concentration, restricting bank borrowing, and reserving certain business activities exclusively for small enterprises. The

45. Jwa (1997).
46. Yang (1994).

initiatives have come to no avail, however. In fact, some initiatives have even yielded entirely unintended results. For example, fearing government restrictions on entry, chaebols may make preemptive moves into new business areas before the impending regulations are imposed.[47] In this case building up a large capacity is a popular tactic to convince the government that they are here to stay and that it is a logical choice to restrict followers to prevent "duplicate and wasteful investment." Business activities susceptible to entry restrictions are often characterized by large fixed costs where economies of scale prevail. Indeed, all chaebol-dominated industries are characterized by high capital intensity.

Another example of a government initiative's resulting in a perverse effect is the promotion of business specialization among chaebols. In 1991 the Korean government ordered chaebols to select three core business lines, promising to provide them with better access to bank credit. Not surprisingly, many chose their most capital-intensive operations, notably those devoted to petrochemicals, which is considered an industry of the past, not the future.[48] We may compare the factor inputs of the manufacturing sectors in Korea and Taiwan to illustrate the point that Korean industry is more capital intensive than Taiwan's. Table 5-7 lists the labor coefficients of the manufacturing sectors in Korea (for the year 1993) and in Taiwan (for the year 1991), based on input-output tables. Except for textiles, where the labor coefficients are identical; telecommunications equipment, where Korea's labor coefficient is marginally higher; and automobiles and parts, where Korea's industry is substantially more labor intensive, in the rest of the manufacturing sectors Korean industry is decisively more capital intensive than that of Taiwan. Although the figures show only direct labor inputs, it is not surprising to see that indirect labor inputs exhibit the same pattern as well because capital intensiveness in Korean industry is pervasive across all manufacturing sectors.

High capital intensity involves a large sum of capital investment that drains the nation's financial resources even if there is a very high savings ratio. These investments were not accompanied by comparable productivity growth, however. In fact, the returns on capital invested in the manufacturing sector, excluding capital gains on land, has been below the cost of debt for most of the period between 1981 and 1995.[49] On the other hand, high capital intensity increases the marginal productivity of labor, making Korea's manufacturing

47. Jwa (1997).
48. Leipziger and Petri (1997, p. 594).
49. Baily and Zitzewitz (1999).

Table 5-7. Labor Coefficients of Korea's and Taiwan's Manufacturing Sectors

Sector	Korea (1993)[a]	Taiwan (1991)[b]
Textiles	0.1349	0.1349
Basic chemical materials	0.0675	0.1040
Synthetic fibers	0.0655	0.0784
Petroleum	0.0290	0.0654
Rubber	0.1466	0.2242
Plastics	0.1383	0.1830
Iron and steel	0.0655	0.0843
Machinery	0.1750	0.2007
Computer products	0.1094	0.1111
Consumer electronics	0.1019	0.1362
Telecommunications equipment	0.1696	0.1611
Automobiles and parts	0.1266	0.1076

Sources: Korean data: Bank of Korea, *Monthly Statistics Bulletin,* March 1996; Taiwanese data: Directorate-General of Budget, Accounting, and Statistics, *1991 Input-Output Tables* (150 sectors).

a. The Korean data are based on the 1993 input-output table (75 sectors).

b. The data for Taiwan are based on the 1991 input-output tables (150 sectors); small sectors are combined into large sectors for comparison, using domestic production values as weights.

wages the highest among the four Asian newly industrialized countries. Unable to pay high wages and crowded out of the financial market, smaller Korean firms that once operated in labor-intensive industries were forced to exit the market, reinforcing the degree of business concentration.

Industrial Structures

Both Korea and Taiwan have undertaken far-reaching industrial restructuring since 1980, particularly since the 1985 Plaza Accord, which sent the currencies of both countries skyrocketing. The change in the industrial structure of these two countries can be gauged by the composition of commodity exports. Tables 5-8 and 5-9 reflect this composition in 1982 and 1992. In both years the total export values of the two countries were comparable, but the composition of exports differed. In 1982 textiles, apparel, and footwear constituted the core of conventional exports for both countries. In Korea the combined ratio was 30.66 percent; in Taiwan the ratio was 29.18 percent. Apart from these textile-related products, the rest of the export structure was distinctly different. In Korea iron and steel (12.64 percent) and shipbuilding (12.96 per-

Table 5-8. The Export Structures of Korea and Taiwan, 1982

| | | Korea | | Taiwan | |
| | | Value (thousands of U.S. dollars) | Share (percent) | Value (thousands of New Taiwan dollars) | Share (percent) |
CCCN[a]	Sector description				
1–24	Agriculture	1,311,882	6.00	64,448,999	7.46
25–26	Mineral products	403,266	1.85	4,540,810	0.53
27	Petroleum products	318,958	1.46	16,446,834	1.90
28–38	Chemical materials	507,621	2.32	12,498,776	1.45
39–40	Plastics and rubber	603,496	2.76	36,539,046	4.23
41–43	Leather products	939,100	4.30	33,784,625	3.91
44–46	Wood products	312,595	1.43	30,435,387	3.52
47–49	Paper products	122,73	0.56	6,298,022	0.73
50–60	Textiles	3,153,870	14.43	127,126,810	14.71
61–63	Apparel	2,238,139	10.24	52,079,883	6.03
64–67	Footwear and apparel accessories	1,309,334	5.99	72,941,739	8.44
68–72	Nonmetal minerals	335,292	1.53	17,960,553	2.08
73	Iron and steel	2,762,018	12.64	37,601,661	4.35
74–83	Metal products	392,185	1.79	27,869,450	3.22
84	Machinery	512.732	2.35	44,478,730	5.15
85	Electrical machinery and electronics	2,116,515	9.69	127,949,763	14.80
86–88	Vehicles	536,525	2.46	21,752,052	2.52
89	Shipbuilding	2,831,724	12.96	19,989,472	2.31
90–92	Precision instruments	583,050	2.67	26,533,465	3.07
93–99	Other	562,819	2.58	82,971,616	9.60
	Heavy and chemical industries[b]	9,586,093	43.87	280,717,288	32.48
	Total	21,853,394	100.00	864,247,693	100.00

Sources: Korea: Republic of Korea, *Statistical Yearbook of Foreign Trade;* Taiwan: Republic of China, Ministry of Finance, *Monthly Statistics of Exports (Imports).*

a. CCCN stands for the Customs Cooperation Council Nomenclature.

b. Heavy and chemical industries include chapters 27, 28–38, 73, and 84–89 of the Customs Cooperation Council Nomenclature.

cent) accounted for sizable exports, whereas in Taiwan electrical machinery and electronics (14.80 percent) and other manufactured goods (such as sporting goods) accounted for a sizable proportion. Korea also exported more chemical materials than Taiwan. The composition of commodity trade faithfully reflects the orientation of the HCI drive in Korea and Taiwan; that is, it reflects that the Korean HCI drive was aimed at promoting exports, whereas the Taiwanese HCI drive was largely of an import-substituting nature. When HCIs are defined broadly—that is, as comprising petroleum products, chemical materials, iron

Table 5-9. Export Structure of Korea and Taiwan, 1992

HS code[a]	Sector	Korea Value (thousands of U.S. dollars)	Korea Share (percent)	Taiwan Value (thousands of New Taiwan dollars)	Taiwan Share (percent)
1–24	Agriculture	2,533,931	3.31	86,003,060	4.20
25–26	Mineral Products	178,933	0.23	1,699,986	0.08
27	Petroleum products	1,742,334	2.27	13,330,747	0.65
28–38	Chemical materials	2,490,467	3.25	44,480,527	2.17
39–40	Plastics and Rubber	3,826,588	4.99	137,114,820	6.70
41–43	Leather products	3,172,214	4.14	29,476,569	1.44
44–46	Wood products	117,508	0.15	21,510,296	1.05
47–49	Paper products	611,931	0.80	19,701,743	0.96
50–60	Textiles	8,316,381	10.85	199,591,312	9.75
61–63	Apparel	5,527,758	7.21	98,023,162	4.79
64–67	Footwear and apparel accessories	3,518,713	4.59	108,785,898	5.31
68–72	Nonmetal minerals	5,148,014	6.72	61,554,949	3.01
73	Iron and steel	1,916,023	2.50	59,564,484	2.91
74–83	Metal products	1,247,198	1.63	79,716,142	3.89
84	Machinery	6,601,278	8.61	400,315,758	19.55
85	Electrical machinery and electronics	17,878,927	23.33	346,113,242	16.90
86–88	Vehicles	4,738,022	6.18	99,365,161	4.85
89	Shipbuilding	4,112,777	5.37	6,250,778	0.31
90–92	Precision instruments	1,284,370	1.68	55,350,114	2.70
93–99	Other	1,668,150	2.18	180,013,250	8.79
	Heavy and chemical industries[b]	39,479,828	51.51	969,420,697	47.34
	Total	76,631,517	100.00	2,047,961,998	100.00

Sources: Korea: Republic of Korea, *Statistical Yearbook of Foreign Trade;* Taiwan: Republic of China, Ministry of Finance, *Monthly Statistics of Exports (Imports).*

a. The HS code is the Harmonized Commodity Description and Coding System code.

b. Heavy and chemical industries include chapters 27, 28–38, 73, and 84–89 of the HS code.

and steel, machinery, electrical machinery and electronics, vehicles, and ship-building—Korea's exports of such products in 1982 reached 43.87 percent of its total exports, compared to 32.48 percent of Taiwan's.

The composition of the commodity trade was completely reconfigured ten years later (in 1992) in both Taiwan and Korea. The share of textile-related products to total exports decreased to 22.65 percent in Korea and to 19.85 percent in Taiwan. In Korea the share of exports accounted for by iron and steel and shipbuilding also decreased significantly, with electrical machinery and electronic products taking their place. The ailing Korean shipbuilding industry was revitalized after the Plaza Accord, although its share of total exports decreased to only 5.37 percent in 1992 due to the lack of a further capacity buildup. The share of steel exports also decreased despite extensive capacity building after 1982, as Korea's downstream automobile industry absorbed a large proportion of the output. On the other hand, Korean exports of chemical materials increased almost five times in absolute value from 1982 to 1992, raising their share of total exports to 3.25 percent in 1992. The most dramatic development occurred in the electronics industry, where semiconductor products became the rising star of Korea's exports, pushing the share of electronics products among total exports to 23.33 percent in 1992.

In general, the composition of the commodity exports of the two countries was more similar in 1992 than in 1982. Broadly defined HCIs accounted for 51.51 percent of Korea's exports compared to 47.34 percent of Taiwan's. It seems that over the longer term the HCI legacy in the 1970s had more of an effect on business structure than on industrial development. This business structure manifests itself in the mix of industrial output. The bulk of Taiwan's HCI exports consisted of computers and parts, which are light and sleek but are classified as (office) machinery (see chapter 84 of the Harmonized Commodity Description and Coding System [HS] code). In fact, in 1992 virtually all categories of exports from Taiwan were less "heavy" than their Korean counterparts. For example, in the case of chemical materials exports, Taiwan had a greater proportion of exports of synthetic fibers, whereas Korea had a greater proportion of exports of basic petrochemical materials. In the case of iron and steel, Taiwan had a greater proportion of exports of steel pipes and sections, whereas Korea had a greater proportion of exports of steel plates and hot-rolled coils. In the case of electronics products and machinery, meanwhile, Taiwan had a greater proportion of exports of computers and computer peripherals, whereas Korea had a greater proportion of exports of semiconductors.

Table 5-10 shows the major electronics exports from Korea and Taiwan in 1992. It can be seen that semiconductors (integrated circuits) constituted 47.3 percent of electronics exports from Korea, whereas computers and parts constituted 70.9 percent of electronics exports from Taiwan. Although Korea also exported a substantial number of computers and Taiwan a substantial number of semiconductors, the content and production methods clearly differ between the two, a discussion of which follows later.

Table 5-10. Major Electronics Exports from Korea and Taiwan, 1992

		Korea		Taiwan	
HS code[a]	Item	Value (thousands of U.S. dollars)	Share (percent)	Value (thousands of U.S. dollars)	Share (percent)
8471–73	Computers and parts	2,945,025	22.2	9,306,299	70.9
8521	Video cassette recorders	1,180,982	8.9	53,092	0.4
8527	Radios and recorders	1,327,274	10.0	270,764	2.1
8528	Television receivers	1,536,527	11.6	1,576,407	12.0
8542	Integrated circuits	6,273,589	47.3	1,915,314	14.6
	Total	13,263,397	100.0	13,121,876	100.0

Sources: Korea: Republic of Korea, *Statistical Yearbook of Foreign Trade* (1992); Taiwan: Republic of China, Ministry of Finance, *Monthly Statistics of Exports (Imports)*.

a. The HS code is the Harmonized Commodity Description and Coding System code.

Trade Patterns

Feenstra, Yang, and Hamilton discuss the relationship between business organization and trade patterns, using Korea and Taiwan as contrasting models.[50] They argue that the chaebol-dominated Korean economy has a tendency to exploit scale economies and the benefits of vertical integration, whereas the small firm–dominated Taiwanese economy has an inclination toward product diversification. Using an index of product diversification, they show that Taiwan's exports are indeed more diversified than Korea's. This lack of variety has exposed the Korea industry to a higher risk of export market fluctuation than has been experienced by Taiwan. For example, a downturn in the dynamic random access memory (DRAM) market since 1996 has significantly worsened Korea's balance of payments. Feenstra, Madani, Yang, and Liang also show, in a sector-by-sector analysis, that increasing the variety of intermediate inputs raises the total factor productivity of industries using these inputs.[51] Korea's gains in scale economies may have been offset by losing opportunities in productivity growth.

In fact, in order to exploit scale efficiency the Korean chaebols not only are vertically integrated, but they also invest excessively in upstream industries, sometimes to the extent that the scale economies are already exhausted.[52] Heavy investment in upstream industries brings the additional benefit of creat-

50. Feenstra, Yang, and Hamilton (1999).
51. Feenstra and others (1999).
52. Truett and Truett (1997).

Table 5-11. Export Ratios for Selected Industries of Korea and Taiwan
Percent

Industry	Korea (1993)	Taiwan (1991)
Textiles	43.80[a]	40.44
Chemical materials	22.54	8.56
Synthetic fibers	16.24	24.76
Petroleum products	11.73	6.10
Rubber	35.44	28.56
Plastics	9.70	48.33
Iron and steel	14.26	6.79
Machinery	11.66	51.94
Computer products	49.80	81.65
Consumer electronics	37.66	70.75
Telecommunications equipment	31.32	47.52
Automobiles and parts	14.16	12.95

Sources: Korea: Bank of Korea, *Monthly Statistical Bulletin* (March 1996), citing input-output tables (1993); Taiwan: Directorate-General of Budget, Accounting, and Statistics, *1991 Input-Output Tables*.

a. The export ratio is the ratio of exports to the total value of output, calculated from input-output tables.

ing a threat to potential entrants and a guarantee of government support. Jwa argues that once a chaebol enters a business that is subject to entry regulation, survival is almost guaranteed.[53] Heavy investment in upstream industries leads to a high export propensity for raw materials, although the transport costs for raw materials are typically high, making the loss from trade as opposed to domestic consumption apparent.

Table 5-11 lists the export ratios of some representative industries in Korea and Taiwan. The differences in export propensity between the two countries reflect the differences in specialization. It can be seen that in upstream and capital-intensive industries such as basic chemical materials, petroleum products, and iron and steel, Korea had a higher export ratio in the 1990s, whereas Taiwan had a higher export ratio in downstream and more labor-intensive industries such as synthetic fiber and plastics. It is noteworthy that, of the mainstay exports of both countries, such as machinery, computer products, consumer electronics, and telecommunications equipment, Taiwan had a higher export ratio.

53. Jwa (1997).

Table 5-12. Selective Tariff Rates of Korea and Taiwan
Percent

HS code[a]	Item	Korea (1999)	Taiwan (1998)
2901.21	Ethylene	5.0	0
2903.21	Vinyl chloride	12.8	1.25
2917.36.10	Terephthalic acid	10.8	1.0
5402.33	Polyester filament	16.5	1.25
5513.43	Polyester woven fabrics	21.5	5
6101.30	Men's overcoats made of artificial fibers	35.0	12.5
7208.10	Hot-rolled coils	10.0/5.0[b]	7.0
8457.10	Machine centers	13	10
8471.41	Computers	9	2.1
8528.12	Color televisions	8	14.0
8542.19	Integrated circuits	0	0.5
8703.31	Small passenger cars	8	30

Sources: Korea: *Tariff Schedule of Korea* (1999); Taiwan: *Customs Import Tariff and Classification of Import and Export Commodities* (1998).

a. The HS code is the Harmonized Commodity Description and Coding System code.

b. The figures are 10 percent for hot-rolled coils thicker than 4.75 mm, 5.0 percent for the rest.

Part of the difference in export propensity is due to trade protection afforded to Korean industries. Table 5-12 compares the tariff rates between Korea and Taiwan for some representative products. It can be seen that Korea had much higher tariff rates for petrochemical products such as ethylene, vinyl chloride, and terephthalic acid. Korea also provided a higher level of protection to its textile sector, from upstream textile fibers to downstream garments. The two countries had similar levels of tariff protection for their steel and the machinery industries, but Korea protected its computer industry more than Taiwan. Korea had a lower tariff rate for consumer electronics such as color televisions, but had prohibited the importation of such products from its chief competitor, Japan, up until the Asian financial crisis. In contrast, Taiwan lifted similar restrictions in 1986. Korea also had a lower tariff rate on automobiles, but imports were effectively shut out by nontariff measures.

Trade protection generates economic rent for chaebols, which dominate the domestic market. This rent enables chaebols to engage in risky business ventures. For example, economic rent reaped from the consumer electronics market was used to subsidize heavy investment in the semiconductor industry, which had endured a sustained period of losses before 1986. For example, Samsung, the leading semiconductor firm in Korea, deliberately put its semiconductor and consumer electronics operations in the same division in order to ensure a continuous flow of funds from consumer electronics to risky semiconductor undertakings.[54] Without opportunities for cross-subsidies, private enterprises in Taiwan lack an incentive to engage in similar types of investment. As a result, in Taiwan the high-tech industries, such as the semiconductor industry, have to be nurtured by state capital.

Market Entry

Market entry strategies have also differed between the two countries because of their differences in business structure. In the semiconductor industry the Korean chaebols have directly attacked mainstream products, namely DRAM, by challenging market-leading Japanese producers. In Taiwan small ventures established by the government have chosen the niche products of logic integrated circuits (ICs) to avoid direct confrontation with market leaders. The former approach necessitates a large sum of investment that will be recovered only if scale economies are realized, whereas the latter approach is viable even with a small amount of capital. The former approach precludes foreign direct investment because multinationals do not enjoy the same kind of subsidies.

The success of the Korean semiconductor industry also partly depends on the misfortunes of Japanese industry. This Korean industry thrived when Japan was forced by the United States to restrict its IC exports in 1986, and it suffered when the Japanese yen depreciated in 1996. In contrast, the Taiwanese approach, the success of which depends on specialized technologies and niche production, provides ample opportunities for joint ventures with multinationals. This is evidenced by the development of Taiwan's semiconductor industry in the late 1990s when joint ventures were established to engage in the production of DRAMs, which had been circumvented by Taiwan's indigenous firms until then.[55]

Industrial Restructuring

Differences in business structure also set apart the courses of industrial restructuring in Korea and Taiwan, especially after the Plaza Accord. Antonelli argues that the restructuring of business firms is a cumulative process and that

54. Mathews (1995, p. 165).
55. Ku (1998b).

Table 5-13. Domestic-Foreign Direct Investment (FDI) Ratios in Korea and Taiwan, 1982–97

	Korea			Taiwan		
Year	Gross fixed investments (millions of U.S. dollars)	FDI (millions of U.S. dollars)	Ratio	Gross fixed investments (millions of U.S. dollars)	FDI (millions of U.S. dollars)	Ratio
1982	17,536	127	0.72	12,316	32	0.26
1983	19,358	126	0.65	11,696	19	0.16
1984	27,063	37	0.14	12,590	72	0.57
1985	26,249	34	0.13	11,717	79	0.67
1986	29,005	110	0.38	14,597	65	0.45
1987	36,227	183	0.51	21,846	705	3.23
1988	46,215	151	0.33	26,091	4,121	15.79
1989	58,497	305	0.52	33,240	6,950	20.91
1990	94,051	820	0.87	35,617	5,249	14.74
1991	102,234	1,357	1.33	41,422	2,054	4.96
1992	95,274	1,048	1.10	48,819	1,967	4.03
1993	97,523	1,056	1.08	52,231	2,611	5.00
1994	108,885	2,075	1.91	55,668	2,640	4.74
1995	126,696	3,120	2.46	57,984	2,983	5.14
1996	130,078	3,934	3.02	56,944	3,843	6.75
1997	106,116	...	...	51,619	5,222	10.12

Sources: Korea: Bank of Korea, *Monthly Statistical Bulletin;* Taiwan: Council for Economic Planning and Development, *Taiwan Statistical Data Book;* Central Bank of China, *Balance of Payments.*

its path depends on the assets that the firms have accumulated in the past.[56] Faced with a changing operating environment characterized by a high currency value and a high wage rate, the options for restructuring include foreign direct investment, automation, outsourcing, and diversification. Studies on Taiwan's textile industry and electronics industry indicate that diversification has not been a favored option in Taiwan.[57] In fact, in both industries Taiwanese firms have chosen to become more specialized rather than more diversified.

For Taiwan's small firms, using FDI to relocate existing production lines to overseas locations for continual exporting is a more viable option. Starting in the second half of the 1980s, Taiwanese firms have made massive direct investments in Southeast Asia and China. Table 5-13 shows the amounts of Korean and Taiwanese FDI. It can be seen that Taiwan has made more FDI than Korea in absolute terms and that it also embarked upon the

56. Antonelli (1995).
57. Chen and Ku (1998); Ku (1998a).

course of FDI earlier. Taiwan has also made more overseas investments relative to domestic investments. Between 1988 and 1996, the average ratio of overseas investment to domestic investment was 9.2 percent for Taiwan, whereas the average ratio for Korea was only 1.4 percent. Leipziger and Petri argue that small Taiwanese firms made more FDIs than large Korean firms because they were less able to maintain their market positions through domestic restructuring.[58] They contend that an inability to maintain market positions makes Taiwanese firms inferior to larger Korean firms.

Through FDI, however, existing product lines and international market access are preserved. FDI provides time and financial resources for domestic production to be restructured. Studies on Taiwan's textile and electronics industries, in which FDI is concentrated, show that firms that have engaged in FDI have been more innovative in restructuring their product lines, whereas those that have stayed away from FDI have tended to concentrate on a few newly emerged, capital-intensive product lines for business realignment.

The essence of restructuring is that resources are released from declining industries and get absorbed into emerging industries. In Taiwan this is accomplished mainly through the exit of old firms from declining industries and the entry of new firms into emerging industries. In Korea restructuring is accomplished within the same group of chaebols that have monopolized economic resources. It has been shown that in Taiwan the turnover of firms is an important mechanism through which industrial productivity is improved, as inefficient firms are eliminated in the process.[59]

In Korea restructuring is largely accomplished through the intrafirm adjustment of chaebols. The restructuring of chaebols in the early 1980s immediately following the HCI drive took the form of mergers and acquisitions. Capacity was reduced and investment scaled back through government-directed mergers and acquisitions. Sometimes the government even awarded the firm surviving a merger and acquisition with a monopoly market position to ensure its further survival.[60] It is unclear whether the overall efficiency of Korean industry was improved after this kind of restructuring. Chaebols are growth oriented, and they have a tendency to rush into emerging industries, reshuffling resources. In the late 1980s, when the Korean government abandoned its "one item, one company" principle in regulating entry to the petrochemical industry, almost

58. Leipziger and Petri (1997).
59. Aw, Chen, and Roberts (1997).
60. Kim (1990).

all the major chaebols rushed into this sector, resulting in a sixfold increase in capacity from 1988 to 1994.[61] Likewise, when the United States–Japan trade agreement to restrain Japanese exports of semiconductors to the U.S. market was reached in 1986, all major Korean chaebols jumped into the semiconductor industry with aggressive investments, concentrating on commodity-type memory chips as a way of diversifying from maturing consumer electronics products. In contrast, none of the major semiconductor firms in Taiwan today is a spinoff from the electronics firms of the 1970s.[62]

Foreign Direct Investment

Korean firms also engaged in FDI, but their pattern of FDI has differed from that of Taiwanese firms in terms of market orientation and production organization. Korean FDI, like its domestic investment, was dominated by large enterprises. Although small firms' involvement in Korea's outward FDI has increased in recent years, small firms usually invested in consortia with chaebols.[63] Unlike Taiwanese FDI, which is export oriented, Korean FDI mostly aims at local markets. Taiwanese FDI is associated with production relocation; Korean FDI largely represents an expansion of domestic production. Relocation sets off a sequence of product restructuring that cannot be matched by expansionary FDI. Taiwan's export-oriented FDI in Southeast Asia and China created a production network to service the traditional export markets that Taiwanese firms are used to servicing from Taiwan. This allowed Taiwan to support a handsome trade surplus with Southeast Asia and China through its supply of machinery and intermediate goods to this regional network. Although Taiwan's trade surplus vis-à-vis the United States has evaporated and its trade deficit vis-à-vis Japan has grown in recent years, Taiwan is still currently able to maintain a stable overall surplus in its external trade. This stands in sharp contrast with Korea's chronic trade deficit, which exists despite the country's efforts to diversify its exports into nontraditional markets such as South Asia and Eastern Europe.

Conclusions

Korea constructed a government-corporate-finance nexus as a mechanism for economic growth during its HCI drive. This nexus had a built-in risk-sharing

61. Kim and Ma (1996, p. 112).
62. Mathews (1995).
63. Sakong (1993, p. 152).

scheme whereby the solvency of the corporate sector depended on the continual injection of funds from the finance sector to support the companies' high rate of growth. This nexus became an impediment to structural adjustment in Korea after 1980. The government's efforts to liberalize the financial market in the 1980s did not significantly improve the allocative efficiency of capital because the dominant players in the corporate sector, the chaebols, were still perceived by banks as the lowest-risk borrowers, although they had already been highly leveraged. Financial liberalization also did not help banks and the other financial intermediates to develop the kind of institutional capability that could regulate the flow of funds in an efficient and prudent manner.

In contrast, Taiwan's commercial banks currently remain mostly state owned, though they choose more diversified lending portfolios than do Korean banks and hence are more independent of business groups. The pace of financial liberalization in Taiwan is similar to that in Korea, but competition from foreign financial institutions seems to improve efficiency in Taiwan's financial sector more than in Korea's. In particular, financial liberalization in Taiwan has not led to the kind of speculative borrowing and concentrated lending seen in Korea because Taiwanese banks have not been hampered by the kind of structural rigidity seen in Korea. They have had fewer nonperforming loans and more dispersed borrowers.

Since 1980 economic development in Korea has been charted by large conglomerates, whereas that in Taiwan has been championed by small and medium enterprises (SMEs). The Korean conglomerates are fond of large-scale, capital-intensive investments, whereas Taiwanese SMEs pursue niche products with flexible production. Compared with that of Korea, Taiwan's industrial structure produces a greater variety of products, lessening the potential dangers of export market fluctuation and increasing the chance of productivity growth.

Small firms, however, are less capable than large ones of undertaking internal restructuring for the purpose of maintaining their market positions. Instead, they are more inclined to relocate production overseas in the face of rising wages at home. This runs the risk of hollowing out domestic industries. The differences in restructuring strategy between Korea and Taiwan are reflected in Taiwan's relatively low ratio of domestic investment and relatively high ratio of overseas investment. Nevertheless, foreign direct investment maintains the profitability of small firms, allowing them to move into new businesses when opportunities arise. Moreover, the production networks constructed through foreign direct investment have enabled Taiwan to benefit from Southeast Asia's and China's booming exports, contributing to a healthy balance-of-payments position that reduces the likelihood of a contagious financial crisis.

Taken together, these findings argue for greater analytical differentiation among the many East Asian economies, a point to be heeded particularly by development economists and institutions alike. In addition, these findings suggest the kinds of industrial priorities and financial structures that helped Taiwan weather the Asian crisis, which should be taken into account as emergent economies seek to avoid financial and economic debacles in the years ahead.

References

Adelman, Irma, and Song Byung Nak. 1998. "The Korean Financial Crisis of 1997–98." Mimeo.

Amsden, Alice. 1989. *Asia's Next Giant.* New York: Oxford University Press.

Antonelli, Christiano. 1995. *The Economics of Localized Technological Change and Industrial Dynamics.* Boston: Kluwer Academic.

Aw, Bee-Yan, Xiaomen Chen, and Mark Roberts. 1997. "Firm-Level Evidence on Productivity Differentials, Turnover, and Exports in Taiwan's Manufacturing." Working Paper, Pennsylvania State University, Department of Economics.

Baily, Martin, and Eric Zitzewitz. 1999. "The East Asian Miracle and Crisis: Microeconomic Evidence from Korea." Mimeo.

Chen, Tain-Jy, and Ying-Hua Ku. 1998. "Foreign Direct Investment and Industrial Restructuring: The Case of Taiwan's Textile Industry." Paper presented at the 1998 National Bureau of Economic Research–East Asia Economic Seminar, Osaka, Japan (June 25–27).

Cho, Yoon Je. 1996. "Government Intervention, Rent Distribution, and Economic Development in Korea." In *The Role of Government in East Asian Economic Development,* edited by M. Aoki, H-K Kim, and M. Okuno-Fujiwara. Oxford: Clarendon Press.

Feenstra, Robert, Dorsati Madani, Tze-Hang Yang, and Chi-Yuan Liang. 1999. "Testing Endogenous Growth in South Korea and Taiwan." *Journal of Development Economics* 60(2): 317–41.

Feenstra, Robert, Tze-Hang Yang, and Gray Hamilton. 1999. "Business Groups and Product Variety in Trade: Evidence from South Korea, Taiwan, and Japan." *Journal of International Economics* 48(1): 71–100.

Hattori, Tamio. 1996. "Kankoku Taiwan Ni Okeru Kigyo Kibo Koso No Henyo" (Changing Business Structures in Korea and Taiwan). In *Kankoku Taiwan No Haden Mekanizumu* (Development Mechanisms of Korea and Taiwan), edited by Tamio Hattori and Yukihito Sato. Tokyo: Institute of Development Economics.

Hwang, Hae-Du. 1997. "Trade and Industrial Policy of Korea Revisited." Mimeo.

Ishizaki, Nao. 1996. "Kankoku No Jukagaku Kogyoka Seisaku" (Korea's Strategies for Developing Heavy Industries). In *Kankoku Taiwan No Haden Mekanizumu* (Development Mechanisms of Korea and Taiwan), edited by Tamio Hattori and Yukihito Sato. Tokyo: Institute of Developing Economics.

Jwa, Sung-Hee. 1997. "Globalization and New Industrial Organization: Implications for Structural Adjustment Policies." In *Regionalism versus Multinational Trade Arrangement,* edited by Takatoshi Ito and Anne Krueger. University of Chicago Press.

Kim, E. Han. 1990. "Financing Korean Corporations: Evidence and Theory." In *Korean Economic Development,* edited by Jene K. Kwon. New York: Greenwood Press.

Kim, Hyung-Ki, and Jun Ma. 1996. "The Role of Government in Acquiring Technological Capability: The Case of the Petrochemical Industry in East Asia." In *The Role of Government in East Asian Economic Development,* edited by Masahiro Okuno-Fujiwara. Oxford: Clarendon Press.

Kim, Ji Hong. 1990. "Korean Industrial Policy in the 1970s: The Heavy and Chemical Industry Drive." Korean Development Institute Working Paper 9015.

Kim, June-Dong. 1998. "The Impact of Investment Rule-Making and Liberalization: The Case of Korea." In *The Impact of Investment Liberalization in APEC: Policy Reviews and Case Studies.* Singapore: Asia Pacific Economic Cooperation (APEC) Economic Committee.

Kong, Myungjai. 1998. "Stock Market Development, Liquidity Constraint, and Investment: A Case of Korean Chaebol and Non-Chaebol Manufacturing Firms in the 1980s." *Asian Economic Journal* 12: 1–22.

Koo, Bohn-Young. 1984. "The Role of the Government in Korea's Industrial Development." Korea Development Institute Working Paper 8407.

Krueger, Anne. 1990. "Asian Trade and Growth Lessons." *American Economic Review* 80: 108–12.

Krugman, Paul. 1994. "The Myth of Asia's Miracle." *Foreign Affairs* 73: 62–78.

———. 1998. "What Happened to Asia." Mimeo.

Ku, Ying-Hua, 1998a. "Foreign Direct Investment and Industrial Restructuring: The Case of Taiwan's Electronics Industry." *Taiwan Economic Review* 26(4): 459–586.

———. 1998b. "The Semiconductor Industry." In *The Impact of Investment Liberalization in APEC: Policy Reviews and Case Studies.* Singapore: Asia Pacific Economic Cooperation (APEC) Economic Committee.

Kwack, Taewon. 1984. "Industrial Restructuring Experience and Policies in Korea in the 1970s." Korea Development Institute Working Paper 8408.

Lau, Lawrence, ed. 1986. *Models of Development: A Comparative Study of Economic Growth in South Korea and Taiwan.* San Francisco: ICS Press.

Leipziger, D. M., and Peter Petri. 1997. "Korean Industrial Policy: Legacies of the Past and Directions for the Future." In *Korea's Political Economy: An Institutional Perspective,* edited by Lee-Jay Cho and Yoon Hyung Kim. Boulder, Colo.: Westview Press.

Mathews, John. 1995. "High Technology Industrialization in East Asia: The Case of the Semiconductor Industry in Taiwan and Korea." Taipei: Chung-Hua Institution for Economic Research.

Park, Daekeun, and Changyong Rhee. 1998. "Currency Crisis in Korea: Could It Have Been Avoided?" Mimeo.

Park, Yung Chul. 1994. "Korea: Development and Structural Change of the Financial System." In *The Financial Development of Japan, Korea, and Taiwan,* edited by Hugh Patrick and Yung Chul Park. Oxford University Press.

Park, Yung Chul, and Dong Won Kim. 1994. "Korea: Development and Structural Change of the Banking System." In *The Financial Development of Japan, Korea, and Taiwan,* edited by Hugh Patrick and Yung Chul Park. Oxford University Press.

Pistor, Katharina, and Phillip Wellons. 1997. *Symposium on the Role of Law and Legal Institutions in Asian Economic Development 1960–1995.* Harvard Institute for Economic Development.

Rodrik, Dani. 1995. "Getting Interventions Right: How South Korea and Taiwan Grew Rich." *Economic Policy* 0(20): 53–97.

———. 1998. "TFPG Controversies, Institutions, and Economic Performance in East Asia." In *The Institutional Foundations of East Asian Economic Development,* edited by Yujiro Hayami and Masahiko Aoki. London: Macmillan.

Sakong, Il. 1993. *Korea in the World Economy.* Washington: Institute for International Economics.

Schive, Chi, and Ming-Wen Hu. 1999. "The Development of Small and Medium Enterprises in Taiwan since 1980." Mimeo.

Scitovsky, Tibor. 1986. "Economic Development in Taiwan and Korea." In *Models of Development: A Comparative Study of Economic Growth in South Korea and Taiwan,* edited by Lawrence Lau. San Francisco: ICS Press.

Shea, Jia Dong. 1994. "Taiwan: Development and Structural Change of the Financial System." In *The Financial Development of Japan, Korea, and Taiwan,* edited by Hugh Patrick and Yung Chul Park. Oxford University Press.

Truett, Lila, and Dale Truett. 1997. "The Korean Metals Industry and Economic Development." *Journal of Asian Economics* 8: 333–47.

World Bank. 1993. *East Asian Miracle.* World Bank.

Yang, Ya-Hwei, 1994. "Taiwan: Development and Structural Change of the Banking System." In *The Financial Development of Japan, Korea, and Taiwan,* edited by Hugh Patrick and Yung Chul Park. Oxford University Press.

Yeh, Ming-Fong, and Chia-Hsing Wu, 1998. "Han-Kuo Chin Jung Feng Pao Fen Hsi" (Analysis of the Korean Financial Crisis). *International Commercial Bank of China Monthly* 17(3): 1–24.

CHAPTER SIX

Taiwan and the Asian Financial Crisis: Impact and Response

Jiann-Chyuan Wang

The Asian financial crisis swept across much of the region and beyond, leaving economic and even political turmoil in its wake. However, Taiwan managed to come out of the crisis relatively unscathed, though it has been widely viewed as one of the "Asian tigers," much like Thailand, Korea, Indonesia, and others that suffered during the upheaval. What set Taiwan apart and allowed it to perform as well as it did in the storm?

To address this question, this chapter proceeds in three principal sections. First, it analyzes the impact of the Asian financial crisis on Taiwan and the response of its monetary authorities. Second, it explores the reasons behind Taiwan's comparatively positive economic performance in the midst of region-wide turmoil, focusing on sound economic fundamentals and certain government policies. Third, it elaborates possible strategies for Taiwanese firms in weathering the storm of the crisis.

The Crisis Comes to Taiwan

Many Southeast Asian countries achieved remarkable economic growth in the 1980s and 1990s. Accompanying the rapid economic growth, huge financial assets were accumulated in the private sector. Excess liquidity then flowed into the real estate and stock markets. These investment bubbles became time

Table 6.1. Exchange Rate and Stock Price Changes in Asian Countries, 1997–98

| | Exchange rate | | | Stock index | | |
| | Currency/ U.S. dollars | | | Index | | |
Economy	June 30, 1997	December 31, 1998	Percent change	June 30, 1997	December 31, 1998	Percent change
Hong Kong	7.7470	7.7455	0	15,196.79	10,396	–31.6
Indonesia	2,432	7,675	–68.3	724.556	404.5	–44.2
Japan	114.600	114.9	–0.5	20,604.96	14,152.95	–31.3
Korea	888.00	1,193	–25.6	745.40	565.27	–24.2
Malaysia	2.5245	3.80	–33.6	1,077.30	550.84	–48.9
Philippines	26.376	38.985	–32.3	2,809.21	1,873.15	–33.3
Singapore	1.4305	1.6493	–13.3	1,987.95	1,397.73	–29.7
Taiwan	27.812	32.237	–13.8	9,030.28	6,558.28	–27.4
Thailand	24.70	36.15	–28.4	527.28	337.17	–36.1

Source: Republic of China, Central Bank of China.

bombs for the financial sectors. As the real estate and stock markets crashed, the problem of accumulated bad loans dragged financial systems down even further.

As a result of malfunctioning financial sectors and worsening current account deficits, the overvalued currencies in the Association of Southeast Asian Nations (ASEAN)-4 countries (Indonesia, Malaysia, the Philippines, and Thailand) were attacked by speculators and eventually left free to depreciate. Currency depreciation triggered panicky capital outflows, and the drain on foreign exchange reserves meant that international payment requests could not be met. Thus financial turmoil broke out and inflicted serious damage on many Asian countries. As is shown in table 6-1, between June 30, 1997, and December 31, 1998, the Thai baht registered a 28.4 percent drop relative to the U.S. dollar. Similar trends of currency depreciation occurred in other ASEAN-4 countries too: the Philippine peso declined by 32.3 percent, the Malaysian ringgit devalued by 33.6 percent, and the Indonesian rupiah plunged a spectacular 68.3 percent over the same period.

In spite of relatively sound economic fundamentals, Taiwan could not prevent speculative attacks against the local currency, the New Taiwan (NT) dollar. As indicated in table 6-2, Taiwan's foreign exchange reserves amounted to U.S.$91.9 billion at the end of December 1998; moreover, in 1998 Taiwan enjoyed a high economic growth rate (4.83 percent) and a low inflation rate

Table 6-2. Comparisons of Economic Indicators among Asian Countries, 1997–98

Unless otherwise specified, billions of U.S. dollars

Item	Taiwan	Singapore	Hong Kong	South Korea	Thailand	Malaysia	Philippines	Indonesia
Foreign exchange reserves (1998)	91.9	75.9	89.6	53.54	28.82	22.98	9.00	22.71
Foreign debts (1997)	1	0	0	110.3	89.2	42.4	41.9	109.3
Current account balance (1998)	4.7	15.4	–0.5	39.6	13.0	7.1	…	5.4
Current account balance/GDP (1998), percent	1.65	15.7	–0.29	8.95	8.44	7.45	…	2.48
Economic growth rate (1998), percent	4.83	0	–5.2	–6.0	–7.2	–6.0	0.3	–13.5
Inflation rate (1998), percent	1.7	–0.1	2.8	7.5	8.1	5.3	9.5	59.5
Ratio of nonperforming loans (1997), percent	4.95[a]	n.a.	2.70	7.00	8.00	3.90	n.a.	8.80

Sources: Republic of China, Central Bank of China (1999); Asia Pacific Consensus Forecasts (1999).

a. Ratio is for 1998.

(1.70 percent). In particular, Taiwan's current account continued to register a surplus of U.S.$4.7 billion for 1998, whereas the ratio of public external debt to the gross domestic product (GDP) stayed very small.

Taiwan's Response

Generally speaking, there is a need for central banks to intervene in the economy in order to shore up confidence in the local currency, especially for export-oriented economies like Taiwan. Therefore, it was understandable when the Central Bank of Taiwan made exchange rate stability its top priority. In August and September 1997 the rate of exchange of NT dollars to the U.S. dollar fluctuated between 28.7 and 28.4. In early October, amid predictions that the NT dollar would depreciate, speculation became rampant, and at one point the daily foreign exchange transactions reached U.S.$1.5 billion. During this period short-term interest rates increased sharply. The Central Bank not only engaged in open market operations at this time, but also lowered the reserve ratios required for demand deposits to alleviate the pressures of capital shortage.

On October 17, however, the Central Bank decided to allow market forces to operate freely based on the following considerations. First, it was recognized that persistent management of the exchange rate was not sustainable, and higher interest rates would hurt local investment. Second, the government understood that speculation about depreciation was too significant to dispel. In late October the NT dollar declined to 30.23 to the U.S. dollar, a depreciation of about 8 percent. The interbank interest rate rose to between 8.6 percent and 11.47 percent, then declined to 6.43 percent after the exchange rate for the NT dollar stabilized. On December 1, 1997, affected by the huge depreciation of the Korean won, the exchange rate for the NT dollar further declined to 32.11.

With regard to the stock market, the stock price index plunged 18.05 percent from June to the end of the year, a relatively small figure compared with those of other Asian countries. However, the major causes of the decline in share prices in Taiwan included a decrease in international stock prices, lower profits in the electronics industry, readjustment in overheated share prices, and a lack of investor confidence. The exchange rate fluctuations should not be entirely blamed for the sluggish performance of the stock market.

In late September 1997 there was serious debate in Taiwan as to whether the government should intervene in the foreign exchange market. Those arguing against government intervention claimed that the exchange rate represented price in the market, which should be determined by market supply and demand. According to this view, even under speculative pressure an overshooting exchange rate will be adjusted by market forces. However, those who favored government intervention argued that, unlike commodity prices, the exchange rate exerts an extensive and profound influence on the economy. A widely fluctuating exchange rate will have an adverse impact not only on commodity prices and foreign trade, but also on inward and outward investments. Moreover, an overshooting exchange rate may not be corrected by the market mechanism because it is characterized by rigidity. Even if there could be a rebound, it would take time. Therefore, as a result, an overvalued or undervalued currency will result in tremendous adjustment costs to the real economy. For these reasons, the noninterventionists argued, it is not inappropriate for a central bank to intervene in the foreign exchange market even under a floating rate regime. However, they also argued that a central bank should implement a mechanism whereby it could intervene in accordance with economic fundamentals and other monitoring indicators.

The Impact on Exports

In the case of an export-oriented economy such as Taiwan's, it is important to understand how the Asian financial crisis affected Taiwan's real economy. From a macroeconomic point of view, under the influence of the crisis the value of Taiwan's exports declined by 9.4 percent in 1998 from its level in 1997. Among Taiwan's major export destinations, Asia was the area where the value of Taiwan's exports decreased the most, registering a 18.50 percent negative growth rate from 1997 to 1998; in the ASEAN countries Taiwan's exports declined by 29.7 percent from 1997 to 1998. In Japan's market Taiwan's imports also declined by 20.2 percent in this period. However, Taiwan's United States–bound exports fared much better, decreasing by only 0.60 percent, and in Europe Taiwan's exports enjoyed a 6.62 percent growth rate during 1997–98 (see table 6-3). Did a sharp decrease in exports imply that Taiwan lost its export competitiveness to other competitors? Two indicators help explain the decrease in exports: the real exchange rate (RER) and the change in market share compared to those of major competitors.

The RER for Taiwan is compared with those of other Asian economies in table 6-4, adjusted by the consumer price index (CPI) and the unit export price (UVX), respectively. As indicated, if we use the United States' RER as a base, we can see that Taiwan's RER increased by 23.40 percent when adjusted for

Table 6-3. Comparison of Taiwan's Export Values by Destination, 1997–98
Billions of U.S. dollars

Destination	1997	1998	Export growth rate (percent)
ASEAN-5[a]	14.88	10.46	−29.7
Asia	61.59	50.19	−18.50
Europe	18.42	19.64	6.62
Hong Kong	28.71	24.83	−13.5
Japan	11.70	9.33	−20.2
United States	29.56	29.38	−0.6

Source: Ministry of Finance, Republic of China, *Import-Export Trade Statistics* (1999).
a. The ASEAN-5 countries are Indonesia, Malaysia, the Philippines, Singapore, and Thailand.

CPI. This change is better than mainland China's 1.55 percent and Singapore's 20.44 percent and comparable to Japan's 23.61 percent. However, the figure is much worse than those of South Korea and the ASEAN countries because the NT dollar depreciated relatively less than their currencies. If we adjust RER by UVX, the result is similar, indicating that Taiwan's export competitiveness was weaker than those of countries whose currencies depreciated sharply; however, its absolute export competitiveness did not deteriorate.

Compared with its performance in 1997, Taiwan's market share in the United States decreased by 0.13 percent in 1998 (see table 6-5). In the same period Singapore's U.S. market share decreased by 0.30 percent and South Korea's by 0.04 percent, whereas mainland China's registered a 0.60 percent increase. The rapid growth of China's share of the U.S. market can be partly attributed to Taiwan's policy regarding China-bound investments, which targets exports to the U.S. market. Based on these figures, it appears that Taiwan's export competitiveness was not significantly damaged by the Asian financial crisis.

At the industry level, traditional industries with very limited profit margins that were based on ASEAN-bound exports of, for example, plastics, textiles, machinery, and petrochemicals were hurt the most by the crisis. However, in the information and electronics industry, of which the major export markets are the United States and Europe, the negative impact was not so severe. In general, the strength of Taiwan's electronics sector lies in its flexibility, its economies of scale resulting from mass production, and its international system for the division of labor. Many Taiwanese companies have invested heavily in

Table 6-4. Export Competitiveness of Taiwan and Its Major Export Competitors, 1997–98

Exporter	Currencies versus U.S. dollar		First six months of 1997 versus first six months of 1998			Changes in real exchange rate (percent)	
	June 1997	June 1998	Exchange rate	CPI^a	UVX^b	Adjusted by CPI^a	Adjusted by UVX^b
Taiwan	27.81	34.35	1.235	1.017	1.082	23.4	11.46
China	8.296	8.280	0.998	0.998	1.060	1.55	−8.070
Japan	114.4	140.8	1.231	1.012	1.021	23.61	17.69
Malaysia	2.524	4.169	1.651	1.050	1.179	59.68	36.70
Singapore	1.430	1.706	1.193	1.006	1.023	20.44	13.91
South Korea	888.1	1,373	1.546	1.085	1.333	44.65	13.17
Thailand	25.79	42.31	1.640	1.097	1.339	51.92	19.60
United States	. . .	. . .	. . .	1.016	0.976	. . .	. . .

Source: Data compiled by Wen-Jung Lien.

a. CPI = consumer price index.

b. UVX = unit export price; the real exchange rate is used as a base here.

Table 6-5. Market Shares of Major Exporters to the United States, 1997 and 1998

Percent

Exporter	1997	1998
Canada	19.30	19.13
China	7.19	7.79
France	2.38	2.63
Germany	4.95	5.45
Hong Kong	1.18	1.15
Japan	13.94	13.35
Mexico	9.86	10.36
Singapore	2.31	2.01
South Korea	2.66	2.62
Taiwan	3.75	3.62
United Kingdom	3.75	3.81

Source: Republic of China, Ministry of Finance, *Import-Export Trade Statistics* (1999).

both ASEAN countries and mainland China. Over two-thirds of such exports consisted of semifinished goods or reexports, which basically remained unaffected by the financial crisis. However, falling asset prices in the Southeast Asian countries following the crisis may have hurt Taiwan's exports to the region. The relatively inexpensive South Korean products resulting from the weak won posed a threat to Taiwan in addition to the ASEAN countries because South Korea has been Taiwan's major export competitor for the past ten years.

Generally speaking, in the short run the depreciation of the Korean won has increased South Korean competitiveness in the areas of steel, textiles, and plastics. As time goes on, however, Korean firms with financial troubles might have difficulty purchasing raw materials without strong credit guarantees, or they may need to pay higher prices for raw materials due to the relatively weak won. As a consequence, their price advantage will be offset.

The Impact on Electronics Exports

With regard to the electronics industry, South Korean firms specialize in the production of dynamic random access memory (DRAM), liquid crystal displays (LCDs), and monitors. Korean-made DRAM products have a direct impact on Taiwanese firms because Korean firms regularly dump their products in Taiwan at prices approaching their variable costs. However, in the monitor industry big U.S. computer firms are not expected to easily switch their contractors because price is not the only factor in a long-term relationship. Contracting firms with stable supplies, as well as good maintenance and other related services, will get stable orders. Switching orders to firms that might fall into financial trouble at any time is a risky business.

In addition to mergers and acquisitions, price cutting is also a popular strategy for consolidating market share in times of overcapacity. Therefore, following the Asian currency crisis it has been commonplace to find personal computers (PCs) carrying price tags of under U.S.$1,000; this trend deserves some attention. There are two major reasons for the popularity of pricing PCs under U.S.$1,000. First, the lack of new applications means that there is less of an incentive for the public to upgrade their PCs. Second, following the currency crisis a global PC oversupply has forced companies to cut their prices in order to compete for survival in the market.

With the proliferation of low-price computers, global PC suppliers (for example, IBM, Compaq, and Dell) have adopted a build-to-order (BTO) strategy in order to maintain their profit margins. In original equipment manufacturing (OEM) contracts Taiwan's OEM manufacturers (for example, Acer and Mitac) project PC demand for the next three or four months and then ship PCs to global PC vendors (Japanese or U.S. suppliers, hereafter referred to as the suppliers). Shipments to the distributors (customers), inventory management, and related costs are under the control of the suppliers. However, in the BTO model marketing agents (distributors) report their PC demand to the suppliers, which in turn place their orders with Taiwan's OEM manufacturers. Taiwan's OEM manufacturers have to deliver the PCs to their overseas warehouses or operating bases located near the suppliers' customers (distributors) within two or three weeks. In a sense, the suppliers delegate responsibility for PC shipments, inventory control, financial leverage, and the preparation of components and raw materials to Taiwan's OEM manufacturers.

In order to fit into the BTO model, Taiwan's OEM manufacturers were forced to establish a global logistics framework. There are several effects associated with the BTO model. First, big firms may swallow up small firms. Without a global logistics ability, smaller OEM manufacturers will be forced to pursue niche markets or become regional suppliers. Second, the profit margin for components suppliers will be squeezed. Since major global PC vendors squeeze every last penny from their OEM manufacturers, these OEM manufacturers then undercut the prices of their components suppliers in order to retain their profit margins. Third, price competition will be more fierce and will bring down their corporate profits; as a consequence, firms without good management may be driven out of the market. In general, following the financial crisis price-cutting strategies became popular with OEM manufacturers in order to gain market share or merely to compete for survival in the market. Under such circumstances lower prices and reduced sales translated into lower corporate profits. This situation may prove particularly acute in Taiwan's electronics industry given its emphasis on original equipment and optimized distribution model (ODM) production.

The statistics suggest that the trend of low-price PCs is bad news for Taiwan's small- and medium-size enterprises (SMEs). First, in Taiwan's desktop PC market the top seven PC firms account for more than three-quarters of the market. Second, the top seven firms' market share of notebook PC exports increased by about 10 percent, from 78.6 percent in 1997 to 87.3 percent in 1998. Third, in Taiwan's SME-dominant integrated circuit (IC) design sector there are about seventy firms, whereas the top ten firms account for 90 percent of total sales; the market share of the top three firms ranges from 40 percent to

50 percent, and these top three design houses are actually affiliates of big enterprises.

In addition, Lee and Yu point out that, in contrast to traditional industries, in the high-tech industry the division of labor between large enterprises and SMEs is not stable because large enterprises can always switch OEM contracts through their stronger bargaining power.[1] SMEs are also in a weaker position relative to large enterprises in recruiting skilled technical personnel and gaining other production necessities such as land and capital. Under such circumstances, the oligopolizing trend in the high-tech industry seems to go against SMEs. Interviews with several industrial leaders have revealed a consensus that in the high-tech manufacturing industry there is only a very limited number of areas, such as IC design, software, and information services, in which SMEs can play a crucial role, whereas in other areas SMEs can become only OEM partners of large firms or regional suppliers in a niche market.

Explaining Taiwan's Escape from the Crisis

At the height of the Asian financial crisis Taiwan's healthy economic fundamentals, including a low level of public external debt, abundant foreign exchange reserves, and a current account surplus, helped erect a wall of defense against the financial onslaught in the region.[2] The major factors in support of this foundation are detailed in this section.

Economic Liberalization and Internationalization

During the 1980s various changes in the domestic and external environment influenced the Taiwanese government's economic policies. On the domestic front Taiwan's industrial sector faced increasing economic pressure related to losing its competitiveness. A labor shortage and rising land and labor costs led firms to relocate their industrial activities offshore to mainland China and Southeast Asia. Externally, persistent trade surpluses in Taiwan were placing

---

1. Lee and Yu (1996).

2. Although Taiwan faced a string of corporate crises beginning in October 1998, the government stepped in by implementing policy measures such as lowering corporate taxes for the banking sector, bringing down the deposit reserve ratio, rescuing a banking sector hit by bad loans, and boosting public confidence in economic recovery. The situation has been under tight government control since February 1999.

heavy upward pressure on the exchange value of the NT dollar. Also, in the 1990s Taiwan was poised to open up its domestic market due to its aspiration to become a member of the World Trade Organization. Therefore, facing both internal and external pressure, the government aggressively pursued economic liberalization and firms producing low value–added products were forced to move offshore to regain their competitive edge, whereas those that stayed in Taiwan engaged in either automation or research and development (R&D) investments or actively pursued setting up subsidiaries overseas to achieve an international system for the division of labor. Their ultimate goal was, of course, to enhance their competitiveness.

Industrial restructuring occurred rather quickly, but turned out successfully. Taiwanese products moved up into difficult market segments in the ASEAN countries and China, enabling Taiwanese firms to meet financial and economic challenges. As the Council for Economic Cooperation and Development claimed, Taiwan's economic development remained on track into late 1997, as it outpaced its Asian competitors after efficiently solving financial and industrial restructuring problems arising from the depreciation of the New Taiwan dollar and the decline in stock market prices.[3]

In contrast, the ASEAN-4 countries achieved remarkable economic growth beginning in the early 1990s, when newly industrialized countries made direct investments in those countries due to their currency appreciation and rising production costs. However, the ASEAN-4 economies still relied on labor-intensive, exported-oriented industries, and industrial upgrading remains in the very early stages. In addition, these countries' high level of economic growth stems from foreign investment, but, entangled with interest groups, the government will step in to allocate resources, resulting in inefficient resource allocation as well as overinvestment and "bubbles" in the real estate and stock markets. Therefore, with the huge depreciation of renminbi (RMB), the currency of mainland China, in 1994 and relatively low production costs, mainland China began to dominate a large portion of the ASEAN-4 counties' export market share in the United States and Europe, eventually resulting in a huge current account deficit in the ASEAN-4 countries. This was also one of the major causes of the ASEAN countries' currency crisis.

On the other hand, Taiwan's economic liberalization drive, especially with regard to financial reforms such as privatization in the banking industry, effectively cut links between banks and interest groups and constrained over-

3. *China News*, December 9, 1997.

extended loans, which are considered a major factor in the recent financial crises in other Asian countries. Although it is true that several years ago Taiwan's credit cooperatives started incurring bad debts, the government stepped in and urged them to merge with commercial banks, and the problem was quickly brought under control.

Medium- to Large-Size Firms and Financial Liberalization

As Taiwan's economy grew, recording an average rate of economic growth of 8.4 percent during the 1990s, the need for financial services significantly increased. In response to these needs, the government implemented a financial liberalization policy that dates back to the early 1980s. In the capital market restrictions on firms' listed shares were greatly relaxed, and, as a result, the number of registered firms on the listed and over-the-counter (OTC) markets quickly expanded. In money markets firms used commercial paper and corporate bonds to obtain short-term and long-term loans, respectively, thereby replacing bank loans.

Following stock market liberalization the size of Taiwan's stock market grew rapidly. The number of listed and OTC companies increased from about 200 in the early 1990s to 490 by July 1997. Market capitalization also increased to NT$350 billion in 1997. In addition, several other financial tools were implemented in the government's financial reforms. These financial tools, such as convertible bonds, corporate bonds, and stock warrants, are attractive investments and funding vehicles, offering low-cost equity for firms. Thanks to such liberalization measures, more and more enterprises could raise funds in the capital market, which has thus become an important source of long-term capital for companies.

Between 1981 and 1995, in terms of private enterprises and individuals (excluding government institutions and those issuing informal credit), external borrowing data show that the ratio of direct finance to total finance was about 21 percent in this period, whereas the ratio of indirect finance to total finance was 79 percent.[4] However, the trend reversed after 1996. The ratio of direct financing rose from 29.63 percent in 1995 to 75.66 percent in 1996 (see table 6-6). The increased emphasis on direct finance in Taiwan not only improved firms'

---

4. Securities issued by enterprises but underwritten by financial institutions are considered in this chapter as a kind of direct finance. This is because enterprises using this method raise financial capital through issuing securities in the capital market.

Table 6-6. Direct and Indirect Finance (Flow Analysis), 1981–96
Billions of New Taiwan dollars

Year	Total finance	Indirect finance[a]	Ratio	Direct finance[b]	Ratio
1981	1,764	1,214	68.82	550	31.18
1982	2,203	1,830	83.07	373	16.93
1983	2,417	2,089	86.43	328	13.57
1984	2,405	1,888	78.50	517	21.50
1985	980	950	96.94	30	3.06
1986	1,493	1,678	112.39	−185	−12.39
1987	4,363	4,011	91.93	352	8.07
1988	3,711	9,161	94.34	550	5.66
1989	10,000	7,743	77.43	2,257	22.57
1990	7,952	5,860	73.69	2,092	26.31
1991	11,494	10,843	94.34	651	5.66
1992	16,315	15,032	92.14	1,283	7.86
1993	14,894	11,565	77.65	3,329	22.32
1994	15,679	12,861	82.03	2,818	17.97
1995	11,234	7,905	70.37	3,329	29.63
1996	9,163	2,230	24.34	6,933	75.66
Average	7,629	6,054	79.22	1,575	20.77

Source: Republic of China, Central Bank of China.

a. Indirect finance is defined as loans made by all financial institutions to the private and public sectors as well as to individuals.

b. Direct finance is defined as stock, certificates of deposit, corporate bonds, and so on, as issued by companies.

financial conditions, but also improved their ability to respond to adverse economic conditions.

The Insignificant Investment "Bubble"

Various studies have focused on the role that bank lending played in the formation of an investment bubble in Japan in the second half of the 1980s. Hirayama claims that increased lending by banks to the real estate sector in the 1980s was one determinant of rapidly rising property prices.[5] It is estimated that close to 40 percent of bank lending went to the real estate industry in Japan at that time. According to Taiwan's Banking Law, there is a 20 percent upper

5. Hirayama (1997).

limit for bank investment in the real estate and stock markets. This restriction serves as a protection against the formation of financial bubbles if the markets crash. Taiwan's real estate prices increased sharply between 1986 and 1989 and have been under correction ever since, reducing the possibility of a serious bubble. Moreover, because banks are held responsible for nonperforming loans, they are very conservative about overextending loans to firms. This attitude has certainly helped preclude the type of financial overexpansion that occurred in South Korea and elsewhere in the region.

The Importance of Small- and Medium-Size Enterprises

Taiwan's economy predominantly consists of SMEs; about 98 percent of local enterprises are so classified.[6] The division of labor between SMEs and large enterprises provides Taiwanese industry with flexibility and timely delivery capability. This flexibility also provides the economy with maneuverability in dealing with financial fluctuations. Big firms enjoy selling standardized products through mass production in economic boom times, but it is harder for them than for SMEs to adjust overcapacity during periods of economic downturn. According to Kim, the increasing rate of total factor productivity (TFP) in South Korea has declined since the late 1980s. This fact helps explain the declining investment efficiency of South Korean firms.[7]

Many analysts point out that the division of labor between SMEs and large enterprises provides national flexibility in dealing with financial fluctuations. However, how the division of labor system managed to protect Taiwan from a severe recessionary impact due to the Asian financial crisis is a question that deserves greater attention. The key contributions of this division of labor system can be summarized in several points.

First, low entry and exit costs create an efficient division of labor system. Taiwan's SMEs often develop into specialized satellite firms with core competence in the production of key components. They do not become subordinate to a specific big enterprise, however; rather, they undertake OEM orders for more than one "center" firm, averting the possibility of bankruptcy if one center firm decides to switch orders. As Aw, Chen, and Roberts have pointed out, a "dense network of firms" specializing in subcontracting and trading

6. Firms with capital assets of less than NT$60 million (U.S.$1 converts to NT$33) or with fewer than 200 employees are classified as SMEs.

7. Kim (1998).

services lowers the start-up losses of new manufacturing firms.[8] Low-threshold entry and exit costs facilitate the rapid transfer of resources from less efficient to more efficient producers within an industry, which makes a significant positive contribution to the growth of industrial productivity. Because of low entry and exit costs and a dense network of firms specializing in subcontracting work, there will be many satellite firms at the center firm's disposal. These satellite firms compete for OEM contracts, and this means that the center firm can always find the most efficient firms to do the work, resulting in flexibility and reduced costs.

In contrast, the industrial networks of South Korea and Japan have created very stable center firm–satellite firm relationships. These have advantages such as good coordination and information exchange in these solid industrial networks; however, there are also two major weaknesses in such networks. As soon as a center firm is hurt by an economic downturn, its dependent satellite firms will also suffer. Besides, in order to maintain stable relationships with satellite firms, a center firm can give contracting work only to members of its network rather than to potentially more efficient firms outside the network.

Second, a division of labor gives firms the collective ability to resist pressures stemming from economic downturns. This point is well illustrated by the fact that the popularity of PCs priced at less than U.S.$1,000 and manufactured by global PC vendors squeezed Taiwan's PC makers' profit margins. Since many satellite firms vie for OEM contracts for these PC makers, the PC makers can undercut the prices of their OEM partners (for instance, producers of key components). Each member of the network absorbs part of the loss, and the network thereby collectively endures price-cutting pressure and retains its market share.

Third, an industrial network such as that in Taiwan offers a delicately balanced division of labor system and production flexibility. Since there are so many satellite firms in the market, each has to find a market niche in order to survive. Hence, components and modules production has become very standardized in the electronics industry in Taiwan. This trend not only provides SMEs with scale benefits in a very specific standardized products segment, but also allows Taiwan's electronics firms to operate through a very closely coordinated relationship. For instance, in most countries a motherboard production operation is a subdivision of a big PC maker and is rarely an independent production entity. In Taiwan, however, many smaller firms specialize in producing

8. Aw, Chen, and Roberts (1997).

motherboards, either exporting them independently or supplying large firms. Owing to cost-effectiveness concerns, most major PC firms in Taiwan have stopped producing motherboards; generally they contract out the production of motherboards to specialized producers. Large-volume orders from big firms provide SMEs with the economies of scale they need to survive; firms handling such orders have created a subindustry in Taiwan.

This delicately balanced division of labor system, then, allows large firms to work on their areas of core competence and to contract out production in other areas to OEM firms. This industrial networking allows large firms to produce a wide range of products for global PC sellers. For example, Taiwan's producers of notebook PCs can always meet global PC vendors' various requests—for example, for contracts for notebook PC OEMs with or without CPUs or with or without LCDs, or for 10,000 units of PCs one month and 100,000 the next. That is to say, the finely synchronized division of labor system allows for timely delivery and flexibility for firms competing for global PC contracts.

Conservative Borrowing Abroad

According to Yang, the priority in financial liberalization should be given to domestic finance liberalization, then to international finance liberalization.[9] A sound domestic financial system should increase efficiency and competitiveness and, as a result, endure sharp capital movements. In this regard Taiwan's policy with regard to foreign capital is more conservative than that of the ASEAN-4 countries. Taiwan's financial reform policy emphasizes the liberalization of the domestic financial market, with gradual relaxation of restrictions on foreign capital movements. Consequently, the ratio of foreign capital to total capital in Taiwan's stock market is only about 3 percent. By contrast, the share of foreign investment in many Southeast Asian countries is over 30 percent. As a consequence, the withdrawal of foreign capital impacts Taiwan less than it does many countries.

Linkages to the U.S. and Chinese Economies

Since the mid- to late 1990s the U.S. and Chinese economies have performed far better than others in the Asia-Pacific area, even in the face of the regional economic downturn. Taiwan has close relationships with these two

9. Yang (1998).

economies in terms of the division of labor and foreign investment. In the high-technology industries Taiwan has become an overseas manufacturing base for big U.S. computer firms. Taiwan has also made heavy investments in China since the early 1990s. As long as the growth momentum of these two economies continues, Taiwan will benefit.

On the other hand, since exchange rates in the ASEAN countries are pegged to the U.S. dollar and remain basically fixed, the large depreciation of RMB overtook ASEAN countries' export share in the U.S. market, resulting in a deteriorating current account balance.[10] China's current account balance in 1998 was U.S.$24.6 billion, whereas Indonesia, Malaysia, and Thailand together registered a current account deficit of U.S.$12.5 billion.

Looking Ahead: Response Strategies for Taiwan's Firms

In the wake of the Asian financial crisis, a global oversupply of electronics products is unavoidable. Therefore, firms should be more cautious about overextending their investments. From a financial perspective, firms should be more conservative in engaging in financial leverage; however, undertaking hedging strategies to avoid exchange rate loss is necessary. On the production side several strategies could be adopted in response to the economic downturn. Given the importance of electronics firms to Taiwan's economic success, it would be particularly prudent for them to adopt these strategies.

Upgrading Production Technology and Process Management

Under the conditions of overcapacity resulting from the Asian financial crisis, fierce price competition has become a popular strategy for firms. Therefore, an upgrading of production technology and process management is urgently needed to bring down costs if such firms are to survive in the market. SMEs must make more efforts to consolidate OEM/ODM contracts. In addition, it is also feasible for SMEs to adhere to a strategy of pursuing niche markets in order to supplement their original markets to combat further potential problems stemming from the crisis.

10. Since January 1, 1994, mainland China has been implementing exchange rate reform, unifying its previous two-tier exchange rate system, which triggered a huge depreciation of its currency. The exchange rate for RMB to U.S. dollars dropped from 5.77 in 1993 to 8.45 on January 1, 1994.

Efficiently Managing Materials, Components, and Inventory

Under the BTO system global PC vendors delegate their shipment, components, materials, and inventory management responsibilities to Taiwan's OEM manufacturers. It is important for these firms to engage in the global logistics system and thereby maintain the efficient management of every process of the value chain in order to prevent their profit margins from diminishing.

Forming Strategic Alliances

In times of economic recession, seeking outside partners to undertake resource complementarity in order to maintain competitiveness is a very common strategy. There are several types of strategic alliance. First, there is the OEM contract security alliance. For instance, the Taiwan OEM manufacturer Acer has formed an alliance with IBM to consolidate its OEM/ODM contract. Other alliances such as the Dell-Compaq and Compaq-Mitac alliances can also be classified as OEM contract security alliances. Meanwhile, components suppliers may cooperate with big OEM manufacturers to secure their center-satellite relationships. Second, there is the bare-bones system, which is designed to prop up competitiveness by bringing down costs. In order to match the needs of the BTO system, key components producers cooperate with computer case producers; this so-called bare-bones system helps preserve profit margins and is a new type of alliance.

Third, sales-production alliances set out to tackle the trend of low-priced computers. In order to develop European and U.S. markets, Taiwan's mid-size firms with good manufacturing ability can cooperate with European and U.S. firms that own marketing networks. This can serve as a win-win strategy for both sides. Fourth, R&D alliances have also become popular in the wake of the Asian currency crisis. For instance, Japan's DRAM- and LCD-producing firms license their royalties to Taiwanese firms that can provide sufficient financial capital.

Diversifying Export Markets

Since the onset of the crisis, Asian countries' purchasing power has been seriously affected. It is therefore necessary for Taiwanese firms to diversify their export markets in order to retain their market share as Asian economic growth slows.

Conclusions and Policy Recommendations

Although Taiwan's healthy economic fundamentals have allowed it to weather the storm of the regional crisis reasonably well, the problems experienced in the region have been shared by all of the Asian developing economies. For example, the global oversupply of PCs, in particular, will result in fierce competition in the computer market, with a profound effect on Taiwan. Under such circumstances the upgrading of production technology, the efficient management of the value chain process, and the formation of strategic alliances, either to preserve profit margins or to maintain market share, are the most readily available methods for combating increasing market competition and economic slowdown.

In addition, there are several measures the governments of Taiwan and other regional economies can undertake to stabilize their financial sectors as well as to help their firms survive the problems posed by regional economic stagnation. In the financial sector important considerations include a number of steps. First, there is a need to establish an exchange rate mechanism with more flexibility while at the same time strengthening financial discipline. The main reasons for the Asian currency collapse are the rigid exchange rate mechanisms (pegged to the U.S. dollar), the malfunctioning of the financial sector, and large external borrowing. Under such circumstances, should governments allow their currencies to float with more flexibility, speculation may be reduced to a certain extent. Moreover, bad loans caused by overinvestment in the property and stock markets, which damage the real sector of the economy, may cause expectations of currency depreciation to increase. As a result, foreign investors will withdraw their investments to protect their profits, and thus a financial crisis will occur. For this reason, it is extremely important to enforce law and discipline in terms of supervising the financial sector to maintain the soundness of economic fundamentals.

Second, there is an urgent need to develop a healthy, well-functioning capital market. A sound capital market can provide firms with needed long-term capital without the need to obtain loans from a bank. This will enhance the allocative efficiency of capital. In particular, when a central bank is faced with sporadic speculation and decides to stabilize the exchange rate, the reduction in the money supply will push up short-term interest rates, resulting in a shortage of capital. This, in turn, will put pressure on the central bank to stick to its foreign exchange policy. Should a country have a sound bond market, firms can still obtain stable long-term capital. This will not only alleviate capital drought, thus preventing firms' investments from being damaged, but also lessen the pressure on the central bank to defend the local currency.

Third, the government should continue to pursue financial liberalization. Financial liberalization has both pros and cons, and since the onset of the Asian currency turmoil many people have lost confidence in the whole idea. They believe that foreign capital tends to opt for short-term financial investment and not long-term productive investment. This will cause damage to the local economy. However, a liberal financial market can in fact provide firms and government with better risk management and is thus a beneficial means for sidestepping financial problems. For a developing economy, too much regulation is inefficient and costly. However, since financial liberalization often takes place very suddenly, the government must implement policy measures to pursue liberalization in a more cautious manner by first gradually expanding the domestic capital market, then lifting investment restrictions. At the same time, the lesson of the Asian financial crisis tells us that a developing economy should not liberalize capital account transactions prematurely when risk appraisal of the financial sector is still inadequate and monetary control difficult.

As for the real sector, governments can implement important policy measures as well. First, governments might seek a more efficient system for the division of labor between large enterprises and SMEs. Such a division of labor and the resulting overall economic flexibility has been one of the major reasons Taiwan has weathered the storm of the Asian currency crisis well. However, following rapid change in the technological environment and the increasing popularity of low-end PCs, the profit margins of SMEs and component firms have been squeezed in Taiwan, and in some cases the firms have been driven out of the market altogether. Under such circumstances the Taiwanese government should organize loans or emergency funds to help SMEs get through these tough times and to preserve the system of the division of labor between large enterprises and SMEs.

Second, in Taiwan the government can seek to strengthen the spill-over effect of electronics technologies into other industries. During the past two years, the information industry has experienced unprecedented expansion, and become the engine of the entire economy. Nevertheless, if this sector encounters negative business tendencies, the entire economy may be profoundly affected. The integration and convergence of the information industry with the entire economy, therefore, is crucial to Taiwan's future economic development. To effect such integration, one possible strategy is to strengthen the electronics industry's spillover into traditional industries—for instance, by applying PC technology to machinery tools and marketing them as PC controlled. Such a spillover will broaden Taiwan's technology base and benefit the whole economy, helping Taiwan achieve sustainable growth.

Third, the government can enforce the relevant regulations to help local firms avoid unfair competition in the domestic market. Following the currency crisis, foreign firms dumped their products on Taiwan due to excessive supply; therefore, it is urgently required that the government impose import relief measures to prevent local firms from being adversely affected by foreign firms' dumping behavior. Additionally, in recent years more and more foreign technology firms have been accusing Taiwanese firms of infringing on their intellectual property rights. Though their accusations might be founded in fact, the Taiwanese firms' behavior likely results from common business practices. Consequently, the Fair Trade Law should be enforced in such cases.

Finally, the government should pursue sustainable growth without pushing too hard for rapid economic growth. Overinvestment and aggressive financial leverage activities are the two major reasons why the Southeast Asian countries and South Korea were so severely affected by the regional financial crisis. Therefore, the Taiwanese government should abide by the principle of "prioritizing economic stability over rapid economic growth" and should keep pursuing a sustainable growth strategy. To effect this it is necessary to enforce prudent financial discipline to improve the financial system and create an environment conducive to firms' R&D investments. Any decision to pursue quick economic growth may result in resource misallocation and put the whole economy in jeopardy.

In sum, further comparative research is needed to analyze Taiwan's continued success in the wake of the regional economic downturn. In particular, this research could provide lessons for other emergent economies and perhaps assist them in avoiding costly problems should future financial storms hit the region.

References

Aw, Bee Yan, Xiaomin Chen, and Mark J. Roberts. 1997. "Firm-Level Evidence on Productivity Differentials, Turnover, and Exports in Taiwanese Manufacturing." National Bureau of Economic Research Working Paper 6235, pp. 1–35.

Hirayama, Kenjiro. 1997. "Japanese Financial Markets in Turmoil: Liberalization and Its Consequences." Paper presented at Financial Development, Good Governance, and Economic Growth: Lessons from Pacific Asia Conference, Bangkok (December 15–16).

Kim, Won-Kyu. 1998. "Total Factor Productivity and Competitiveness in Korea." Paper presented at Source of Productivity Growth Meeting, Singapore, May 18–21.

Lee, J. F., and Y. J. Yu. 1996. "A Study of Dynamic Networking Organization in High-Tech Industry." Paper presented at the Technology and Industrial Network Conference, Taipei, at National Chen-Chi University (in Chinese).

Yang, Ya-Hwei. 1998. "Government Should Not Rush for Financial Liberalization." *Economic Outlook* 57: 28–31. In Chinese.

CHAPTER SEVEN

Taiwan's Active Role in the Global Production Network

Shin-Horng Chen and Da-Nien Liu

B efore the financial crisis hit the Asia-Pacific region, the kind of export-led strategy that characterized economic development in the region was an article of faith among neoclassical development economists and international organizations, despite criticism about its limitations.[1] Balassa claimed that because of the positive and dynamic interaction between open trade strategy and economic performance, export-oriented industrialization in East Asia led to better growth performance than did import substitution industrialization in South America.[2] However, the past two years prove that the East Asian newly industrializing countries (NICs), like their South American counterparts, are not immune from financial crises. The question we must ask ourselves now is: how should the countries concerned come to terms with this reality?

Although the Asian financial crisis may be largely attributable to the un-sound management of the macroeconomic environment and financial sectors in the affected countries, its underlying causes are of a different hue.[3] In the early 1990s Krugman argued that the "miracle" of economic development in the Asia-Pacific region was based more on perspiration, through augmentation and mobilization of economic inputs, than on inspiration, which would entail an

1. Cline (1982); Krugman (1994).
2. Balassa (1978).
3. McLeod and Garnaut (1998); Mai (1998).

increase in total factor productivity resulting from technological innovation.[4] Whether or not history is on the side of Professor Krugman is a matter that deserves special scrutiny. In that spirit of inquiry, this chapter adds the perspective of technological innovation to the examination of economic development in the region in the postcrisis period.

In addition, since the 1980s there has been an overall trend toward the internationalization or globalization of economic activities.[5] The prominent tendency toward internationalization of production is reflected in the higher rate of growth in the pace of foreign direct investment as opposed to international trade, though the extent of internationalization of research and development (R&D) is widely debated.[6] As a result of internationalization or globalization, not only is production now reorganizing on a global scale, but local economies are also becoming increasingly interdependent, as is evident in the "contagion effect" of the Asian financial crisis. Similarly, emerging de facto integration in the Asia-Pacific region reflects growing trade, investment ties, and regional interdependence, which encompasses the outreach of the developing countries, particularly NICs, in the region.[7] To address the economic prospects of the region, it seems more appropriate to focus on linkages across local economies rather than on the strategic trade policies of individual economies, as is seen in the conventional debate on export-oriented versus import-substitution industrialization.

In light of these points, this chapter examines the way in which regional economies can co-evolve to sustain development in the postcrisis period, with a particular emphasis on the role of Taiwan. During the initial phases of the crisis Taiwan registered respectable growth rates of 6.77 percent (1997) and 4.83 percent (1998) and remained relatively unaffected. Nonetheless, Taiwan is a stakeholder in the region, and shrinking demand in Asia has hurt Taiwan's export capacity, which is considered the engine of economic growth. Therefore, Taiwan and its neighboring countries share the same concerns as to how to revitalize the regional economy. Without denying the importance of having to restructure the local macroeconomic environment and financial sectors as a remedy to the crisis, this chapter, taking into account technological innovation and regional integration, approaches this issue in terms of industrial restructuring on a regional and a global basis.

4. Krugman (1994).
5. Michalet (1991); Sigurdson (1990).
6. Howells (1992); OECD (1992, pp. 211–15); Westney (1990).
7. Naya (1997).

In taking this approach, the chapter proceeds in four principal sections. First the chapter reviews Taiwan's developmental path in order to highlight the trend toward increasingly integrating Taiwan with other regional economies, particularly those in Southeast Asia. Next it clarifies the role played by technological innovation in Taiwan's economic performance. Such regional integration has already been envisaged in Taiwan's midterm economic development blueprint, as exemplified by the Asia-Pacific Regional Operations Center (APROC) plan, which is discussed in the third principal section of the chapter. According to this plan, Taiwan is striving to promote itself as a key regional base or as the regional headquarters for multinationals in the production and distribution of high value-added goods, turning Taiwan into a node of the global production network.

The fourth part of the chapter examines the progress of the information technology industry in order to shed some light on the future development of Taiwan and its neighbors. Attention is drawn to the emergence of so-called global logistics, a variant of global production networks in the information technology industry. Global logistics contracting has resulted from profound changes in interfirm competition and in the personal computer (PC) manufacturing industry, where there is a trend among world-class PC firms to extensively use subcontracting. With such a development, the drive to reduce production costs, lead time to market, and inventory costs has prompted Taiwanese PC firms to establish production and logistics networks to serve their customers. As a result, the totality of the PC production system in Taiwan has come to resemble a "just-in-time" system on a global scale. On the basis of these findings, the chapter offers some conclusions and policy recommendations in a concluding section.

Taiwan's Path of Development

Over the past few decades quite often Taiwan's developmental path was characterized by an export-led strategy, although Taiwan had adopted import substitution measures as a prelude to entry into the global market. As a result, Taiwan joined the league of NICs, mainly because the export-led strategy brought about beneficial learning effects engendered by competition in overseas markets.[8] Due credit for this process should be given to foreign direct

8. Balassa (1978); Keesing (1967).

investment in Taiwan, particularly for its contribution of technology transfer and spillover effects.[9] Although the export-led strategy is labeled an outward-looking orientation, the profile of Taiwan's international economic relations prior to the mid-1980s was limited in scope, with the United States and Japan as major partners. More details on this process are given later.

Factor Productivity

Krugman argues, based on the findings of Kim and Lau and Young, that the remarkable record of economic growth in the East Asian NICs has little to do with total factor productivity or technological change, but much to do with the rapid increase in factor inputs.[10] Contrary to the theory propounded by Krugman, Liang, after taking into account the heterogeneous characteristics of inputs, has shown that there was an improved performance in Taiwan's total factor productivity in 1982–87 and 1987–93, which increased at rates of 4.31 percent and 2.74 percent, respectively.[11] He even produced evidence to show that between 1982 and 1987 Taiwan outperformed the United States and Japan in terms of total factor productivity in thirteen out of twenty sectors. Dessus, Shea, and Shi also confirm the acceleration of Taiwan's productivity catch-up after the early 1980s and attribute it to import of capital goods whose production involves foreign technologies and indigenous research and development rather than just to education and foreign direct investment.[12]

Integration with the Region

Since the late 1980s Taiwan has been in the process of increasingly integrating with other economies in the region, particularly those in Southeast Asia. Before 1986 Taiwan's international economic relations were connected mainly with Japan and the United States. Japanese technologies, materials, and parts were imported to Taiwan to produce goods, and from its home base Taiwan exported goods to the United States. After 1986 Taiwan's outward investment started to take off. By March 1997 foreign direct investment in Southeast Asia by Taiwanese firms had reached U.S.$28.7 billion, making Taiwanese firms the

9. Wang (1998).
10. Kim and Lau (1994); Krugman (1994); Young (1994).
11. Liang (1995).
12. Dessus, Shea, and Shi (1995).

Table 7-1. Structure of Taiwan's Merchandise Exports, 1987–97
Percent

Year	ASEAN-5	Indonesia	Japan	Hong Kong	Malaysia	Philippines	Singapore	Thailand	United States
1987	5.5	0.8	12.9	7.6	0.5	0.9	2.5	0.8	44.2
1988	6.8	1.0	14.5	9.2	0.7	1.0	2.8	1.2	38.7
1989	8.3	1.4	13.7	10.6	1.0	1.2	3.0	1.7	36.2
1990	10.0	1.8	12.4	12.7	1.6	1.2	3.3	2.1	32.3
1991	9.8	1.6	12.1	16.3	1.9	1.1	3.2	1.9	29.3
1992	10.0	1.5	10.9	18.9	2.0	1.3	3.1	2.2	28.9
1993	11.0	1.5	10.5	21.7	2.0	1.2	3.4	2.4	27.7
1994	11.4	1.5	11.0	22.9	2.4	1.3	3.6	2.6	26.2
1995	12.5	1.7	11.8	23.4	2.6	1.5	3.9	2.8	23.7
1996	12.2	1.7	11.8	23.1	2.5	1.7	3.9	2.4	23.2
1997	12.7	1.9	9.6	23.5	2.6	1.9	4.0	2.3	24.2

Source: Taiwan, Council for Economic Planning and Development, *Taiwan Statistical Data Book* (1998).

foremost foreign investors in these countries.[13] More recently China has over-taken the Southeast Asian economies as the biggest host country for Taiwanese outward investment, altogether registering U.S.$30 billion inward investment from Taiwan. As a result, the profile of Taiwan's international trade has changed to some extent. Between 1987 and 1997 the share of Taiwan's exports to the United States decreased from 44.2 percent to 24.2 percent. In contrast, although the five countries of the Association of Southeast Asian Nations (ASEAN)—Thailand, Malaysia, the Philippines, Indonesia, and Singapore—accounted for only 3.0 percent of Taiwan's exports in 1987, their combined share climbed to 12.7 percent by 1997.

Still more significant is Taiwan's indirect trade, conducted via Hong Kong, with China, which accounted for 23.0 percent of Taiwan's exports in 1997, as opposed to 7.6 percent in 1987 (see table 7-1). There are signs that Taiwan's foreign direct investment in Southeast Asia has led to a vertical division of labor between Taiwan and its neighboring countries in a number of industries. A study commissioned by Taiwan's Bureau of Industry revealed that Taiwan's foreign investment in China and the ASEAN-5 countries had helped generate U.S.$19.63 billion in exports from the host countries, which was almost equivalent to Taiwan's exports to the markets of the United States, Japan, and Europe replaced by those countries.[14] By investing in ASEAN countries Taiwanese

13. Chung-Hua Institution for Economic Research (1995).
14. Wang and Lee (1997).

firms have transferred a substantial set of industrial resources, including technology, markets, production facilities, and human resources, to the host countries.[15] These points clearly illustrate the extent of Taiwan's economic integration.

Although Taiwan's outward investment in the ASEAN countries was driven initially and primarily by the inexpensive labor in the host countries, factor endowment may not yet sufficiently explain the current pattern of the division of labor in the Pacific Basin.[16] This is a point to which the chapter will return later.

A New Development Prospect: The APROC Plan

In 1995 Taiwan began implementing its Asia-Pacific Regional Operations Center (APROC) plan as its midterm economic development blueprint. The APROC plan has two major facets. First, it aims to promote Taiwan as a hub in the Asia-Pacific region by attracting multinationals to make Taiwan their regional operational base for investment and business activities. Second, APROC helps foster a highly liberalized and internationalized economy in Taiwan. To achieve its designated goals, the APROC plan emphasizes liberalization and internationalization as the two key principles of macroeconomic adjustments in Taiwan. Along similar lines, it also entails the development of Taiwan into a manufacturing, sea transportation, air transportation, financial, telecommunications, and media center for the Asia-Pacific region.

Key Components of the APROC Plan

Several key points provide the policy framework for implementing Taiwan's APROC plan. First, in terms of macroeconomic adjustment the plan focuses on promoting trade and investment liberalization, reducing entry and exit restrictions on personnel, removing restrictions on capital movement, and establishing an appropriate legal environment for an information society. Second, with regard to the manufacturing sector, the APROC plan envisions fostering an overall environment for upgrading manufacturing industries and estab-

15. Chung-Hua Institution for Economic Research (1995).
16. Chow (1997).

lishing intelligent industrial parks to turn Taiwan into a science and technology–based island. Third, in terms of the financial sector the plan foresees the development of a dynamic financial center focusing on integrating a foreign exchange market, an offshore banking unit, and a foreign currency market; promoting the expansion and internationalization of the bond and securities market; developing a derivatives market; enhancing the gold market; and developing the insurance market.

Fourth, with regard to sea transportation the plan intends to vigorously improve services and facilities and expand cargo transportation operations. This includes enhancing the overall development of Kaohsiung Harbor and the expansion of its transportation capacity. Fifth, in terms of air transportation the plan works to develop express cargo and passenger transportation centers while building an aerospace city and implementing plans for building a new international airport.

Sixth, as for telecommunications, the APROC plan expects to vigorously promote telecommunications liberalization and the development of a center for private business networks. This includes expanding cable connections and creating an improved telephone connection and customer service center, restructuring the telecommunications regulatory framework, developing an international-class telecommunications industry, and promoting the National Information Infrastructure Development plan in coordination with the development of the telecommunications center. Finally, with regard to the media the plan aims to improve the general environment for the media industry and establish a high-tech media park.

Implementing the APROC Plan

This is an ambitious plan, and it will require continued careful implementation. How can Taiwan overcome potential obstacles to seeing it through? For example, in the ongoing process of globalization multinationals and their overseas investments have played a very important role in stimulating economic development in countries around the globe. However, on occasion multinationals can be so footloose as to undermine the sustainability of host countries' economic development, especially when their overseas investments do not involve substantial sunk costs. In the 1970s, for example, peripheral regions in Western Europe were very active in attracting multinationals' to their regions as part of their developmental strategy. In response, multinationals set up "branch plants" that tended to be functionally unsophisticated. When those regions' labor costs increased or when the multinationals themselves were beset by economic downturns, the multinationals tended to scale down their branch plants or even withdraw completely from these regions. As a result, economic development in the peripheral regions of Western Europe came to a sudden halt. This scenario is termed the "branch plant syndrome" in the literature.[17]

In light of such developments it is fair for developing economies to ask how they can "anchor" multinationals as well as indigenous firms, keeping them committed while persuading them to continuously upgrade their local operations over time. To address this question the APROC plan calls for the reengineering of Taiwan's economy such that multinationals and indigenous firms will tend to use Taiwan as a key regional base or as their regional headquarters for the production and distribution of high value-added goods. It is well documented that corporate high value-added operations and headquarters of various kinds tend to be concentrated in localities where financial resources are easily accessible and where transportation and telecommunications infrastructures are well developed.[18] In order to meet this challenge the APROC plan strives to upgrade soft as well as physical infrastructures in Taiwan to ensure the free flow of capital, goods, services, information, and human resources. In light of this, the second facet of the APROC plan amounts to a large-scale liberalization program, or a "competitiveness policy," in Gassmann's terms, emphasizing the fostering of conditions to form a framework for industry.[19]

In addition, the APROC plan has an international dimension. As mentioned earlier, the idea of developing Taiwan as a manufacturing center in the Asia-Pacific region aims at encouraging multinationals as well as indigenous firms to choose Taiwan as their regional base for the production and distribution of high value-added goods. Under this process a more efficient division of labor with other regional economies may be achieved, and Taiwan may more efficiently use its own resources so as to better integrate itself into the regional economy. This prospect appears to fit very well with the need for the revitalization of the regional economy in the postcrisis period.

17. Firn (1975).
18. Bosman and de Smidt (1993); Goddard and Pye (1977); Goddard and Smith (1978).
19. Gassmann (1994); Gonenc (1994).

Intraindustry Integration

A look at the degree to which Taiwan has developed regional intraindustry relationships gives an indication of the island's progress in integrating itself within the region, an important foundation for the APROC plan. Although Taiwan's outward investment in the ASEAN countries was driven initially and primarily by the inexpensive labor the host countries, factor endowment may yet not sufficiently explain the current pattern of the division of labor in the Pacific Basin. For example, as Chow argues:

> The pattern of international division of labor among these countries is primarily based on technology hierarchy which is subject to dynamic changes in accordance with their comparative advantages at various stages of production. . . . [In turn], their comparative advantages at various stages of structural transformation have been undergoing dynamic changes in accordance with their respective technological sophistication and industrial developments. . . . Facilitated by intra-regional FDI flows, and the segmentation of the production network on a regional/global scale, the emphasis of trade flows within the region had shifted from inter-industry to intra-industry trade. Therefore, vertical rather than horizontal division of labor dominated the trade pattern within the Pacific Basin.[20]

Taking the computer industry as an example, table 7-2 shows a substantial increase in intraindustry trade and the vertical division of labor between Taiwan and its ASEAN neighbors between 1990 and 1996, lending some support to Chow's arguments.

In addition, the production system in the region is probably part of a global production network or a cross-national production network (CPN), in the terms of Borrus and Borrus. As these two authors point out:

> CPNs permit and result from an increasingly fine division of labor. The networks permit firms to weave together the constituent elements of the value-chain into competitively effective new production systems, while facilitating diverse points of innovation. But perhaps more importantly, they have turned large segments of complex manufacturing into a commodity available in the market.[21]

They go further, arguing that although CPNs originated in the electronics industry, they will diffuse more widely into other industries.

20. Chow (1997, pp. 2, 5, and 24).
21. Borrus and Borrus (1997).

Table 7-2. Intraindustry Trade between Taiwan and Selected East Asian Economies in the Computer Industry, 1990 and 1996

Thousands of New Taiwan dollars

Production code	Country	1990 Exports	1990 Imports	1996 Exports	1996 Imports
HS 8471[a]	ASEAN[b]	4,465,612	7,076,312	12,126,043	23,565,445
	Brunei	4,466	0	14,260	0
	Hong Kong	3,216,469	368,968	9,280,913	343,752
	Indonesia	153,128	2,393	266,214	1,161,507
	Malaysia	447,975	132,235	2,368,128	4,681,039
	Philippines	295,145	446,748	932,839	3,644,976
	Singapore	3,064,655	5,383,110	6,775,389	8,542,889
	Thailand	500,243	1,111,826	1,769,213	5,535,034
	Vietnam	18,243	0	289,798	7
	Total[c]	107,913,028	27,413,036	293,702,534	58,814,622
HS 8473[d]	ASEAN[b]	5,071,066	845,517	16,631,791	4,970,366
	Brunei	961	0	3,403	0
	Hong Kong	1,854,045	2,456,103	23,653,988	1,466,367
	Indonesia	159,378	7,587	669,065	1,061
	Malaysia	984,511	139,411	1,422,555	1,015,019
	Philippines	253,832	33,237	5,484,310	271,689
	Singapore	2,543,750	617,979	5,503,189	2,867,981
	Thailand	1,128,634	47,303	3,549,269	814,616
	Vietnam	9,219	0	194,242	0
	Total	61,417,014	11,604,115	217,872,957	20,394,042

Source: Board of Foreign Trade, Ministry of Economic Affairs, Taipei, Taiwan, *Monthly Statistics of Export and Import* (magnetic tapes).

a. HS 8471 = computers and peripheral products.

b. ASEAN includes Brunei, Indonesia, Malaysia, the Philippines, Singapore, and Thailand and does not include Hong Kong or Vietnam.

c. Total represents Taiwan's total exports/imports of the specified products.

d. HS 8473 = components and parts.

Taiwan's Place in the Global Production Network

Having discussed Taiwan's future developmental framework as promoted by the APROC plan, this section goes on to examine the progress made by the APROC plan in the context of the information industry in order to shed some light on the future development of Taiwan and its neighbors. Before doing so, however, some background should be given on the development of Taiwan's information industry.

The Development of Taiwan's Information Industry

Since the 1980s the information industry has increasingly become the engine of economic growth in Taiwan. Although progressive development in the information sector is widely seen throughout the world, in Taiwan the industry has outgrown the majority of its international counterparts. Currently Taiwan ranks as the third largest producer of information products worldwide. This outstanding performance has gained its momentum mainly from the PC and peripheral equipment subsectors. Quite a number of Taiwan-made products within these two sectors, such as motherboards, scanners, monitors, keyboards, and notebook computers, enjoy a significant global market share (see figure 7-1). What underlies this success are the well-regarded production and design capabilities of Taiwanese firms, which have made Taiwan a major source of contract work for internationally prominent information technology (IT) companies. On the basis of Taiwan's success in this sector, it is argued, Taiwan is well equipped to become a "one-stop shopping center" for IT products.

The development of Taiwan's information industry was driven initially by foreign direct investment, but the momentum has now shifted to local firms.[22] Although production by multinationals' subsidiaries accounted for 40 to 50 percent of Taiwan's IT exports in the mid-1980s, this percentage substantially decreased to 15 percent or so in 1995. This trend toward a diminishing production share of foreign-owned subsidiaries implies a shift in the role played by multinationals, from active participation in local production to channeling indigenous production into the global market via international procurement. In addition, Taiwan's IT firms have continuously devoted themselves to R&D. As a result, Taiwan and South Korea together account for 85 percent of dynamic Asian economies' patent applications in the IT field in the United States.

Beginning in the late 1980s, Taiwanese IT firms started to engage in outward investment, initially directed toward Southeast Asia, and more recently toward China and elsewhere in the world. As a result, the offshore IT production of Taiwan-based firms grew from U.S.$973 million in 1992 to U.S.$14.52 billion in 1998, accounting for 43 percent of the IT production by Taiwan-based firms. There are also signs that the recent surge of Taiwanese IT firms' investments in Europe, which account for 80 percent of Taiwan's outward investment in the region, has more to do with the integration of regional production and marketing operations than with the establishment of individual function sites. There-

22. Hobday (1995).

Figure 7-1. Taiwanese Firms' 1996 World Market Share in PC-Related Products

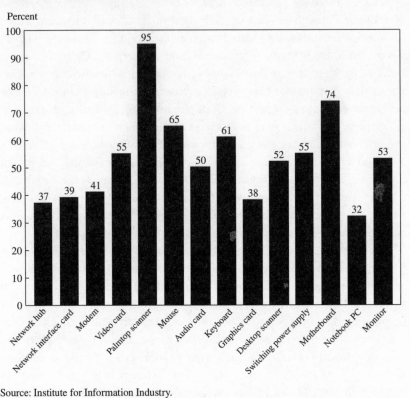

Source: Institute for Information Industry.

fore, although the outreach of Taiwan's IT firms was driven initially by a motivation to reduce production costs, it has increasingly become part of a process of establishing cross-border production and distribution networks in response to current global restructuring in the industry.[23] This point is discussed further later.

The Emergence of Global Logistics Networks

Since the late 1980s, as the ability to manufacture PCs has diffused widely throughout the world and as price competition has intensified and profit mar-

23. Chen and Liu (1999).

gins have narrowed for most mature computer technologies, the PC industry has witnessed a profound change in interfirm competition and in its manufacturing systems. In this process PC firms in the United States have sought to establish new sources of competitive advantage by accelerating the pace of new technology development and increasingly using external subcontractors. As a result, component technology is sourced from a global network of suppliers, whereas the final assembly of PCs tends to be done in each of the major market areas of North America, Europe, and Asia.[24]

More specifically, recent developments have led to the emergence of a variant of global production networks: global logistics.[25] In their efforts to withstand market encroachment by low-cost clone suppliers, large U.S. firms, led by Compaq, Hewlett Packard, and IBM, now tend to concentrate on R&D and marketing while outsourcing production and logistics operations from, for example, Taiwan-based firms. Specifically speaking, Compaq pioneered the so-called optimized distribution model (ODM), which, in essence, can provide customers with options as to what, when, and how they want at the lowest prices.

This operational model has three facets. First, in order to narrow the gap between supply and demand, production is required to meet orders (build-to-order) rather than forecasts (build-to-forecast). Second, in order to meet the variety of customer demands, build-to-order practices are extended to configuration-to-order practices, under which customized products are produced in specific quantities. Third, Compaq's vendors are required to undertake final assembly, bringing together a set of modular subassemblies produced and delivered by Compaq's subcontractors. From Compaq's perspective the adoption of the ODM enables it to concentrate on its own core competencies of R&D and marketing while leaving the rest of the value chain to its subcontractors in Taiwan and to vendors. Meanwhile, the latter two types of firms have come to resemble members of Compaq's "virtual business," providing the ammunition requisite for Compaq to compete effectively in the global market. Borrus even suggests that the revival of the U.S. electronics industry in the 1990s vis-à-vis its Japanese counterpart in the 1990s has rested in significant part on the American firms' connection with Asian production networks.[26]

---

24. Angel and Engstrom (1995); see also Borrus and Borrus (1997).
25. Chen and Liu (1999).
26. Borrus (1997).

What does such a new model of contracting mean when its comes to the development of Taiwan's PC industry? The new contracting relationships of Taiwanese IT firms with leading U.S. firms, along with the drive to reduce production costs, lead time to market, and inventory costs, has prompted these Taiwanese firms to establish international production and logistics networks to serve their customers. For example, by implementing the ODM Compaq has completely handed its inventory costs over to its subcontractors. The latter are also required to produce and deliver subsystem products in line with tight schedules and the variety of market demand. Therefore, they have to ensure that everything is synchronized up and down the supply chain. To do so these subcontractors, such as those based in Taiwan, have had to establish a well-structured, fast-response global production and logistics network by means of internalization or the formation of strategic alliances. Often they have also asked their suppliers of components and parts to follow suit in order to smoothly link up the supply chain. As a result, the totality of PC production systems has increasingly come to resemble a "just-in-time" system on a global scale. Therefore, the commercial fortunes of all the firms involved, which are located in different countries, will be bound up together. So, too, will be the fortunes of all the economies concerned.

Therefore, the relationship between Taiwanese IT firms and their customers—owners of world-class PC brand names—has gone beyond that of the traditional original equipment manufacturing (OEM) model. Under OEM contracting Taiwanese IT firms acted merely as providers of finished products to their customers. In contrast, emergent global logistics contracting requires Taiwanese subcontractors to take on a larger responsibility by participating in supply-chain management, logistics operations, and after-sale services. In addition, both sides of the contracting relationship now have to work closely together in order to create "across-the-board" competitive advantages in all mainstream activities in the industry, engendering escalating interdependence between them and hence a "locked-in" effect. Aided by such relationships, Taiwanese firms may be able to broaden the scope of their value chains, upstream to R&D and downstream to distribution and logistics, in a less risky manner. Moreover, with a global production and logistics network at their disposal that will satisfactorily meet the needs of their customers, Taiwan-based IT firms may preempt the entry into the network of their counterparts in many countries. As a result, from Taiwan's viewpoint owners of world-class PC brand names, which are international core firms in the industry, can be "anchored" to Taiwan's economy.

The Impact on the Region

Southeast Asian countries remain important partners for Taiwan in this context. In undertaking subcontract work for global logistics, the Taiwan-based firms need to strive not only to reduce their production costs, but also to gain flexible production and fast response capabilities. When they can do so, their overseas subsidiaries will tend to function as more than low-cost production sites, taking on larger responsibilities for competitiveness. This will often require a higher degree of responsiveness, which will be better served by using local creative resources.[27] As a result, Taiwanese firms' subsidiaries will integrate more with their host economies in Southeast Asia.

In addition, there is an emerging international dimension to Taiwan's national innovation system. The term *national innovation system* refers to a complex set of relationships among actors producing, distributing, and applying various kind of knowledge within a national border.[28] There is a growing body of literature on national innovation systems, but whether innovation systems are bounded by national borders is a subject of debate.[29] Numerous studies have shown the role played by governmental policies and government-sponsored research organizations in stimulating and promoting Taiwan's IT industry.[30] Another issue is that previously Taiwanese firms could rely mostly on local firms and networks, stretching from Keelung to Hsinchu, in their production of PCs; however, under the global logistics systems they now have to mobilize resources from their global networks to do so.[31] This arguably will add a new international dimension to Taiwan's national innovation system, in the sense that PCs delivered by Taiwan-based firms will be the result of innovation in a variety of countries. As regards countries in the Asia-Pacific region, as production systems become an integral part of cross-national production networks, the fortunes of all economies concerned will be bound up together. Ideally, the economic and industrial development of these economies can and should co-evolve in a dynamic and balanced manner.

27. Sigurdson (1998 p. 13).
28. McKelvey (1991); OECD (1997).
29. Sigurdson (1998).
30. For example, see Hou and San (1993) and Kraemer et al. (1996).
31. Kawakami (1996); Kraemer et al. (1996).

A Region-Based Way Forward

The contagion effect of the Asian financial crisis has something to do with the increased interdependence among regional economies resulting from globalization and regional integration. It shows the downside of regional integration, as regional economies went down like a house of cards when one of them was toppled by the backlash of financial mismanagement. By the same token, however, there is a hope that the countries of the Asia-Pacific region may revitalize themselves together. To address the prospects of the regional economy, it would therefore appear to be more appropriate to focus more on cross-national economic linkages than on the strategic trade policies of individual countries.

As far as Taiwan is concerned, its economic prospects lie substantially in the de facto regional integration that is currently taking place, in which Taiwan may be able to act as an essential node of global production networks. In terms of industrial development, Taiwan and its neighboring partners need to address the issue of how to "anchor" multinationals as well as their indigenous firms, keeping them committed and encouraging them to continuously upgrade their local operations over time. From a macroeconomic perspective, Taiwan can promote this process by ensuring the free flow of capital, goods, services, information, and human resources. By introducing these new competitive parameters, Taiwan can promote itself as a key regional base or as the regional headquarters for multinationals in the production and distribution of high value-added goods. Can this approach be extended regionally?

Some hope rests with the proliferation of global production networks, which, though they originated in the electronics industry, have the potential of diffusing more widely into other industries. Specifically, global logistics contracting in the PC industry is a variant of the operation of global production networks. In their efforts to withstand market encroachment by suppliers of low-cost PC clones, large U.S. PC firms now tend to concentrate on R&D and marketing while outsourcing production and logistics operations from, for example, Taiwan-based firms. Under such a system the drive to reduce production costs, lead time to market, and inventory costs has prompted Taiwanese firms to establish cross-regional production and logistics networks to serve their customers. In addition, they have to ensure that everything is synchronized up and down the supply chain. As a result, PC production systems have overall come to resemble a global "just-in-time" structure. Admittedly, PC firms in the United States are in the driver's seat, but Taiwan-based PC firms, by mobilizing their global networks, may preempt the entry into the network of their counterparts in many countries.

Even so, Southeast Asian countries will remain important partners for Taiwan. Under the process of global logistics contracting Southeast Asian industries will become more than low-cost production sites; they will take on a larger share in ensuring competitiveness in the industry overall. By increasingly relying on local innovative resources, Taiwan and its neighboring countries will experience a greater degree of integration and address their mutual interests in growth. In other words, PCs delivered by Taiwan-based firms will be the result of the productive and innovative efforts of a variety of firms and economies in the region. Therefore, global logistics contracting and the establishment of global production networks not only weave together the cross-national constituent elements of the value chain into competitively effective new production systems, they also facilitate the development of diverse points of innovation, a key component in the development of any emergent economy. Based on Taiwan's experience, this approach points to a promising way forward for regional economies seeking to meet their potential in the wake of the Asian financial crisis.

References

Angel, D. P., and J. Engstrom. 1995. "Manufacturing Systems and Technology Change: The U.S. Personal Computer Industry." *Economic Geography* 71(1) (January): 79–102.

Balassa, B. 1978. "Exports and Economic Development." *Journal of Development Economics* 5(2): 181–89.

Borrus, M. 1997. "Left for Dead: Asian Production Networks and the Revival of U.S. Electronics." In *The China Circle: Economics and Electronics in the PRC, Hong Kong, and Taiwan,* edited by B. Naughton. Brookings Institution.

Borrus, M., and Z. Borrus. 1997. "Globalization with Borders: The Rise of Wintelism and the Future of Global Competition." *Industry and Innovation* 4(2) (December): 141–66.

Bosman, J., and Marc de Smidt. 1993. "The Geographical Formation of International Management Centers in Europe." *Urban Studies* 30(6): 967–80.

Chen, S. H., and D. N. Liu. 1999. *Strategic Alliances in the Context of Competition Policy.* Final report to the Bureau of Industry, Taipei. Taipei: Chung-Hua Institution for Economic Research. In Chinese.

Chow, P. 1997. "Technology Hierarchy, Globalization of Production Networks, and International Division of Labor among Pacific Basin Countries." Paper presented at the First International Business Management Conference, National Chi Nan University, Taiwan.

Chung-Hua Institution for Economic Research. 1995. *Taiwan's Small and Medium-Sized Firms' Direct Investment in Southeast Asia.* Taipei: Chung-Hua Institution for Economic Research.

Cline, W. R. 1982. "Can the East Asian Model of Development Be Generalized?" *World Development* 10(2): 81–90.

Dessus, S., J. D. Shea, and M. S. Shi. 1995. *Chinese Taipei: The Origins of the Economic Miracle.* Paris: Development Center of the Organization for Economic Cooperation and Development.

Firn, J. R. 1975. "External Control and Regional Development: The Case of Scotland." *Environment and Planning A* 7: 393–414.

Gassmann, H. 1994. "From Industrial Policy to Competitiveness Policy." *OECD Observer* 187: 17.

Goddard, J. B., and R. Pye. 1977. "Telecommunications and Office Location." *Regional Studies* 11: 19–30.

Goddard, J. B., and I. J. Smith. 1978. "Change in Corporate Control in the British Urban System." *Environment and Planning A* 10: 1073–84.

Gonenc, R. 1994. "A New Approach to Industrial Policy." *OECD Observer* 166: 8–12.

Hobday, M. 1995. *Innovation in East Asia: The Challenge to Japan.* Aldershot, Vt.: Edward Elgar.

Hou, C. M., and G. San. 1993. "National Systems Supporting Technical Advance in Industry: The Case of Taiwan." In *National Innovation Systems: A Comparative Analysis,* edited by R. Nelson. Oxford University Press.

Howells, J. 1992. *Going Global: The Use of ICT Networks in Research and Development.* Working Paper 7. Newcastle upon Tyne: Newcastle University, Newcastle PICT Center.

Kawakami, M. 1996. *Development of the Small- and Medium-Sized Manufacturers in Taiwan's PC Industry.* CIER Discussion Paper Series 9606. Taipei: Chung-Hua Institution for Economic Research.

Keesing, D. B. 1967. "Outward-Looking Polices and Economic Development." *Economic Journal* 77(306): 303–20.

Kim, J. I., and L. J. Lau. 1994. "The Sources of Economic Growth in the East Asian Newly Industrializing Countries." *Journal of the Japanese and International Economics* 8(3) (September): 235–71.

Kraemer, K. L., J. Dedrick, and others. 1996. "Entrepreneurship, Flexibility, and Policy Coordination: Taiwan's Computer Industry." *The Information Society* 12: 215–49.

Krugman, P. 1994. "The Myth of Asia's Miracle." *Foreign Affairs* 73(6) (November/December): 62–78.

Liang, C. Y. 1995. "Productivity Growth in Asian NIEs: A Case Study of the Republic of China, 1961–93." *APO Productivity Journal* (Winter).

McKelvey, M. 1991. "How Do National Systems of Innovation Differ? A Critical Analysis of Porter, Freeman, Lundvall, and Nelson." In *Rethinking Economics:*

Markets, Technology, and Economic Evolution, edited by G. M. Hodgson and E. Screpanti. Aldershot, Vt.: Edward Elgar.

McLeod, R. H., and R. Garnaut, eds. 1998. *East Asia in Crisis: From Being a Miracle to Needing One.* New York: Routledge.

Mai, C. C., ed. 1998. *The Asian Currency Crisis: The Taiwan Experience.* Taipei: Chung-Hua Institution for Economic Research.

Michalet, C. A. 1991. "Strategic Partnerships and the Changing Internationalization Process." In *Strategic Partnerships: States, Firms, and International Competition,* edited by L. K. Mytelka. London: Pinter.

Naya, S. F. 1997. "Interdependence and Asia-Pacific Economic Cooperation." In *Hedging Bets on Growth in a Globalizing Industrial Order: Lessons for the Asian NIEs,* edited by L. J. Cho and Y. H. Kim. Seoul: Korea Development Institute.

Organization for Economic Cooperation and Development (OECD). 1992. *Technology and the Economy: The Key Relationship.* Paris: OECD.

————. 1997. *National Innovation Systems.* Paris: OECD-STI.

Sigurdson, J. 1990. "The Internationalization of R&D: An Interpretation of Forces and Responses." In *Measuring the Dynamics of Technological Change,* edited by J. Sigurdson. London: Pinter.

————. 1998. "The Role and Bounds of National Science and Technology Policies." Paper presented at the Taipei Workshop for the OECD Project on National Innovation Systems in Catching-up Economies, Taipei (April 20–22).

Wang, S., and Y. Lee. 1997. *Ten-Year Summary Report.* Final report to the Bureau of Industry, Taipei, Taiwan. In Chinese.

Wang, W. T. 1998. *Foreign Direct Investment, Spillovers, and Catching Up: The Case of Taiwan.* CIER Economic Monograph Series 39. Taipei: Chung-Hua Institution for Economic Research.

Westney, E. D. 1990. "Internal and External Linkages in the MNC: The Case of R&D Subsidiaries in Japan." In *Managing the Global Firm,* edited by C. Barrtlett, Y. Doz, and G. Hedlund. New York: Routledge.

Young, A. 1994. "The Tyranny of Numbers: Confronting the Statistical Realities of East Asian Growth Experience." Working Paper 4680. Cambridge, Mass.: National Bureau of Economic Research.

Part Four

LESSONS LEARNED

CHAPTER EIGHT

What We Have Learned from the Asian Financial Crisis

Peter C. Y. Chow

The East Asian miracle, characterized by a "flying geese" pattern of export-led growth, was devastated by the 1997–98 financial crisis.[1] Japan, the leading goose of the flock, suffered an unprecedented recession, with the other countries such as Korea and the countries of the Association of Southeast Asian Nations (ASEAN) following behind. Their typically rapid growth in exports and gross domestic product (GDP) came to a halt in mid-1997 as the currency depreciation in Thailand led to a debt crisis that spread throughout the region. Why did the decades-long Asian economic miracle turn into a financial disaster within such a short time? Now that analysts have had time to reflect, what lessons can be learned from the experience and applied in ways that not only will help the region recover more effectively, but also will help ensure that future crises can be alleviated or avoided altogether?

With few exceptions, most studies on the Asian financial crisis have focused on the causes and consequences of financial crisis within individual economies rather than on a regional comparison across several economies. A comparative study of why the financial crisis hit some economies but only glanced off others not only would enhance our understanding of the role of the financial

---

1. The International Monetary Fund (1998) classified four major categories of financial crisis—currency crisis, banking crisis, foreign debt crisis, and systemic financial crisis. This chapter adopts the general term *financial crisis*.

sector in economic development, but also would allow us to develop policy lessons for developing countries both inside and outside the region. Drawing on the comparative and individual economy studies in this volume, this concluding chapter provides a more comprehensive, cross-economy analysis of financial developments and crisis management in the region than have the previous chapters. Specifically, it zeroes in on why economies such as Taiwan's emerged from the crisis relatively unscathed, whereas other ostensibly similar economies bore the full brunt of the crisis.[2] Rather than arguing over whether the financial crisis resulted from economic fundamentals or merely from financial panic, this chapter takes a different approach by answering the question of why it occurred in some economies but not in others.[3]

To do this, the remainder of the chapter is organized into four major sections. The first offers a comparative overview of six features commonly shared across the region that helped fuel the financial crisis in the first place. The next section provides additional details, especially comparative details, on the specific cases of Thailand, Indonesia, and Korea. A third major section draws com-

2. Taiwan seems to be an appropriate subject for comparative study for a number of reasons. First, Taiwan was one of the few economies—along with China, Singapore, and to some extent Hong Kong—that, in comparison to the region overall, managed to weather the storm of the financial crisis. However, even Hong Kong, which managed to back up its money supply and maintained its pegged rate exchange system, suffered sluggish growth with declining real estate and security markets. China's financial market is highly segmented and insulated from the rest of the world. In spite of increased capital inflows after its economic reform, China's foreign capital has come mainly from foreign direct investment and long-term foreign loans, whereas portfolio investments on securities have been negligible. Moreover, China insulates foreign portfolio investment by limiting foreign investors to the "B shares" of its security market. China's currency, the renminbi (RMB), is a nonconvertible currency on the international market. With regard to comparative management of financial crisis, it is more fruitful to focus on Singapore and Taiwan. In this light, the present chapter focuses on Taiwan.

3. There were two major schools of thought as to the causes of the Asian financial crisis. The first was the "fundamentalist school"—Krugman (1979, 1998); Corsetti, Pesenti, and Roubini (1998); and Goldstein (1998)—which holds that weak macroeconomic fundamentals under a fixed exchange rate regime became vulnerable to speculative currency attack. The second is usually referred to as the "expectation school" or "financial panic school"—Radelet and Sachs (1998) and Stiglitz (1998)—which argues that lack of investor confidence led to a liquidity crisis and bank insolvency. Both schools have merit, but neither one can fully explain the onset of the Asian financial crisis.

parisons to Taiwan's financial development and monetary policy during and after the crisis. Based on these findings and those in the volume as a whole, a concluding section provides policy lessons to be gained from the Asian financial crisis.

Why Did the Economic Miracle Turn into a Financial Crisis?

Although the causes of financial crisis varied by degrees among the affected economies, it is clear from the research of this volume that six characteristics were commonly shared.

Uneven Development between the Financial and Real Sectors

First, the research in this book and elsewhere exposes weak financial institutions and shallow financial markets in the region due to the legacies of rapid growth of trade and GDP. In the literature Patrick divides the patterns of interactions between economic and financial development into two models: the "demand-following model," in which the growth of the real sector creates the demand for financial services, inducing the development of financial institutions and markets, and the "supply-leading model," in which the development of the financial sector provides sufficient capital for the growth of the real sector.[4] Regardless of the sequential order of development, the real sector and the financial sector, which are similar to the front and rear wheels of an automobile, must be balanced for smooth and long-term sustainable development in any economy.

However, in developing East Asian countries the growth of the real sector—trade, industrial development, and output—had outperformed that of the financial sector and created a pattern of uneven development between the real sector and the financial sector. The legacies of such uneven development in Asian economies became more evident with the integration of their fragile financial sectors with more efficient and well-functioning financial sectors among developed economies, which began with the globalization process in the late 1980s and early 1990s. Despite enviable growth records in many East Asian countries in past decades, their financial sectors were still rather backward as reflected by the existence of unorganized curbed money markets, the shallow-

---

4. Patrick (1966).

ness of their financial development, and the overregulation of their financial sectors (state banks as well as deposit and lending rates) until the second half of the 1980s.[5] The unbalanced growth between the real and financial sectors was doomed to eventually fail as a globally integrated financial system started to operate in the 1990s.

Most economies in East Asia displayed robust growth between 1991 and 1997, enjoying high saving and investment ratios, moderate inflation, and tolerable budget and trade deficits. But behind these macroeconomic indicators there were hidden problems such as increasing foreign debts, overinvestment, excessive capacities with government-guided commercial loans, general ignorance of risk inherently connected with crony capitalism and gigantic conglomerates, and a lack of risk management of exchange rate exposures in foreign loans mostly denominated in U.S. dollars. Each of these factors sowed the seeds of financial disaster, threatening long-term sustainable development even without the onset of the crisis.

Absence of Sound Banking and Supervisory Systems

Most developing Asian countries integrated their nascent domestic financial markets with those in developed countries after the Uruguay Round, which was started in 1986 and concluded in 1992.[6] Policymakers overseeing these fledgling financial sectors still exercised implicit or explicit influence on bank lending activities, allowing a de facto credit rationing of domestic financial sectors while deregulating the foreign sector by liberalizing capital flows across national boundaries, and thus proceeded contrary to well-known frameworks for the sequential order of financial liberalization.[7] In addition, it has

5. For information on growth records, see Young (1995). According to McKinnon (1984), there is a positive correlation between financial growth and real growth. Some typical indicators of financial deepening are the ratio of M2 to the gross national product (GNP), the ratio of deposit money to the total money supply, and the ratio of claims in the banking system to national income. By 1980 the ratio of M2 to GNP was 1.39 in Japan, 0.83 in Singapore, 0.75 in Taiwan, 0.34 in Korea, and 0.21 in the Philippines. Data source: International Monetary Fund, *World Economic Outlook* (various issues).

6. Among the industrialized countries, the United States pushed hard for trade liberalization in three major sectors in which it has a comparative advantage in the world market: the agricultural sector, high-tech industries, and services (such as banking, finance, and insurance).

7. McKinnon (1991); Shaw (1973).

been argued that a sound banking system and the ability of monetary authorities to control money supply were prerequisites for liberalizing capital account trans-actions.[8] But many East Asian countries liberalized their capital flows before they equipped themselves with those prerequisites.

De facto credit rationing guided by implicit or explicit government lending policies (administrative orders) not only distorted capital efficiency, but also misled foreign lenders with an implicit government guarantee on their loans. Hence, a "moral hazard" syndrome emerged long before the crisis. For example, even though Korea's tolerance for preferential lending to achieve industrialization may be socially justifiable for driving rapid industrial growth in the short term, the lack of capital efficiency and persistent predatory pricing in Korea's export promotions proved to be unsustainable in the longer term. After an appreciation of the Korean won began in mid-1995, when Korea was also faced with the devaluation of the Chinese renminbi and the Mexican peso in 1994 as well as the sharp rise in Taiwan's semiconductor exports to the world market, Korean exports stagnated.[9] Economies previously overheated between 1990 and 1995 left less leverage for many East Asian countries such as Korea to adopt tight monetary policies to check the inflows of foreign capital and constrain overinvestment. When export recessions hit, excessive capacities along with outstanding foreign loans sparked the financial crisis.

In the case of Thailand, financial liberalization without appropriate oversight led foreign capital to unproductive assets such as real estate and stocks. Lifting restrictions on capital accounts enabled the Bangkok International Banking Facility (BIBF), which had been established in 1993 primarily to attract foreign capital to relend to domestic banks and financial companies, to dramatically expand the country's portfolio of foreign indebtedness.[10] Much of this foreign

8. Kwan (1997).

9. In 1996 Taiwan was ranked the second largest exporter of integrated circuits and the third largest exporter of information industry in the world. The growth rate for the Taiwanese information industry was 20.8 percent in 1995–96. Data source: Taiwan, Bureau of Foreign Trade, Ministry of Economic Affairs.

10. By August 1997 the out-in loans of the BIBF totaled U.S.$22.3 billion, whereas the out-out loans totaled only U.S.$10.4 billion. (Out-in loans are those made to concerns inside a country using money borrowed from outside the country. Out-out loans are loans made using money borrowed from outside the country and lent to concerns outside the country.)

capital was directed to Thailand's stock and property markets for speculative projects. The speculative bubble in Thailand was exemplified in 1992–96 by the oversupply of new housing units by a ratio of nearly 2 to 1 in terms of housing supply to demand. As an obvious result, builders who were unable to sell or lease their properties later faced troubles in retiring their loans. Edison, Luangaram, and Miller point out that "excess credit creation can easily raise values above equilibrium; but when disequilibrium is being corrected, credit constraints can set in motion a vicious downward spiral in asset price."[11] What had been a potential crisis became a real one when Thai exports slowed in the face of strong competition from China and Mexico, both of which devalued their currencies in 1994.

Exchange Rate Misalignment and Capital Flow Reversals

Strong economic performances in these countries masked the backwardness of their financial institutions for an extended period, which, as the research in this volume shows, sowed the seeds of economic vulnerability long before the crisis occurred. But the problem became truly apparent only after domestic financial sectors were integrated with the dynamic global financial market. This is evidenced in particular with regard to the pegged exchange rates regimes in several East Asian economies. There are two principal legacies of misalignment of the exchange rates. First is the incompatibility of pegging exchange rates and a monetary autonomy to maintain macroeconomic balances when capitals are freely moved across national boundaries after liberalizing capital accounts in many of these countries (a standard model traced back to Mundell-Fleming). Second, with the prolonged use of pegged exchange rates regimes, economic authorities neglected prudential hedging and risk assessment against undue exposure when foreign loans were denominated in key foreign currencies. Under these conditions countries with high debt-service ratios, larger current account deficits, and lower ratios of foreign exchange reserves to total GDP were particularly hard hit by the financial crisis.

Given these structural defects in the exchange rates system of nascent regional financial systems, the swing of exchange rates between the Japanese yen and the U.S. dollar in the 1990s created difficulties for these financial

11. Edison, Luangaram, and Miller (1998).

systems. Between 1990 and 1995 there was a depreciation of the real effective exchange rates in countries that pegged their currencies to the U.S. dollar when the Japanese yen was strong against the dollar. Kwan argues that there is a synchronization between the yen-dollar rate and the overall growth rate of Asian economies (though this argument is not entirely applicable to certain industries and certain countries).[12] Hence, double-digit export growth rates were accompanied by a real depreciation of domestic currencies in most Asian countries in the first half of the 1990s when the yen was strong against the dollar.[13]

Export-led economic booms, owing to the misalignment of exchange rates (undervalued currencies) in those countries, were further stimulated by foreign capital inflows, first in foreign direct investment (FDI), then in speculative capital inflows.[14] Moreover, due to rising labor costs in certain Asian newly industrializing countries (NICs) beginning in the 1980s, a strong yen in Japan shifted the destination of Japanese FDI (especially that destined for labor-intensive light manufactured products produced for Japanese multinational corporations) from the first tier of "flying geese" (Asian NICs such as South Korea, Hong Kong, and Taiwan) to the second tier (such as the ASEAN countries), especially after the Plaza Accord in the late 1980s.[15]

Capital flows between developed countries of the Organization for Economic and Cooperation Development (OECD) and developing Asian countries resulted from both push and pull factors. With fiscal deficit reductions in the OECD, relatively lower interest rates, and a strong yen but a stagnant economy in Japan, there were push forces of capital flight from industrialized countries to economies in the East Asian region. These push factors were complemented by pull factors that attracted foreign capital to the soon-to-be-troubled region.

12. Kwan (1997).

13. The average annual growth rate of exports was 10.8 percent in Indonesia, 13.4 percent in Korea, 14.4 percent in Malaysia, and 14.2 percent in Thailand between 1990 and 1995 period. The growth rate for the Philippines was 9.4 percent. See World Bank (1997).

14. Kaminsky and Reinhart (1998) argue that there were more FDI inflows and fewer short-term capital inflows into East Asia than into Latin America before 1996. But the composition of foreign capital inflows in East Asia reversed after 1996. After that, there were more short-term capital inflows and fewer FDI inflows into East Asia.

15. Kohama and Urata (1988); Urata (1993).

Essentially, financial liberalization undertaken in these countries was accompanied by robust growth in trade and outputs, sensible government budgets, low inflation, and seemingly stable exchange rates in recipient countries. As a result, capital flows to the developing regional economies increased over the course of the 1990s. Regrettably, the lack of adequate financial infrastructures coupled with poor oversight made it not a question of whether a financial crisis would strike, but when. Therefore, rather than condemning the globalization of financial markets per se as the crisis scapegoat, it is important to recognize as well that the lack of appropriate channels to guide foreign capital to productive activities was primarily responsible for the financial turmoil.[16]

Given high saving ratios and relative weak consumer loans in many Asian countries, the foreign capital channeled by bank lending was mostly directed to two major types of projects. First, capital typically flowed to the projects of favorite firms patronized by the government, such as the chaebols in Korea and those enterprises tied to crony capitalism in Indonesia. The second type of project included speculative, nonproductive initiatives such as those in the real estate and other nonexport sectors.[17] Meanwhile, export booms and persistent trade surpluses in many East Asian economies undermined the ostensibly cautious lending behavior of foreign commercial banks. The lack of appropriate supervision and transparency in commercial lending policies misled foreign capital flows to concentrate either in overexpanding enterprises such as the chaebols in Korea or in nonproductive financial assets and real estate. Therefore, the problem of borrowing short and lending long became apparent long before the actual onset of the financial crisis in the region.

By 1995–97 the depreciation of nearly 50 percent for the yen caused real exchange rate appreciation and resultant declining export competitiveness for many economies in East Asia. Moreover, increasing local labor costs and the rising export competition from China (which devalued its currency nearly 40 percent in 1994 and has a high degree of export overlap with its ASEAN neighbors) led to current account deficits and economic recession in all the ASEAN countries (with the exception of Singapore) as well as Korea.

16. McKinnon and Pill (1998) argue that the financial crisis was not caused by overconsumption, but was due to overinvestment in poor-quality projects.

17. Banking loans to enterprises accounted for nearly three-quarters of credits, whereas consumer credit was less than 12 percent in Korea in 1993. See Bank for International Settlements, *Annual Report 1993*. On the other hand, nonperforming property loans accounted for nearly half of the assets in the Bangkok Bank of Commerce in 1996.

In general, during the first half of the 1990s interest rates in the ASEAN countries were relatively higher than those in the OECD countries, especially Japan. Therefore, it was considered profitable for domestic banks in the region to make out-in loans (loans made using money borrowed from outside the country, but lent to concerns within the country) by borrowing from Japan and other OECD countries and lending to domestic enterprises during the first half of the 1990s. Given the interest rate differentials and the coverage of exchange risk by denominating loans in foreign currencies, it was also beneficial for foreign lenders to extend loans to the ASEAN countries. Among the various categories of foreign capital flows into Asian countries, short-term capital outpaced long-term capital. Moreover, foreign portfolio investment increased more rapidly than FDI in the early 1990s.

The situation changed dramatically, however, with the cutoff of short-term capital inflows after the yen depreciated against the dollar in 1996–97. What followed was a significant reversal of short-term capital flows in 1996–97. In 1996 the net capital inflows into Indonesia, Korea, Malaysia, the Philippines, and Thailand totaled U.S.$95 billion, amounting to nearly a third of worldwide capital flows into emerging market economies. But the trend reversed in 1997 with a net capital outflow of U.S.$12 billion from these five troubled economies alone; the turnaround in capital flow represented approximately 10 to 12 percent of GDP for these five economies. As the research in this volume details, the reversal of capital flows stands out as one of the catalytic elements causing the financial crisis.

The Impact of Regional Trade Patterns

In addition to the contagious effects of currency rate fluctuations and capital flows in the region, two aspects of regional trade patterns should also be addressed. The first aspect relates to the "export ladder" that determines the division of labor within the region by dictating that Japan and technologically more advanced countries such as the Asian NICs export capital goods and semifinished intermediate goods to less developed ASEAN countries.[18] These intermediate inputs are then further processed and assembled before shipping completed products to export markets. Hence, there is an increasing trend toward intraregional trade within the Asia-Pacific region. For example, intraregional trade in Asia increased from 31.4 percent of total world exports in 1989 to 40.4 percent in 1996 in spite of the strong growth of exports to other

18. The concept of an export ladder can be attributed to Meier (1995).

regions. Increasing intraindustry relations also greatly enhanced economic interdependence in the Asia-Pacific region. Under such circumstances, volatile exchange rates in any country could cause a chain reaction of exchange rate fluctuations throughout the region.

The second important regional trade pattern is the lopsided distribution of finished product exports destined for markets in developed countries, especially the United States. A heavy concentration in certain export markets is reflected particularly in the high percentage of regional exports that go to the United States. Moreover, there is a high degree of export overlap among Asian economies as reflected in the indices of their "export similarities" and the high correlation coefficients of their "revealed comparative advantage."[19] Given that they were exporting similar groups of commodities to the same market, a sudden and sharp currency depreciation in any one economy would motivate others to do the same to maintain competitiveness.

Commercial Lending, Crony Capitalism, and Conglomerates

The institutionalization of crony capitalism in Indonesia and conglomerates in Korea hindered financial reforms. Essentially, strong economic performances in recent decades covered over the political and economic legacies of rent seeking in the commercial lending policies of those countries. Foreign sources of capital underestimated the potential risks in dealing with those borrowers who were implicitly protected by recipient governments. A sense among lenders that such enterprises were "too big to fail" did much to undermine prudent lending practices. Some argued that an inherent "moral hazard" arose, especially among Western and Japanese banks, based on the mistaken assumption that loan defaults would be bailed out by governments. However, there has been no clear consensus as to the precise role of this moral hazard problem in generating the financial crisis in Asia.[20]

19. The similarity index (S) of Finger and Kreinin (1979) is calculated by means of the following formula: $S = \Sigma \min (S_{iac}, S_{ibc})$, where S_{iac} and S_{ibc} are the shares of the ith export commodity from country a to c and from country b to c, respectively. The higher the similarity index, the greater the overlapping of export commodities between exporting countries a and b in the c market. Regarding the "revealed comparative advantage" of the Asian economies, see Chow (1993).

20. Lipsky (1998) argues that the moral hazard problem, though important in designing a future international financial system, was overexaggerated as a driving force behind the crisis.

Predatory Speculation

The fluctuations in yen-dollar exchange rates, the associated fluctuations of short-term interest rates in Japan and the OECD, as well as the integration of the global financial market, caused sudden and sizable flows of arbitrage funds into and out of the region that were too large and too speedy to stop. In fact, predatory speculation in a world of free capital mobility could affect healthy economies with strong real sectors, too. Despite their relatively healthy real sectors, Hong Kong and Taiwan were vulnerable to speculative capital flows that were far faster and of much greater volume than the volume of trade flows. Hence, in a globally integrated financial market some protections, such as a cap on the percentage of foreign ownership allowed on domestic securities, may be necessary to insulate weak financial systems from predatory speculations.

In summary, excessive, mostly short-term foreign debts, though undertaken in different forms in different countries, were one of the most commonly shared features of the financial crisis in the region. The crisis was not due to over-consumption, but rather due to overinvestment financed by excessive foreign borrowing from abroad. Moreover, these investments were concentrated in poor-quality projects. But regardless of the rationales for foreign borrowing, all the countries in the region ended up with similar macroeconomic imbalances in which investment exceed savings. The short-term capital inflows that filled up the savings-investment gap and the cumulative trade deficits under pegged exchange rates regimes overwhelmed foreign exchange reserves, another root problem in precipitating the crisis. State interventions related to banks' lending support for large conglomerates under conditions of crony capitalism not only distorted the efficiency of the capital market, but also led to implicit assumptions of government support in case of financial failures. Therefore, there was not financial liberalization per se, but rather liberalization undertaken in a somewhat unorthodox sequence (due to external pressure) and the lack of sound banking and supervisory systems. These structural weaknesses were often known, but their condition was greatly exacerbated with their integration into the global financial market beginning in the early to mid-1990s.

The Cases of Thailand, Indonesia, and Korea

As noted here and in the other chapters of this volume, excess development in the real estate sector in Thailand, overinvestment in the Korean chaebols, and the politically oriented connections of bank lending in Indonesian were only the most prominent features of the financial crisis for these troubled countries. In looking more closely at each case, we can see additional commonalities among the countries.

Thailand

Thailand liberalized its domestic financial sector by lifting the interest rate ceiling in the late 1980s. Bangkok then liberalized foreign exchange transactions out of the current account in 1990, followed by liberalization of the capital account. In 1993 the Bangkok International Banking Facility (BIBF) was established to attract foreign capital. To some extent the sequential order of financial liberalization to deregulate the domestic sector before the foreign sector (in accordance with McKinnon and Shaw) was adopted by the Thai government, but Thailand deregulated its capital account without completely liberalizing its domestic financial sector and allowed the existence of a two-tier financial institution (described further later). This important violation of the principle related to the sequential order of financial liberalization greatly contributed to the Thai crisis.

Before the establishment of the BIBF, the fifteen commercial banks in Thailand had 3,000 branches. But Thailand's financial and securities companies were prohibited from opening branches. Thai banks could operate several deposit services, but financial and securities companies were restricted to issuing promissory notes only. By the end of 1995 all fifteen Thai banks, but not financial and securities firms, had access to foreign funds through licenses from the BIBF. Therefore, Thailand's commercial banks, but not its financial and securities firms, had the advantage of widening the spread between deposit and lending rates by obtaining lower-cost loans from the BIBF. Therefore, financial liberalization aggravated the discriminatory treatment of domestic banks versus financial firms. Facing stronger competition from commercial banks after liberalizing capital flows, Thai financial firms had no alternative but to expand as much as they could in anticipation of receiving the same treatment as commercial banks in accessing foreign loans.

Moreover, those high-risk borrowers turned down by commercial banks had to deal with financial institutions at higher interest rates. According to one report, property credit accounted for only 8.8 percent of total bank lending, but made up 24.4 percent of the total credits extended by financial companies.[21]

21. Vajragupta and Vichyanond (1998).

Therefore, financial companies were much more vulnerable to speculative bubbles in the real estate sector. With more than 40 percent of new housing units built in Bangkok between 1992 and 1996 vacant, builders had trouble repaying their loans, helping to precipitate the financial crisis.[22]

As noted earlier, competition from a 40 percent devaluation of the Chinese renminbi in 1994, a 35 percent appreciation of the real effective exchange rate for the Thai baht between spring 1995 and mid-1997, and a significant shift of FDI away from ASEAN and toward China led to a recession caused by declining export growth. As the current account deficits increased from 4.3 percent of GDP in 1994 to 6.2 percent in 1995 and 5.7 percent in 1996, the speculative bubble burst and financial companies collapsed as nonperforming loans started to pile up. Foreigners started to withdraw their loans, and the Bank of Thailand, with only U.S.$39.2 billion in foreign exchange reserves in early 1997, addressed attacks from speculative hedge funds by betting U.S.$10 billion of baht on spot, forward, and options markets. After an unsuccessful attempt to defend the baht and the imposition of selective capital controls in the spring of 1997, Bangkok decided to shift from a basket-pegged exchange rates system to a managed float regime on July 2, 1997. As a result, the baht depreciated more than 30 percent, and by the end of August Thai foreign exchange reserves declined to U.S.$32.4 billion.

Thailand's case offers an important lesson that the liberalization of a country's capital account without full-scale deregulation in its domestic financial sectors could lead to a greater vulnerability to financial viruses. Moreover, even after the liberalization of the capital account, long-term capital inflows should be preferred to short-term, and FDI is preferable to portfolio capital inflows. FDI should be channeled toward more productive enterprises rather than speculative nontradable sectors such as real estate. Unfortunately for Thailand and the region, just the opposite occurred.

Indonesia

Among the three countries under discussion in this section, Indonesia probably best represents the so-called Dutch disease, as it has suffered from persistent current account deficits since the mid-1980s due to the decline of international oil prices and the pegging of its currency to the U.S. dollar. Prior to the plummeting of oil prices the government relied on the oil and gas sectors as

22. Parnsoonthorn (1997).

major source of tax revenues.[23] However, in the wake of falling oil prices the government imposed a three-tier system in the mid-1980s, with tax rates of 14 percent, 25 percent, and 35 percent on both business and personal income. But with nearly 85 percent of household incomes below the minimum level of taxable income (equivalent to U.S.$3,000 in 1984), the government considered foreign borrowing and foreign aid as part of government revenues.

Financial deepening in Indonesia was poorly developed in comparison to that in either Malaysia or Thailand.[24] As for bank credit expansion, Indonesia was also far behind its neighbors: bank credit as a percentage of total GDP amounted to only 57 percent in 1997. By contrast, this figure stood at 64 percent in Korea, 95 percent in Malaysia, and 105 percent in Thailand in the same period.[25] In terms of attracting capital inflows, financial intermediaries in Indonesia were also less effective than those in other Asian countries because offshore borrowing in Indonesia was done directly by the private sector. As a result, private foreign debts increased relatively faster than government foreign debts; the share of private foreign debt was 32.75 percent in 1991, but it increased to 53.83 percent in 1997. By March and April of 1998 it even accounted for 60 percent of total foreign debt. But foreign borrowing by the private sector without appropriate hedging was exposed to the risk of fluctuating exchange rates. Therefore, the foreign liabilities of Indonesian commercial banks as a percentage of GDP, though fairly stable at an average of 6.03 percent between 1990 and 1996, really underestimated potential risks. The ratio of short-term foreign debt to foreign reserves reached 1.7 to 1.8 between December 1996 and mid-1997, which was higher than the 1.2 to 1.5 ratio in Thailand in the same period. Total external debts as a percentage of exports reached 202.9 percent in 1995, and debt service ratio reached 30.9 percent of exports in 1995, one of the highest in the region.[26]

23. Tax receipts from the oil and gas sectors accounted for an average of 56 percent of Indonesian tax revenues between 1979 and 1983. Data source: "Central Government Budget," *Government Finance in Indonesia.* Internet edition, http://lcweb2.loc.gov/cgi-bin/query/.

24. The average ratio of M2 as a percentage of GDP in 1990–96 was 45.99 percent in Indonesia, but this figure was 83.49 percent in Malaysia and 76.49 percent in Thailand. Data source: International Monetary Fund, *International Financial Statistics* (various issues).

25. Bank for International Settlement, *68th Annual Report.*

26. From World Bank (1997, table 17).

The distribution of bank credits was biased toward the service sector, with a growth rate of 40.8 percent, 32.6 percent, and 38.9 percent for three consecutive years before the financial crisis in 1997. A large share of these credits (33.5 percent in 1996 and 60.8 percent in 1997) were extended to real estate companies, and credits extended to "others" were related to speculative activities.[27] The high level of foreign borrowing, combined with a high proportion of bank credits to real estate and speculative activities at the time of political uncertainty, all combined to burst the bubble.

Meanwhile, the ratio of short-term foreign debt to foreign reserves reached 1.7 between June 1996 and June 1997. With foreign reserves equivalent to only three months of its import bills, Indonesia could not adopt the Hong Kong model of having a currency board to stabilize its exchange rates. The Indonesian currency depreciated from 4,650 rupiah to the dollar at the end of 1997 to a low of 16,000 rupiah to the dollar in March 1998. Eventually the exchange rate stabilized at 7,970 rupiah to the dollar by the end of April 1998. The "conditionality" of the International Monetary Fund (IMF) imposed fiscal austerity, which forced the government to eliminate subsidies for basic energy costs and public utilities. Hence, there was a 70 percent jump of basic energy costs on May 4, 1998. With the decline in Indonesia's economy, the percentage of the Indonesian population living under the poverty line increased from 11.3 percent in 1996 to 38.8 percent in 1998.[28]

In addition, crony capitalism in Indonesia led to a high concentration of economic power in the hands of enterprises closely tied to political families. The lack of transparency in accounting standards and lending policies under this system, though long a part of economic transactions in Indonesia and elsewhere, was more vulnerable to external shocks once the country's domestic financial sector was integrated with the global financial market. Financial restructuring for sustainable development in Indonesia is long overdue. But it was pushed by external forces because, prior to IMF conditionality (and even during the imposition of the IMF programs in 1997–99), the incumbent government had no strong incentive to wipe out the long tradition of rent seeking, corruption, and back-door business practices.

27. Bank of Indonesia, *Annual Report 1996–97, Annual Report 1997–98.*

28. Data are from the Indonesian Central Bureau of Statistics. The poverty line was defined as 52,470 rupiah and 41,588 rupiah (roughly about U.S.$5.00 at the current exchange rate) per capita per month in urban and rural areas, respectively, in 1998.

Korea

The chaebols in Korea developed rapidly after the economy took off in the 1960s. Typically the chaebols were clustered around one holding company, which was usually controlled by one representative family.[29] They held shares in each other, and interlocking directorates were not uncommon among them.[30] The degree of concentration is exemplified by the percentage shares of top chaebols in Korean GDP and exports.[31] But Korean chaebols differed from Japanese keiretsus in several ways. First, contrary to Japanese keiretsus, which are centered around large financial institutions or banks, Korean chaebols did not have their own financial institutions. Given that equity financing is not well developed in Korea, the chaebols relied more on preferential lending from state banks guided by the government. Even after the privatization of state banks in the mid-1970s, chaebols were still prohibited from owning large shares of commercial banks. Therefore, the Korean government could push for rapid industrialization by directly controlling the policy and direction of chaebols through credit rationing by the state banks.[32] In 1995 the ratio of debt to equity averaged 387 percent in the top thirty chaebols and more than 500 percent in the top five chaebols before they went into bankruptcy in 1997.[33] Second, rather than being organized with vertical integration in the same industry as the Japanese keiretsus were organized, Korean chaebols, much like typical American conglomerates, spread across industries. Third, Korean chaebols had more formal structures and centralized control than Japanese keiretsus, which have a more informal networking system based on interpersonal relationships.

29. Korean chaebols are more family oriented, whereas Japanese keiretsus are oriented to wider social groups. Superchaebols that employ millions of employees are all associated with prominent family leaders such as Chung Ju Yung at Hyundai, Lee Byung Chul at Samsung, Kim Woo Ching at Daewoo, and Koo Bon Moo at Lucky Goldstar.

30. According to Goldman Sachs (1998), the families that controlled the top thirty chaebols controlled on average 27 percent of their listed group affiliates and 65 percent of nonlisted group affiliates through direct ownership of equities by family members, cross-holding of equities between group affiliates, and treasury stock holdings.

31. The production of the top thirty chaebols accounted for 40.5 percent of Korea's GDP in 1995 according to Yoon (1999).

32. Amsden (1989).

33. By way of comparison, the debt-equity ratio was only 87 percent in Taiwan, 160 percent in the United States, and 207 percent in Japan for the same period. Data source: Bank for International Settlement, *Annual Report* (various issues).

As Korea became the eleventh largest economy in the world, financial restructuring was long overdue. Given its big business enterprises and backward financial sector, its equity financing was relatively low in comparison to the direct finance ratios in developed countries. As a result, the Korean chaebols had to rely on policy loans, which took about 50 percent of total bank loans. They increasingly consisted of foreign short-term capital, especially after the movements to liberalize capital in the late 1980s. Alliances among the government, chaebols, and state banks led to preferential loans for the chaebols.[34] Though such a system had been in place for two to three decades, it was no longer compatible with integration into the global financial market. In the past the practice of granting government subsidies via preferential capital financing, though it substantially distorted the efficiency of capital markets, probably was socially justifiable in the short run for the sake of rapid industrialization.[35]

Problems of economic rent seeking for low-cost loans, moral hazards, and even corruption, though inevitable, were still manageable under the authoritarian regimes that dominated Korea until the late 1980s and early 1990s. In particular, when the Korean Central Bank could still serve as the last resort for all banks, preferential loans to chaebols did not cause a liquidity or banking crisis. But as Korea transformed in the 1990s into an industrial democracy and integrated its financial sector with a globalized financial market, the preferential lending policy with substantial short-term foreign capitals was no longer feasible for at least two reasons. First, under an authoritarian regime government bureaucrats were relatively autonomous in setting up industrialization policy objectives and were able to resist the "pork barrel politics" of more open democratic systems. Lack of transparency in government lending, though apparent under the authoritarian regime, was further complicated by illegal election campaign contributions after democratization, especially in the absence of well-developed oversight structures. Second, the mismanagement of foreign capital by extending soft loans to chaebols led to a chain reaction of

34. The government usually subsidizes the chaebols by discounting lending rates by about 50 percent or more. De facto regulation of the banking sector is illustrated by the discrimination between the chaebols and small- and medium-size enterprises in commercial lending and by the high concentration of business loans in the top chaebols.

35. Lee (1999, p. 67) argues that "the fundamental weakness of the Korean economic system lies in its reliance for too long on the government-led development strategy."

liquidity, banking, and debt crises when the Central Bank could no longer serve as the last resort for insolvency. Hence, government-guided investment policies that had functioned well for rapid industrialization could not be sustained at a time of financial integration with the global economy.

Specific details about Korean financial liberalization help explain this situation. Interest rate deregulation began in Korea in November 1991, first for long-term rates, then for short-term ones.[36] As a result, the spread between deposit and lending rates was narrowed and banks' profits declined. Privatization of the commercial banks was undertaken in 1993–94, but some state banks were maintained. Beginning in 1994, the conversion of short-term financial companies into investment banks provided new sources of foreign borrowing. The foreign exchange bank was also privatized in 1996. Therefore, financial liberalization led two major developments in Korea: first, commercial banks sought alternative investment opportunities for more profits, especially in real estate and construction businesses, and second, given the interest rate differentials between developed countries and Korea, commercial banks increased their foreign borrowing on dollar-denominated short-term interbank loans. Both developments contributed to Korean vulnerability to external shocks.

When Korea joined the OECD in 1996, the entry price included the simultaneous deregulation of Korea's current account and capital account. With this move the Korean government required financial institutions to report only their long-term foreign debts, but not short-term ones, which were considered trade-related financing. Moreover, outward FDI was switched from an "ex ante" (prior permission) to an "ex post" (report afterward) basis in August 1997. Therefore, the figures for foreign debts were not precisely known even by the government. Following liberalization, risky transactions with foreign exchanges took a number of forms.[37]

First, there was more aggressive borrowing via foreign short-term loans in an integrated international financial market. Though borrowing from abroad to finance rapid industrialization is socially desirable, it is necessary to apply risk management to those foreign loans. But most of these foreign loans were short-term debts denominated in foreign currencies without an appropriate hedge. Continued government support of industrialization through foreign debt was not accompanied by any improvement in the transparency of accounting

36. Park (1996).

37. The following statements summarize interviews with officials at the Bank of Korea and the Ministry of Finance and Economy in April 1998.

standards in the leveraged chaebols. This is what Lee referred to as the "break-down of the corporate governance mechanism."[38]

Second, liberalization of foreign exchange transactions on the current account allowed exporters to avoid depositing their foreign exchange revenues with the Central Bank. As a result, foreign exchange deposits in the commercial banks declined to U.S.$4.5 billion by December 1997, one year after the liberalization. Third, the ill-experienced managers in merchant banks and financial companies were prone to allowing high-risk exposure due to their lack of capability in managing short-term foreign capital. Prior to the crisis, in early 1997, J. P. Morgan sold U.S.$10 billion of Indonesian and Singaporean commercial paper to some Korean financial companies staffed by young and ill-experienced financial managers. As default loans spread, foreign creditors declined to roll over their loans.

Fourth, in the second half of 1997 speculators on the Hong Kong dollar and investment bankers in New York and Europe cut down their portfolio investments in the Korean stock market. Moreover, a sudden recall of loans from Japan, Korea's largest creditor, decreased confidence among foreign investors and creditors. Fifth, economic recession and declining exports aggravated trade deficits. Current account deficits as a percentage of GDP increased more than fourfold, from 0.73 percent in 1994 to 3.95 percent in 1996.

Sixth, political instability postponed the policy action necessary to prevent the crisis in Korea. Kim Young Sam's government submitted new financial reform bills to the National Assembly just after the Thai currency crisis. But, with the presidential election scheduled for December 1997, no action was taken between August and December 1997, and the legislation was not passed until the financial crisis had set in by the end of year (the financial reform legislation was passed on December 29, 1997).

Finally, the lack of supervision of commercial banks after financial liberalization enabled them to accumulate short-term foreign loans. It aggravated bank insolvency with the downturn in the fortunes of their clients. With commercial lending concentrated in the chaebols, nearly 20 percent of all bank loans was extended to the ten biggest chaebols in 1997–98. The leverage ratios in many superchaebols exceeded 500 percent. As the financial crisis spread, nonperforming loans of the thirty-one commercial banks accounted for up to 30 percent of all banking credits. As the creditworthiness of private banks was

38. Lee (1999).

in jeopardy, only state banks with government guarantees could obtain credits from the international money market.[39]

How Did Taiwan Weather the Storm?

After more than three decades of economic development, Taiwan's economic growth decelerated to an average of 6.5 percent in the first half of the 1990s.[40] In terms of sectoral balance in the macroeconomy, Taiwan maintained a current account surplus, high savings ratios over and above investment, and modest government deficits in the 1990s. The amount of foreign bank claims was less than 10 percent of its GDP, and Taiwan had nearly U.S.$90 billion in foreign exchange reserves in 1997.[41] The amount of foreign assets in consolidated financial institutions was more than seven times its foreign liability by the end of 1997. These healthy conditions differentiated Taiwan substantially from the countries affected so dramatically by the crisis.

In addition, with more than 90 percent of Taiwan's enterprises classified as small- and medium-size enterprises, equity financing was much less significant than debt financing. Taiwan's capital market is dominated by equity rather than bonds. By the end of July 1997, there were only 393 companies listed at the stock market. Financial liberalization undertaken since the 1980s still left the Taiwanese stock market relatively less open than others in the region. Foreign portfolio investment in Taiwan stocks had an adjustable ceiling managed by the government.[42]

39. From May to October 1997, only those state banks such as the Korean Development Bank, the Korean Export-Import Bank, the Industrial Bank of Korea, and the Korean Housing and Commercial Bank could raise funds from international money markets.

40. Galenson (1979); Kuo, Ranis, and Fei (1981); Myers (1984).

41. In Taiwan foreign bank claims' percentage of GDP was 8.5 percent, 8.4 percent, and 7.5 percent by the end of 1995, 1996, and 1997, respectively. By comparison, the figures over the same period for the other three countries were, respectively, 18.3 percent, 22.5 percent, and 22.2 percent for Korea; 24.8 percent, 25.6 percent, and 39.1 percent for Indonesia; and 55.4 percent, 53.7 percent, and 49.5 percent for Thailand. Data source: Bank for International Settlement, *Annual Report* (various issues).

42. Foreign investment firms were permitted to participate in the domestic security market in 1991. Restrictions on foreign holdings of domestic equity were relaxed gradually. The ceiling on foreign investment in a listed company was successively raised

However, after decades of an "outward-oriented" development strategy, Taiwan's economy was very "open," with the foreign sector (exports plus imports) accounting for 95 percent of its GDP in the 1990s. The financial liberalization drive was accompanied by internationalization as well. Major steps toward financial liberalization that had been undertaken since the 1980s included interest rate liberalization, management of float exchange rates, licensing of private banks, the ongoing privatization of state banks, the abolition of exchange controls on current account, and, in 1987, the gradual lifting of control on capital flows.[43] According to economic freedom rankings compiled by the Heritage Foundation and the *Wall Street Journal* in 1997, Taiwan was number 7, whereas Japan ranked number 12, Korea 26, and Malaysia and Thailand 28 out of 156 economies in the survey.[44] As for internationalization, offshore banking units were set up in 1984 and were gradually deregulated. The domestic capital market was also internationalized by authorizing the Asian Development Bank to issue "dragon bonds" denominated in U.S. dollars, Japanese yen, and New Taiwan dollars. Moreover, domestic firms were allowed to issue "global depository receipts" and convertible bonds overseas. In general, financial liberalization in Taiwan was moving more or less in accordance with the sequential order proposed by McKinnon and Shaw.[45]

Though there was room for further improvement in Taiwan's financial system, its banking system was basically healthy, with nonperforming loans

---

from 20 percent on March 1, 1996, to 25 percent in November 1996 and 30 percent in early 1998. In March 1996 portfolio investment was opened to foreign residents and overseas Chinese. Data source: Securities and Exchange Commission (1998).

43. In June 1992 sixteen private commercial banks were authorized by the Ministry of Finance (MOF). In 1993 the MOF also liberalized the establishment of bank branches. Initially outward remittance of foreign exchange was set at U.S.$5 million, and inward remittance was limited to U.S.$50,000 per person in July 1987. But regulation set both of these amounts at U.S.$5 million in 1992. Taiwan's foreign direct investment policy has since changed from an ex ante (permission first) system to an ex post (report afterward) system except for those cases of investment in mainland China over U.S.$50 million. Data source: Taipei, Central Bank of Taiwan, *Statute for Foreign Exchange Regulation.*

44. From the *Wall Street Journal,* December 1, 1997. Each country was rated in five specific categories in ten broad areas: trade policy, taxation, government intervention, monetary policy, capital flows and foreign investment, banking, wage and price controls, property rights, regulation, and the bill market.

45. Shaw (1973); McKinnon (1991).

accounting for only 4.7 percent of credits in the first quarter of 1997.[46] By contrast, this figure stood at 19 percent in Thailand, 15 percent in Korea, and 16 percent in Malaysia during the peak of the financial crisis. In Moody's ratings of banks in the world, Taiwanese banks were ranked behind those in Singapore and Hong Kong, but were ahead of banks in the Philippines, Japan, and other Asian countries.[47] In rankings of financial strength performed in 1997, the Switzerland-based International Institute for Management Development ranked Taiwan number 23 in the world, behind Malaysia, which it ranked at 19, but well ahead of the Philippines (28), Thailand (29), Indonesia (39), and Korea (43).

Table 8-1 provides a more representative definition of financial development in Taiwan. One criterion reflects the country's amount of loanable funds or financial deepening and the scale of financial institutions. In terms of financial deepening, in the mid-1990s Taiwan reached a level comparable to the levels of most mature industrial economies, with the ratio of M2 to GDP exceeding 170 percent (column 1). (M2 is money, broadly defined, including net currency, net checking account deposits, passbook deposits, passbook savings deposits, and quasi-money.) The scale of Taiwan's financial institutions, as represented by total assets in consolidated financial institutions as a percentage of GDP, increased from 58 percent in 1970 to more than 220 percent in the mid-1990s (column 2).

Another measure of financial development is the success of financial institutions in serving as intermediaries to mobilize savings and channel them into capital investments. There are two indicators of this aspect of development. The first is the ratio of saving deposits in major financial institutions to total national savings. As shown in columns 3 and 4 of table 8-1, this figure increased from 24 to 28 percent in 1970 to more than 80 percent on average between 1991 and 1995, before it dropped to 60 percent in the second half of the 1990s. The second indicator is the percentage of commercial loans and investments in gross fixed capital formation. As shown in column 5, it in-

46. Two major improvements are still needed. The first is to eliminate overlapping responsibilities of financial supervision between the Central Bank and the Ministry of Finance. The second is to restructure the credit departments of civic organizations such as farmers' and fishermen's associations.

47. Each rating represented the opinion of Moody's Investors Service related to the likelihood that a nation's banks will require outside financial assistance as well as its financial fundamentals, franchise value, and business and asset diversification. It did not reflect the ability of the country to aid its banks. See "Rating the World's Banks," *Wall Street Journal,* August 14, 1998, A13.

Table 8-1. Indicators of Financial Development in Taiwan

Year	M2/GDP[a]	Total assets/GDP	D1/S[b]	D2/S[c]	L[d]/Gross capital formation
1970	36.99	57.98	28.51 (28.22)[e]	24.06 (23.77)[e]	25.87
1980	56.89	97.17	29.14 (28.38)	30.23 (29.47)	43.47
1990	132.26	184.06	46.70 (48.53)	46.88 (48.72)	65.77
1991	140.65	196.59	76.27 (75.72)	80.66 (80.12)	100.52
1992	150.39	208.85	97.28 (96.28)	88.63 (87.62)	133.23
1993	159.63	216.51	83.22 (82.17)	79.73 (78.68)	104.89
1994	171.58	226.06	93.57 (92.59)	88.77 (87.79)	94.91
1995	177.55	227.62	62.29 (62.06)	61.96 (61.72)	70.21
1996	179.51	223.78	60.28 (60.84)	62.77 (63.33)	59.90
1997	177.35	222.97	57.77 (58.09)	55.20 (55.51)	66.10
1998	178.23	224.97	60.06 (60.74)	60.69 (61.37)	54.98

Sources: Taipei, Council for Economic Planning and Development, *Taiwan Statistical Data Book* (1998); Taipei, Central Bank of China, *Financial Statistics Monthly*.

a. M2 = broadly defined monetary stock; the figure is at the end of June each calendar year, whereas GDP is the inflow of output for that year.

b. D1 = increments of deposits of major financial institutions, including government deposits from previous year; S = gross national savings.

c. D2 = increments of deposits of major financial institutions, excluding government deposits from previous year; S = gross national savings.

d. L = increments of loans and investments of major financial institutions from previous year.

e. Figures in parentheses exclude the amount in checking accounts.

creased from 25.8 percent in 1970 to more than 100 percent by the early 1990s before dropping to 66.1 percent. Though financial dualism still exists in Taiwan, private lending has decreased.[48] The ratio of private lending to business investment decreased from more than 25 percent in the 1960s to less than 20 percent in the 1990s.[49] Therefore, financial development in Taiwan has enhanced the degree of its financial deepening, increased the scale of its financial institutions, and mobilized more domestic savings that was channeled into investment. Still, with regard to internationalization Taiwan lags well behind Hong Kong and Singapore. The amount of foreign bank claims as a

48. Chow (1987). The declining trends in columns 3–5 after 1994–95 reflected the development of more savings and investment channels.

49. The figures include lending to all public and private enterprises. Since state banks had a priority scheme to extend their lending to public enterprises, the figures may have overestimated the percentage of commercial lending in overall investment.

percentage of GDP was only 7.5 percent in Taiwan in 1997, far less than those in Hong Kong and Singapore, where the figure was more than 270 percent in the same period. The high ratios in Hong Kong and Singapore reflected their role as regional financial centers, a role Taiwan had attempted to assume since the 1990s.[50] In terms of volume of foreign exchange transactions, Singapore and Hong Kong ranked behind London, New York, and Tokyo; their daily foreign exchange transactions reached nearly U.S.$100 billion in the late 1900s. In contrast, the average daily transactions for foreign exchange in Taiwan reached only around U.S.$4 billion per day in Taipei the past few years. Given the goal of internationalization, Taiwanese policymakers realistically understood the correct order of priorities: the drive for internationalization could proceed only after the domestic financial sector had become internationally competitive.[51] Taiwan's government expects to completely liberalize its offshore financial markets in the year 2000 and to gradually deregulate its domestic markets as much as feasible.

In spite of these sturdy financial foundations, the 1997–98 financial storm in Taiwan caused a 14 to 16 percent currency depreciation and a steep drop in the stock market. Taiwan's experience offered a lesson to many developing countries that even a well-performing economy was vulnerable to financial turmoil and shocks from abroad. Even with economic growth at 5 to 6 percent, a surplus in the current account equaling 4.5 percent of GDP, abundant foreign reserves equivalent to nearly ten months of its import bills, and a tolerable government budget deficit of about 7.6 percent of GDP but virtually no foreign debt in the public sector, Taiwan's economy was subject to sudden speculative attacks. The experience also implied that healthy economic fundamentals must also be accompanied by sound corporate governance and cautious bank lending, especially with regard to foreign loans.

Following the financial crisis Taiwan responded with a three-phase monetary policy.[52] The first phase lasted from July to October 16, 1997. During this

50. Schive (1995).

51. The following statements made by Mr. Y. D. Sheu, the late governor of the Central Bank in September 1995, are pertinent on this point: "We should be very careful in opening up our capital markets. A careless step might ignite a horrible financial crisis and cause damage to our society. . . . Before taking actions to open markets we should cautiously evaluate their potential advantages and disadvantages and we should establish a well-developed financial infrastructure and a sophisticated monitoring system beforehand." From Sheu (1995).

52. Hu and others (1999).

phase monetary authorities intervened heavily in the foreign exchange market to stabilize the exchange rate between the New Taiwan dollar and the U.S. dollar. With decades of conservative fiscal policy and limited monetary instruments for open market operations, the Central Bank lowered the required reserve ratio as a means of sterilization.[53] As a result of incomplete sterilization, the Central Bank sold nearly U.S.$7 billion in foreign reserves, and the growth of the money supply decelerated from an annual rate of 15.5 percent in July 1997 to 8.4 percent in December 1998.[54] The exchange rate stabilized in the first phase of the policy, fluctuating between NT$27.846 to the U.S. dollar on July 2, 1997, and NT$28.48 to the U.S. dollar on October 15, 1997. The index at the Taiwan stock exchange dropped from 9553.26 in July 1997 to 7983.28 at the end of October 1997.[55]

On October 17, 1997, the Central Bank realized that the Asian crisis would not end quickly, and it decided not to intervene heavily in the foreign exchange market and let the domestic currency float. However, the Central Bank continued to intervene modestly during the yearlong second phase of the monetary policy, which lasted from October 17, 1997, through October 1998. It intended to counter some external shocks such as the plunge of the yen and the pessimistic speculation of foreign investors due to political unrest in Indonesia. One major action undertaken by the Central Bank was to close the nondelivery forward (NDF) transactions—forward contracts made for foreign exchanges without requiring deposits—in May 1998.[56] Though it was criticized as a step

53. Treasury bills and government bonds are rather limited in Taiwan due to conservative fiscal policies and a low level of public debt. To accommodate the accumulated trade surplus, the Central Bank started to issue savings bonds and certificates of deposit (CDs) as additional monetary instruments in the 1990s.

54. Taiwan defined foreign currency deposits in commercial banks as a component of quasi-money (savings deposits) in M2. Therefore, the capital squeeze may not be totally reflected in the growth rate of the money supply. But tightening credit due to intervention related to the foreign exchange rate could be identified by the increasing rate for the money market (91 to 180 days of commercial paper), which rose from 6.8 percent in July 1998 to 7.94 percent in December 1998. Data source: Taiwan, Central Bank of China, *Financial Statistics Monthly* (various issues).

55. Taipei, Directorate-General of Budget, Accounting, and Statistics, Executive Yuan, *Monthly Bulletin of Statistics of the Republic of China* (various issues).

56. NDF transactions, partly motivated by speculation, increased substantially after the Asian financial crisis. Even though the Central Bank stipulated that the number of NDF positions in a bank could not exceed a third of its foreign exchange positions,

backward in terms of financial liberalization, blocking NDF transactions reduced speculative pressure on the foreign exchange market and allowed Taiwan to avoid further currency depreciation.[57] As a result, the exchange rates depreciated only 15 percent during the second phase of the monetary policy, and the stock exchange index experienced only a modest 10 percent decline in this period. Apparently facing the uncertainty of the financial crisis, domestic investors liquidated their stock market securities and deposited the proceeds in dollar-denominated banking accounts. From the end of July 1997 until the end of December 1997, Taiwan's foreign currency deposits in financial institutions increased 55.21 percent, whereas the total trading value of the stock market decreased by 36 percent.

Phase three of Taiwan's monetary policy, which lasted from October 1998 to mid-1999, sought to address the decline in export growth due to currency devaluations in Southeast Asia and in Korea by maintaining growth at around 5 percent, promoting domestic demand, and reducing interest rates. Major policy actions included enhancing domestic consumption and boosting the number of build, operate, and transfer (BOT) projects such as the high-speed railway, power plants, and some high-tech industries. The Central Bank pumped more money into the market by channeling postal savings and lowered the interest rates on secured loans. Taiwan managed to maintain an impressive economic growth rate of 4.76 percent for 1998.

If one combines the rates of currency depreciation and the stock market index as a composite "misery index" and applies it to all the countries in the region with globally integrated financial markets, Taiwan was the economy least affected by the financial crisis. In terms of crisis management, the government probably could claim credit for limiting its intervention in foreign exchange markets and restoring the market mechanism once the market resumed its normal function. Therefore, the decision of the Central Bank to let the New Taiwan dollar float on the foreign exchange market was probably the right one.

---

many foreign branch banks in Taipei exercised loopholes by swapping NDF transactions with DF transactions and purchasing U.S. dollars on spot to maintain the margin set by the Central Bank. Therefore, it caused additional pressures on the foreign exchange rate.

57. The other reason, probably even more significant than the cancellation of NDF transactions, why Taiwan avoided further currency depreciation was that the United States and Japan took joint action to stabilize the exchange rate of the yen to the U.S. dollar in May 1998.

Looking ahead, the Taiwanese government plans to establish a cabinet-level financial regulatory body—similar to the Financial Supervision Commission in Korea—to monitor all financial institutions including those in the banking, finance, insurance, and securities industries. Another proposal would increase the degree of transparency by releasing financial transaction data regarding the board members of business enterprises to the public and to those who hold more than 10 percent of a given company's shares. Taiwan's financial system could be further strengthened through further improvements in financial supervision (especially of the credit departments of civic organizations such as farmers' and fishermen's associations); more transparent accounting systems, especially for corporate foreign loans; clear-cut auditing and supervision of banking accounts; and better coordination between monetary authorities and fiscal agents. Once Taiwan's financial sector becomes stronger, the real sector should be further accelerated in the next century and beyond.

Externally, Taiwan is willing to assist the international community by sharing its development experiences with other developing economies and by contributing resources through international organizations such as the IMF, the Asian Development Bank, and the Asia-Pacific Economic Cooperation Group. However, many of its cooperative initiatives on the international level cannot be realized until Taiwan gains greater recognition and acceptance as a full-fledged member of the international community.

Lessons Learned from the Financial Crisis

The financial crisis accentuated the importance of the financial sector as a critical factor for long-term sustainable development. Financial restructuring is essential for further development in the new globalized financial market. In addition to the seven pillars offered by Michel Camdessus, other important financial lessons for developing economies can be offered here.[58] First, the

58. Camdessus (1998). The seven pillars given by Camdessus are as follows: (1) Provide good governance and intensify the fight against corruption; (2) continue to look for ways to make surveillance more effective and to enhance transparency; (3) strengthen the financial and banking systems, as well as their supervision; (4) promote more effective regional surveillance; (5) continue to liberalize international capital flows; (6) see whether better ways can be found, in crisis situations, to involve the private sector in official efforts to resolve the debt crisis and avoid the problem of moral hazard, perhaps through orderly

proper sequential order of financial liberalization should be followed.[59] Financial liberalization was often undertaken in the countries of the region without following a proper sequential order. Many economies fell under considerable external political pressure to open their fragile financial markets to well-ordered and well-functioning financial systems in the developed world without adequate time to build necessary supervisory structures. Therefore, the benefits of globalization were not equitably shared between developed and developing countries. Korea liberalized its trade and its capital account almost simultaneously to meet the requirements of its OECD membership. Thailand deregulated its capital account without completely liberalizing its domestic financial sector by allowing the existence of a two-tier financial institution. Whether these mistaken policies resulted from internal forces, external forces, or both, they were undertaken contrary to well-known orthodoxies concerning the sequential order of financial liberalization.

Second, greater attention must be given to building the government and corporate institutions necessary to foster more prudent oversight and risk management. Therefore, financial liberalization is not the same as a laissez-faire policy. Although liberalization and less government intervention are socially desirable, financial institutions need to be well supervised after liberalization. The Financial Supervision Commission, a cabinet-level institution set up by the Korean government after the crisis, is a role model for other countries to consider. In addition, corporate transparency and accountability need improvement in ways to make them less vulnerable to the sudden withdrawal of foreign funds. For example, the turbulence of external shocks could be minimized if there were a cap on foreign portfolio investments.

Third, industrialization through preferential lending must be accompanied by sound oversight mechanisms. Much of the Asian financial crisis was caused by overinvestment in low-quality projects.[60] The overinvestment of foreign capital coincided with a liquidity crisis in the economic downturn rather than signifying fundamental structural deficiencies.

---

mechanisms for settling and restructuring debt; and (7) significantly strengthen multilateral institutions by ensuring more equitable representation of all countries on their boards, bolstering their authority and enhancing their resources.

59. Camdessus (1998) argues that "it was not capital account liberalization that contributed to the destabilization of Asian economies, but disorderly capital account liberalization."

60. McKinnon and Pill (1998).

Fourth, the lack of monetary instruments is a handicap in many Asian countries when they are managing financial crises. They often lack the monetary autonomy to manage internal and external balances in their macro-economies due to a pegged exchange rates system and free capital mobility after financial liberalization. Moreover, unilateral or asymmetrical policy actions undertaken by any troubled country with regard to its pegged currency alone, without parallel coordination with its trading partners in the developed world, would not work. It is important to recognize that policy coordination among monetary authorities in all trading countries is necessary to maintain the efficacy of the pegged exchange rates system. If this system is to continue, then development of a system with a basket of currencies—such as the dollar, the yen, and the Euro, based on their relative trade and financial flows in each country—is an alternative to mitigate the dramatic exchange rate swings observed in the 1990s.

Additional policy instruments are necessary to achieve the multiple targets of monetary policy. Comparing the experience of some troubled countries and Taiwan between July 1997 and October 1997 suggests that a sterilization policy under either pegged exchange rates or managed floating rates would need more monetary instruments to uphold it. Otherwise the efficacy of monetary policy will be undercut at the time of financial crises. Taiwan sterilized its money supply by lowering the required reserve ratio, whereas Korea used the rediscount rate because of its lack of leverage in open market operations. Even so, such economies would need to develop more monetary instruments for stabilization.

Fifth, in terms of closing the savings-investment gap in developing countries, FDI should be preferred to foreign loans and long-term loans should be preferred to short-term ones. Public scrutiny of preferential policy loans, whether from foreign or domestic sources, is necessary to avoid the "over-borrowing syndrome."

In summary, the Asian financial crisis offered several important lessons relevant to all developing countries. Generally speaking, transparency, accountability, and credibility are the keys to financial development in any country, developed or not. As the world financial system has become more and more integrated in a global economy, the task of financial liberalization is imperative in developing countries. Hence, it is necessary for developing countries to learn from the Asian financial crisis and to speed up their financial development accordingly.

References

Amsden, Alice. 1989. *Asia's Next Giant.* Oxford University Press.

Camdessus, Michel. 1998. "Reflections on the Crisis in Asia." Address to the extra-ordinary meeting of the G-24 in Caracas, Venezuela, February 7.

Chow, Peter C. Y. 1987. "Money Market Segmentation and Financial Liberalization: A Reversed Financial Repression Thesis in Taiwan." *Journal of Chinese Studies* 4(1): 99–116.

————. 1993. "Revealed Comparative Advantage and International Division of Labor in East Asia." Taipei: Council of Economic Planning and Development. In Chinese.

Corsetti, Giancarlo, Paolo Pesenti, and Nouriel Roubini. 1998. "Fundamental Deter-minants of the Asian Crisis: A Preliminary Empirical Assessment." Paper prepared for the JIMF-Fordham University conference, Perspectives on the Financial Crisis in Asia (June). To appear as "Fundamental Determinants of the Asian Crisis: The Role of Financial Fragility and External Imbalances" in the forthcoming book, *Regional and Global Capital Flows: Macroeconomic Causes and Consequences,* edited by Takatoshi Ito and Anne O. Krueger (University of Chicago Press).

Edison, Hail J., Pongsak Luangaram, and Marcus Miller. 1998. "Asset Bubbles, Domino Effects, and 'Lifeboats': Elements of the East Asian Crisis." International Finance Discussion Papers 606. Washington: Board of Governors of the Federal Reserve System.

Finger, J. M., and M. E. Kreinin. 1979. "A Measure of Export Similarity and Its Possible Use." *Economic Journal* 89: 905–12.

Galenson, Walter, ed. 1979. *Economic Growth and Structural Change in Taiwan.* Cornell University Press.

Goldman Sachs. 1998. "Korea Chaebol Restructuring: Which Way Forward?" *Korea Research.* New York: Korea Stock Price Index 508.43 (March 25).

Goldstein, Morris. 1998. *The Asian Financial Crisis: Causes, Cures, and Systemic Implications.* Policy Analysis in International Economics 55. Washington: Institute for International Economics.

Hu, S. C., and others. 1999. "The Asian Financial Crisis: A Comparative Analysis of Taiwan's Experience." Paper presented at the joint session of the American Economic Association in New York, January 3–5.

International Monetary Fund, 1998. *World Economic Outlook* (May). Washington: International Monetary Fund.

Kaminsky, Garciela L., and Carmen M. Reinhart. 1998. "Financial Crises in Asia and Latin America: Then and Now." *American Economic Review* 88(2): 444–48.

Kohama, Hirohisa, and Shujiro Urata. 1988. "The Impact of the Recent Yen Apprecia-tion on the Japanese Economy." *The Developing Economies* 25(4): 323–40.

Krugman, Paul. 1979. "A Model of Balance of Payments Crises." *Journal of Money, Credit, and Banking* 11: 311–25.

————. 1998. "What Happened to Asia." Massachusetts Institute of Technology, Department of Economics. Internet edition, www.mit.edu/krugman/DISINTER.html.

Kuo, Shirley, Gustav Ranis, and John C. H. Fei. 1981. *The Taiwan Success Story.* Boulder, Colo.: Westview Press.

Kwan, C. H. 1997. "The Thai Currency Crisis: Implications for Asian Economies and the Formation of a Yen Bloc." *Asia Pacific Economic Insights.* Tokyo: Nomura Research Institute.

Lee, Jisoon. 1999. "An Understanding of the 1997 Korean Economic Crisis." *EXIM Review* 19(2): 41–87.

Lipsky, John. 1998. "Asia's Crisis: A Market Perspective." *Finance and Development* 35(2). Internet edition.

McKinnon, Ronald I. 1984. *Pacific Growth and Financial Interdependence: An Overview of Bank Regulation and Monetary Control.* Stanford University, Center for Research in Economic Growth.

————. 1991. *The Order of Economic Liberalization: Financial Control in the Transition to a Market Economy.* Johns Hopkins University Press.

McKinnon, Ronald I., and H. Pill. 1998. "The Overborrowing Syndrome: Are East Asian Economies Different?" In *Managing Capital Flows and Exchange Rates: Perspectives from the Pacific Basin,* edited by Reuven Glick. Cambridge University Press, pp. 322–55.

Meier, Gerald. 1995. *Leading Issues in Economic Development,* 6th edition. New York: Oxford University Press.

Myers, Ramon. 1984. "The Economic Transformation of the Republic of China on Taiwan." *China Quarterly* 99: 540–52.

Park, Woo Am. 1996. "Financial: The Korean Experience." In *Financial Deregulation and Integration in East Asia,* edited by Takatoshi Ito and Anne O. Krueger. *NBER-East Asia Seminar on Economics,* vol. 5. University of Chicago Press, pp. 247–76.

Parnsoonthorn, Krissana. 1997. "Greed Reaps Grim Reward," Bangkok *Post: Economic Review,* Year-end 1996 (January 1997): 62–63.

Patrick, Hugh T. 1966. "Financial Development and Economic Growth in Under-developed Countries." *Economic Development and Cultural Change* 14(2): 174–89.

Radelet, Steven, and Jeffrey Sachs. 1998. "The Onset of the East Asian Currency Crisis." National Bureau of Economic Research Working Paper 6680 (April). Internet edition, www.hiid.harvard.edu.

————. 1999. "What Have We Learned, So Far, from the Asian Financial Crisis?" Harvard Institute for International Development, January 4. This paper was part of the project contracted with the U.S. Agency for International Development (contract PCE-Q-00-95-00016-00, delivery order 16, *Next Steps in the Asian Financial Crisis.*

Sachs, Jeffrey. 1997. "The Wrong Medicine for Asia." *New York Times,* November 3. Internet edition, www.asia_sachs_op-ednyt.1197.html.

Schive, Chi. 1995. *Taiwan's Economic Role in East Asia.* Washington: Center for Strategic and International Studies.

Securities and Exchange Commission. 1998. *Securities and Exchange Act.* Taipei: Ministry of Finance, Securities and Exchange Commission.

Shaw, Edward S. 1973. *Financial Deepening in Economic Development.* Oxford University Press.

Sheu, Y. D. 1995. "The Background and Approach to Developing Taipei into a Regional Financial Center." Presentation at the 20th Annual Convention of the Chinese American Academic and Professional Society, New York, September 9–10.

Stiglitz, Joseph. 1998. "Bad Private Sector Decisions." *Wall Street Journal,* February 4, A22.

Urata, Shujiro. 1993. "Japanese Direct Foreign Investment and Technology Transfer in the Asia-Pacific Region." Paper presented at the Conference on Internationalization of Taiwan's Industry, Taipei, Chung Hwa Institution for Economic Research, July 3.

Vajragupta, Yos, and Pakorn Vichyanond. 1998. "Thailand's Financial Evolution and the 1997 Crisis." Bangkok: Thailand Development Research Institute.

World Bank. 1997. *World Development Report.* World Bank.

Yoon, Bong Joon. 1999. "Korean Financial Crisis, the Chaebol, and Economic Reform." *Korea Observer* 30(3): 411–41.

Young, Alwyn. 1995. "The Tyranny of Numbers: Confronting the Statistical Realities of the East Asian Growth Experience." *Quarterly Journal of Economics* 110 (August): 641–80.

Contributors

Shin-Horng Chen is a research fellow and deputy director of the International Division, Chung-Hua Institution for Economic Research, Taipei, Taiwan.

Tain-Jy Chen is a professor of economics at National Taiwan University.

Peter C. Y. Chow is a professor of economics at the City College and Graduate Center of the City University of New York.

Frank Flatters is a professor of economics at Queen's University, Kingston, Canada.

Bates Gill is a senior fellow in Foreign Policy Studies and director of the Center for Northeast Asian Policy Studies at the Brookings Institution in Washington, D.C.

Ying-Hua Ku is a research fellow at the Chung-Hua Institution for Economic Research.

Da-Nien Liu is a research fellow and director of the International Division, Chung-Hua Institution for Economic Research, Taipei, Taiwan.

Steven Radelet is a fellow at the Harvard Institute for International Development, the director of the institute's Macroeconomics Program, and a lecturer at the Kennedy School of Government.

Jiann-Chyuan Wang is presently a research fellow at the Chung-Hua Institution for Economic Research and associate professor of economics at the Chinese Culture University in Taiwan.

Tatsuo Yanagita is a professor at the Graduate School of Frontier Sciences, the University of Tokyo.

Index